POLARIZATION
WHAT EVERYONE NEEDS TO KNOW®

NOLAN McCARTY

OXFORD
UNIVERSITY PRESS

OXFORD
UNIVERSITY PRESS

Oxford University Press is a department of the University of Oxford. It furthers the University's objective of excellence in research, scholarship, and education by publishing worldwide. Oxford is a registered trade mark of Oxford University Press in the UK and certain other countries.

"What Everyone Needs to Know" is a registered trademark of Oxford University Press.

Published in the United States of America by Oxford University Press 198 Madison Avenue, New York, NY 10016, United States of America.

© Oxford University Press 2019

Library of Congress Cataloging-in-Publication Data
Names: McCarty, Nolan, author.
Title: Polarization : what everyone needs to know / Nolan McCarty.
Description: New York, NY : Oxford University Press, 2019. |
Includes bibliographical references.
Identifiers: LCCN 2018058213 | ISBN 9780190867782 (hardcover) |
ISBN 9780190867775 (paperback)
Subjects: LCSH: Political culture—United States. |
Polarization (Social sciences)—Political aspects—United States. |
Social structure—United States. | BISAC: POLITICAL SCIENCE / General. |
POLITICAL SCIENCE / History & Theory.
Classification: LCC JK1726 .M399 2019 | DDC 306.20973—dc23
LC record available at https://lccn.loc.gov/2018058213

1 3 5 7 9 8 6 4 2

Paperback printed by Sheridan Books, Inc., United States of America
Hardback printed by Bridgeport National Bindery, Inc., United States of America

POLARIZATION

WHAT EVERYONE NEEDS TO KNOW®

To Keith and Howard

CONTENTS

6 How Does Electoral Law Affect Legislative Polarization?   101

7 What Are the Consequences of Polarization for Public Policy and Governance?   134

8 Is the Trump Presidency a New Normal or More of the Same?   156

ACKNOWLEDGMENTS

The years that I have been studying the polarization of American politics overlap exactly with my years as a scholar. My first research paper in my first summer of graduate school was an effort to produce measures of candidate divergence from the campaign contributions of interest groups. While that paper made only a modest contribution to the research I discuss in this book, its real impact on me was the opportunity to begin a career-long collaboration with Keith Poole and Howard Rosenthal. They, of course, were the pioneers, substantively and methodologically, of the entire enterprise. Their 1984 article "The Polarization of American Politics" is arguably the earliest warning of the political winds that were to shape the last quarter of the twentieth century and the first quarter of the twenty-first. Their development of the D-NOMINATE scale fired the first shot of a measurement revolution in political science that redefined how we study political representation.[1] It's been my great honor to tag along for the rest of the ride.

Our first explicit collaboration was the development of DW-NOMINATE, a model that plays a prominent role in what follows. The first application of that model was our short monograph for the American Enterprise Institute on polarization and the realignment of the American political system.[2] It was here that we first discovered the correlation between polarization and income inequality that we would explore in more depth in two editions of *Polarized America*.[3] Along the way we wrote articles on the role of party discipline and gerrymandering on polarization and applied our insights to the political economy of financial crises.[4] I could not have asked for more out of a collaboration. I learned something from each and every email (and there were lots of emails!).

My work on polarization has led to collaborations with many of political science's finest scholars. Most significant has been my work with Boris Shor. Many years of effort went into our compilation of over twenty-five years of roll-call voting in state legislatures. As I discuss in this book, the resulting polarization measures are proving very valuable in addressing a large number of questions about causes and consequences of polarization. The debt of gratitude is not small for Michelle Anderson, Peter Koppstein, and the many others who have contributed to that project.

Special acknowledgment goes to Keith's and Howard's best student, Adam Bonica. He may have been the only person who read that paper I wrote in my first summer. But I am delighted that he picked up my fumble and carried it forward. His use of campaign finance data to measure the preferences of politicians and donors has made a huge impact on the knowledge that I report in this book.

My other polarization collaborators are a veritable *Who's Who* in the study of American politics: Michael Barber, Chris Berry, Tim Groseclose, Frances Lee, Seth Masket, Eric McGhee, Jonathan Rodden, Steve Rogers, Eric Schickler, Chris Tausanovitch, John Voorheis, and Chris Warshaw. Their fingerprints are all over this book.

I would also like to thank Julian Dean, Jake Grumbach, Andy Guess, Howard Rosenthal, Sepehr Shahshahani, Danielle Thomsen, and two anonymous readers for their very helpful comments on various parts of the book.

POLARIZATION

WHAT EVERYONE NEEDS TO KNOW®

1

INTRODUCTION

The months following the election and inauguration of Donald J. Trump have been a time for reflection about the state of American politics and its deep ideological, cultural, racial, regional, and economic divisions. But one aspect that contemporary discussions often miss is that these fissures have been opening over several decades and are deeply rooted in the structure of American politics and society. Indeed long before the historically divisive presidential election of 2016, the polarization of American politics has been an important concern of scholars, journalists, and elected officials.

Unfortunately, there have been few, if any, efforts to synthesize these debates in ways that are accessible to the general public. A few monographs on polarization such as Morris Fiorina's *Culture War?* and Thomas Mann and Norman Ornstein's *It's Even Worse Than It Looks* have directed their arguments about specific aspects of polarization to the general public.[1] A number of edited volumes have been published that cover the range of issues related to political polarization, but the target audiences have been researchers in the social sciences and law. There have been few attempts to explain what social scientists know and don't know about the origins, development, and implications of our rising political conflicts to a general audience. This volume is intended to fill this gap.

The second chapter begins with foundational questions, such as "What is polarization?" and "How is it different than partisanship?" I define polarization as the increasing support for extreme political views relative to the support for centrist or moderate views. Partisanship, on the other hand, is reflected as a strong bias in favor of one's party and strong dislike or prejudice against other parties. Although polarization can contribute to partisanship, and possibly vice versa, the two concepts are clearly distinct. Yet they are often conflated in the popular discourse. I argue that these distinctions are not purely "academic" but have important implications for how we understand and evaluate the performance of our political system. While I primarily focus on polarization, I address issues related specifically to partisanship throughout the book.

In chapter 3, I discuss what we know about the extent to which political elites such as elected officials, judges, and the media have polarized. The bulk of this examination focuses on the US Congress, both because its polarization has been the most studied and is arguably the most consequential. A very important part of that discussion focuses on how political scientists measure polarization. Specifically, I explain in non-technical terms how the polarization of Congress can be measured using a variety of data including roll-call votes, legislative text, and bill co-sponsorship. I also discuss how polarization of the general public is computed using public opinion polls. Importantly, I provide the necessary caveats related to the interpretation of these measures. Because some of the details are technical in nature, I include an appendix that goes into considerably more depth.

Chapter 3 establishes several important findings about elite polarization. The first is that the current era of polarization in Congress began in the middle-to-late 1970s. After several decades in which the average ideological differences between the parties were relatively stable, partisan disagreement in Congress has increased almost every term since 1978. The current period is almost the mirror opposite of the period from the

1920s to the 1950s when partisan polarization fell dramatically. Second, the trends in the US House and the Senate since the late 1800s are extremely similar. This pattern suggests that many of the forces that have generated polarization are common to both chambers of Congress. A third important finding about polarization is the extent to which the trends have been asymmetric across the parties. During the period of increased polarization, the main driver has been the increasing conservatism of the Republican party. Since the 1970s, almost every new class of GOP legislators has compiled a more conservative voting record than the party's returning members. The pattern for the Democratic party has been quite different. Almost all leftward movement in the party can be attributed to an increased number of black and Latino/a representatives who tend to have positions located on the left wing of the party. The average position of other Democrats has not moved substantially. Finally, the chapter provides evidence that other elites have polarized as well. Studies similar to those conducted on Congress show that state legislatures, judges, and news media outlets have all polarized to some extent.

Chapter 4 evaluates the extent to which regular citizens and voters are as polarized as the elites discussed in chapter 3. Here we will see that the evidence is more mixed. It is true that there is much more disagreement on policy issues between voters who identify with the Democratic party and those who identify with the Republican party. But how to interpret that fact is open to considerable disagreement. Many scholars argue that it is indeed evidence that voters have polarized in the sense of adopting more extreme views. But other scholars are equally insistent that it reflects the fact that voters are simply better *sorted* into parties so that most conservative voters are now Republican and most liberal voters are now Democratic— something that was far from true in earlier eras. This chapter unpacks those debates and explores their implications for the debate about whether it is the elites or the voters that are to blame for polarization.[2] Several conclusions about voters are noteworthy. The first is that the partisan polarization or sorting of voters occurred considerably later than the polarization of the political elites and activists. This suggests that the polarization we observe from the elites is probably not a simple reaction to changes among the electorate. Indeed it is more plausible that the positions and partisanship of the voters are a reaction to the polarization of elected officials and other elite actors. Second, despite the widely held belief that voters are polarized along a set of hot button social issues, such as abortion and gay rights, political scientists have routinely found that positions on economic and social welfare issues better predict the partisanship of voters. There are sharp disagreements, however, to the extent to which preferences on social welfare issues are in turn derived from differences in racial attitudes. Finally, I discuss the related concept of *affective polarization* that focuses on the increased salience of partisanship as a social identity. As a consequence of heightened party identification, citizens now show considerably more animus to supporters of the other party. I discuss the roles of ideological and policy polarization as well as the partisan sorting on other social identities in the rise of affective polarization.

Chapters 5 and 6 focus on the possible causes of congressional polarization. In doing so, I try to distinguish those causes that might have plausibly triggered the initial rise in polarization in the late 1970s from those factors that may have exacerbated or amplified those trends once polarization began. The causes discussed in chapter 5 include several of what we might call "macro" explanations. The most prominent of these is the realignment of southern white voters from the Democratic party to the Republican party in the decades following the 1964 Civil Rights Act and the 1965 Voting Rights Act. I explain about how the racial politics in the pre–Civil Rights era reduced polarization on many issues, while the racial politics in the post–Civil Rights era have worked to reinforce it. Then I consider large-scale economic and social change as explanations as well as important developments in the media environment, including cable television, the Internet, and social media. In particular, I discuss how these changes might have upset the less polarized political system as it existed in the middle of the twentieth century, and in some cases how those explanations might help us to understand the earlier era of polarization from the 1870s to the 1920s. Finally, I also discuss the role of legislative institutions and leadership in creating and exacerbating polarization. Of particular interest are the effects of the intense competition for majority control of Congress.

Chapter 6 engages prominent debates about how certain features of our electoral system, such as gerrymandered legislative districts, partisan primary nomination systems, and the private campaign finance system, may increase polarization in Congress and state legislatures. The evidence I present, however, largely rejects the idea that these institutional features are major triggers of increased polarization. Importantly, districting was less legally constrained, primaries were more partisan, and campaign finance was less regulated during the era of low polarization than today. But I give careful consideration of the extent to which these electoral features may have exacerbated some of the trends we have seen. The evidence of exacerbation, however, is not very strong in the case of redistricting and primaries, but there is mounting evidence of a substantial effect of campaign finance. But contrary to common concerns about the role of business and corporate contributions in the aftermath of the *Citizens United* decision, the real culprits are ideologically-minded individual donors whose numbers have increased dramatically over the past couple of decades. I also tackle whether major reforms, such as proportional representation or single-transferable voting, would mitigate the polarization of elected officials. While such reforms merit serious consideration, we should beware of unintended consequences related to how such reforms would work with other parts of our constitutional system.

Chapter 7 delves into questions related to the impact of polarization on policy outcomes and governance. The focus is on how polarization has affected the level and quality of policymaking in the legislative, executive, and judicial branches. The heart of the problem, I argue, is a decline in the capacity of Congress and other legislative bodies to solve problems. While Congress's decline might create opportunities for other actors, such as presidents and judges, to assert influence and power, good policymaking in our constitutional system requires a well-functioning lawmaking and oversight body.

The volume concludes with a discussion of the 2016 election and the Trump presidency. In many ways, Donald Trump's ascendancy seems to contradict many of the trends outlined in this book. His election campaign was anything but that of an orthodox conservative. He ran on rewriting trade deals long supported by Republican presidents and legislators. He promised to protect Medicare and Social Security from the sorts of reforms that have been staples of the GOP agenda for decades. One of his signature proposals was a massive increase in spending on infrastructure, despite his party's long-voiced opposition to larger deficits. Even his tough-on-immigration stance and support for the "Wall" challenged the orthodoxy of establishment Republicans, including the party's previous president and nominees. On many of these issues (but not immigration), President Trump might have found common ground with congressional Democrats. Yet as of this writing, nothing remotely bipartisan has happened since Trump was inaugurated.[3]

Instead, the outcomes of the Trump era have been entirely Republican orthodoxy. The major legislative achievement was a large tax bill. While a revenue-neutral restructuring of the corporate tax system would have garnered significant Democratic support, the bill morphed into an exercise in tax cutting and deficit increasing. The "reform" part of the bill meant the elimination of deductions relied on by Democratic constituencies, such as the deduction for state and local taxes. The other major achievements of Trump's first two years in office were the successful confirmations of Neil Gorsuch and Brett Kavanaugh to the Supreme Court after the GOP-led Senate eliminated the filibuster on Supreme Court nominations. But Gorsuch and Kavanaugh are the sort of Federalist Society–backed jurists that would have been on the shortlist of any Republican president. And the GOP Senate's refusal to hold hearings on President Obama's nomination of Merrick Garland in 2016 shows that they certainly did not need Donald Trump to stiffen their spine to play hardball on Supreme Court nominations. So in the end, the Trump presidency may be an example of the more things change the more they stay the same.

2

WHAT IS POLITICAL POLARIZATION?

Commentators use few words to describe the American political scene as frequently as they use the word "polarized." But unfortunately, the terms polarized and polarization have taken on such a wide variety of meanings among journalists, politicians, and scholars that they often confuse, rather than clarify, the problems that our political system faces. So one of my main tasks in this volume is to be more precise in the terminology in hopes of better explaining contemporary American politics. The formal definition of polarization is derived from that of *polarity*, which is the "state of having two opposite or contradictory tendencies, opinions, and aspects."[1] There are usages of polarization that span almost all possible political "tendencies, opinions, and aspects." The public has variously been described as polarized over cultural norms and practices, religion, attitudes toward subgroups, policy preferences, and partisan attachments. In some cases, the definition is stretched to encompass social and political divisions involving more than two groups—such as when polarization is used to describe conflicts among social, ethnic, and racial identities.

This book, however, focuses on a much narrower set of definitions of polarization. I focus on those political phenomena where the public and its leaders have become increasingly divided. These areas include preferences over public policy, ideological orientations, and partisan attachments. The primary reason for this narrowing is that policy, ideological, and partisan polarization are those areas that have received far more attention from political and other social scientists and therefore have a set of arguments and findings that I believe "everyone needs to know." Of course, there are links between cultural and social polarization that are important for understanding political polarization so I do not completely neglect these other forms of conflict.

Let me unpack the various forms of polarization: policy, ideological, and partisan. I start with policy polarization. A simple definition of *policy polarization* is a process where extreme views on some matter of public policy have become more common over time. As an example, consider attitudes toward government policies related to abortion. To simplify the discussion, let's assume that voters are asked to evaluate three distinct policies related to abortion access. Under policy 1, abortion is legal under all circumstances and is not restricted in any way. Under policy 2, abortion is legal in most circumstances but restricted in some others. Policy 3 holds that abortion is illegal under all circumstances. We would say that policy preferences over abortion were polarizing if support for the two most extreme policies (policies 1 and 3) were growing over time relative to the centrist policy 2. Thus, polarization is distinct from uniform movements of attitudes in either a pro- or anti-abortion direction. We would not say opinion is polarizing if support for policy 3 was increasing while support for policy 1 was decreasing. Another implication of this example concerns how we measure polarization. When policy preferences are very polarized, the two extreme attitudes will have more support than the middle one. In the terminology of statistics, the distribution of polarized opinion is *bimodal*, as there are two distinctive, most common answers. Alternatively, we say opinion is unpolarized or centrist if it is *unimodal*, in that the centrist policy 2 is the single most common position. Polarization may also be related to how much *variation* there is in policy positions. In statistical terms, the variance of opinions represents the typical deviation of individual opinions from the average (or mean) opinion. In a situation of low polarization, most voters choose the same policy position and so the statistical variance is low. In the extreme case, where voters are equally divided between policies 1 and 3, the variance is quite large.

In addition to analyzing polarization on specific policies, political scientists often discuss it in terms of broader ideological differences among voters. For now, let us think of ideology as a general orientation to politics and governance. In the United States, we often imagine ideological orientations falling on a continuum from liberal positions to conservative ones and orient them so that they range from "left" to "right."[2] Conceptually, ideological polarization is similar to policy polarization. If most voters fall toward the ideological center, we'd say there is little ideological polarization. But to the extent to which liberal and conservative ideologies become more common relative to those of the center, we'd call that polarization. As before, we can identify polarization statistically by looking to see whether ideologies have become more bimodal or more variant in the population.

Figure 2.1 may be helpful in understanding what political scientists mean by polarization. The figure shows two curves representing different distributions of ideological orientations. The solid line represents what we might call a centrist distribution of preferences. In this case, the most typical position is one of moderation. Extreme liberal or conservative views are quite rare. The dashed line, however, represents a more polarized distribution. It is clearly bimodal in that the most common positions are distinctly conservative or liberal. Now moderate views are relatively less likely and extreme liberal or conservative views are no longer rare.

While these figures present polarization solely in terms of the distribution of ideological preferences, researchers often focus on how the positions of voters and politicians vary across political parties. Consequently, we can use *partisan polarization*

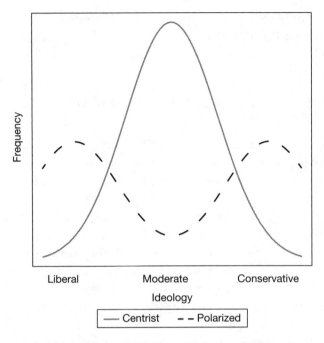

Figure 2.1: Centrist and Polarized Distributions of Preferences Solid figure shows a hypothetical centrist or unimodal distribution of ideological orientations. The dashed line shows a polarized or bimodal distribution.

to refer to situations where polarization is organized around parties. Most often, scholars use party polarization to describe situations where the policy and ideological differences between members of the Democratic and Republican parties have grown. However, as I soon discuss, this usage is controversial because it conflates two distinct trends about voters. Partisan ideological differences may grow either because there is ideological polarization between the liberals who tend to be Democrats and the conservatives who tend to be Republicans. Or partisan differences could increase without ideological polarization if there is a tendency over time for liberals to move into the Democratic party as conservatives move into the Republican party. These different trends and patterns have important implications for how we interpret the increased divergence of opinions across the parties and the likely consequences of those changes.

2.1 What is the difference between partisanship and polarization?

The terms *polarization* and *partisanship* are often used interchangeably, but such usage often obscures important differences. As discussed earlier, polarization generally refers to differences on policy issues, ideological orientations, or value systems, while partisan polarization may refer to these differences across members of different parties. Partisanship, however, can be more general in that it may refer to any partiality one feels toward one's own party regardless of whether polarized preferences and attitudes are the source. In recent years, many scholars have argued that the rise in partisan conflict is best thought of as a rise in general partisanship that is unrelated to rising ideological or policy polarization. Many explanations have been offered as to why high levels of partisanship can persist even without underlying polarization. With respect to Congress and political elites, Frances Lee argues that the intense competition for majority control of the US House and Senate induces high levels of intra-party competition and inter-party conflict, which she dubs "teamsmanship."[3] Given the importance of majority control in setting policy and allocating patronage, this instrumental form of partisanship has been an important feature of American politics throughout its history. But in the current era of partisan parity, it has become much more salient.

Others have argued that partisanship at the mass level is less instrumental and is instead based on strong psychological attachments and social identification.[4] From this perspective, the observed rise in political conflict in the United States is a reflection of the strengthening of "in-group" loyalties and "out-group" animosities. While partisan polarization might underpin these rising animosities, many scholars argue that differences on policy positions across the parties are caused by partisanship, as party loyalists adopt the positions favored by their own party.[5] In chapter 4, I report on the research that has sought to explain the rising salience of partisanship and partisan identities.

2.2 What is the difference between mass and elite polarization?

Any discussion of polarization, its sources, and its consequences should distinguish between *elite* and *mass* polarization. Social scientists use elite polarization to refer to divisions among office holders, party officials, policy intellectuals, and activists. Alternatively, mass polarization refers to that associated with normal voters and citizens. While most people assume that elite and mass polarization are closely related, that is often not the case. As long as the political elites are not perfectly representative of the electorate or not responsive to ordinary voters, we could observe increasing political conflicts among elites that are not mirrored in the broader public. The politics of abortion are a good example of this pattern. Elected politicians tend to take polarized views on the subject. Most Republican leaders have adopted a pro-life position that provides for abortions only in exceptional circumstances, such as when the life of the mother is in jeopardy.[6] Many Democratic officeholders take the near-opposite position that there should not only be few if any restrictions on the practice but that abortion services for the poor should be supported by tax dollars. A plurality of voters reject these positions, however, preferring instead that abortion be available in most circumstances but accepting restrictions based on term. Support for public funding is low.[7] While voters' views on abortion correlate with their partisan identification, large numbers of Democratic voters are pro-life while many Republican voters are pro-choice.[8]

Alternatively, society could become quite divided, but an elite consensus could persevere. A good example of this might be the Vietnam War. Attitudes about the continued conflict in Vietnam became polarized in the public well before the bipartisan elite consensus in favor of US involvement broke down. By May 1967, the American public was evenly divided over the question of whether it was a "mistake" to send troops to Vietnam, but the leadership of both parties remained committed to the war until after the Tet Offensive in 1968.[9]

As I discuss in chapters 3 and 4, polarization of political elites and the masses began at very different times and have followed distinct trajectories. Specifically, the current era of elite polarization appears to have begun in the mid-to-late 1970s, while similar changes in the mass public do not emerge clearly until the 1990s. Given these differences, distinguishing between elite and mass polarization is crucial for understanding the underlying causes and the likely consequences.

2.3 What is partisan sorting and is it different from polarization?

In discussions about polarization, it is often noted that Democratic and Republican voters have increasingly divergent opinions on many matters of public policy. For example, in a recent report, the Pew Research Center notes that the gap between Democrats and Republicans on the value of open immigration has grown markedly.[10] Eighty-four percent of Democrats agreed that "immigrants strengthen the country with their hard work and talents," whereas only 42% of Republicans shared this view. This 42-point gap grew from only a 2-point gap in 1994.

There are two logical ways in which such a partisan gap in views on immigration can emerge. The first is voter polarization. It might be the case that partisans have increasingly taken the extreme positions. Democrats may have increasingly adopted very pro-immigrant positions while Republican voters have become much more anti-immigrant. These changes of voter attitudes lead to the large partisan gap on the question about the contributions of immigrants.

But it is also possible that opinions about immigration have not polarized. Perhaps voters have just sorted into parties so that voters with pro-immigration attitudes now overwhelmingly identify as Democrats while immigration restrictionists have migrated into the Republican party. Such a pattern of *party sorting* can account for the increased differences across partisans even if the distribution of immigration attitudes in the population remains unchanged or moves uniformly in one direction or the other. In this case, it is clear that attitudes have shifted in a pro-immigration direction. Roughly 30% agreed that immigrants strengthened the country in 1994. In the 2017 survey, 65% did. So the most likely cause of the partisan gap is sorting.

Partisan sorting can arise in two different ways. First, voters can choose parties based on their agreement with the party's position on salient issues. In the immigration example, an anti-immigrant Democrat might recognize that the Republican party has increasingly adopted positions closer to her own, and therefore she decides to switch her party allegiance. I call this *ideology-driven* sorting. Since party switching is relatively rare,[11] ideology-based sorting is probably most pronounced for new voters entering the electorate. A new anti-immigrant voter in 1994 may not have recognized an important difference between the parties on immigration, but one entering the electorate in 2017 clearly would. Those who see immigration as a sufficiently important issue might use these differences in deciding which party to support.

The second mechanism is that partisans may decide to adopt the policy positions of their preferred party. So an anti-immigrant Democrat might alter her views about immigration to correspond to the dominant viewpoint of her party. The same might be true for pro-immigrant Republicans. This *party-driven* sorting mechanism is probably most pronounced in those cases where voters do not have strong views about immigration and are therefore susceptible to persuasion and social pressure from other partisans and party elites. To the extent party is an important social identity, many voters may simply decide that maintaining that identity requires supporting their party's dominant view.

Throughout the remainder of the book, I try to distinguish between conclusions related to voter polarization and those related to sorting. But in many cases, it is not clear which of the mechanisms is responsible for the diverging views of partisans. I describe such findings as *partisan divergence*, which of course can be caused by either polarization or sorting.

2.4 What is belief constraint and ideological consistency?

Many scholars of public opinion are interested in another concept closely related to polarization. *Ideological consistency* is the propensity of a voter to have either all liberal, all moderate, or all conservative views. Since the seminal work of Philip Converse, this phenomenon is also called *belief constraint*, which Converse defines as "the success we would have in predicting, given initial knowledge that an individual holds a specified attitude, that he holds certain further ideas and attitudes." For example, if we could predict a person's position on tax cuts from her position on free trade or from that on gay rights, we'd say that those beliefs exhibit constraint and that the voter is ideologically consistent.

While the concepts are distinct, increases in ideological consistency and belief constraint have manifestations that are similar to polarization and sorting. A consistent liberal is not only likely to have liberal views across the board but is also likely to only support liberal politicians and is therefore likely to join the Democratic party. They disagree strongly with consistent conservatives. However, if beliefs were less constrained and consistent, the typical voter might support liberal positions sometimes and conservative ones at others. She might be likely to split her votes between Democratic and Republican politicians. Moreover, pairs of opposed partisans are more likely to agree on at least some issues.

Chapter 4 reviews the evidence about the ideological consistency of voters and how it has changed over time.

2.5 Who is polarized—the public or the politicians?

As I stressed earlier, it is important to distinguish between mass and elite polarization. This is true not only because they are distinct phenomena, but because the evidence points to a much weaker relationship between polarization at the two levels than many people presume. The academic consensus that political elites have polarized over the past forty years is quite strong and is bolstered by both qualitative and quantitative evidence. Noteworthy are qualitative accounts, which often combine historical research and participant observation.[12] There are also several excellent histories of the intraparty battles among partisan elites that culminated in our polarized party system.[13]

As I explain in some detail in chapter 3, the starting point for many quantitative studies of polarization is the robust observation of rising partisan differences in roll-call voting behavior in Congress. The bipartisan coalitions of the 1950s and 1960s have given way to the party-line voting of the twenty-first century. Also discussed in chapter 3, similar patterns of elite polarization have been documented for state legislatures, the judiciary, and large campaign donors. Both the quantitative and qualitative evidence suggest that the late 1970s were a turning point. To be sure portents of the intra- and inter-party conflicts that led to polarization and sorting were in play much earlier, but the predominance of the liberal wing of the Democratic party and the conservative wing of the Republican party was not cemented until the late 1970s.[14]

The extent to which the mass public is polarized is a topic of somewhat more vigorous academic debate that is taken up in detail in chapter 4. Longitudinal studies of voter opinion generally do not provide much evidence of polarization or significant sorting until the 1990s.[15] Consequently, it is hard to sustain claims that mass polarization is the primary cause of elite polarization given that elite polarization precedes it by about fifteen years. Yet it does not appear that the centrist, unsorted electorate placed too many constraints on the efforts of the parties to reorganize themselves along ideological lines. The comparison of the 1964 and 1980 presidential elections is instructive, if imperfect. In both cases, a very conservative Republican candidate challenged a Democratic president from the moderate wing of the party. In the first instance, Barry Goldwater lost forty-four states plus the District of Columbia. In the second, Ronald Reagan won forty-four states. While there are many differences in the context of the two elections, it seems clear that the electorate was far more tolerant of a conservative message in 1980, despite the apparent lack of polarized public opinion.[16]

The debates about the magnitude and timing of mass polarization focus on how to interpret the increased difference between Republican and Democratic voters in terms of general ideological orientations and specific policy preferences. One school of thought, led by Morris Fiorina, argues that these differences can be explained almost entirely by the ideological sorting of voters into the parties.[17] Fiorina and his coauthors often point to the fact that most voters remain fairly moderate in their expressed policy positions.[18] Moreover in studies that produce estimates of voter issue positions that are comparable to legislator positions, representatives are generally found to take positions that are considerably more extreme than those of their constituents.[19] Since voters do not seem to increasingly take on extreme positions, the partisan differences are likely caused by sorting, with liberal voters aligning with the Democratic party and conservative voters aligning with the Republican party.

This sorting interpretation has been challenged by Alan Abramowitz who observes that while many citizens are moderate, those most likely to participate in politics increasingly take extreme policy positions.[20] The greater the level of engagement the more polarized are the preferences. Highly informed voters also appear to be polarized. While some moderate voters have chosen middle-of-the-road positions for substantive policy reasons, many others are uninformed, unengaged, or apathetic, checking off the middle position on surveys due to the lack of an opinion. Of course, at very high levels of voter engagement and sophistication, the lines between elite and mass begin to blur.

Despite the lack of evidence that voter polarization causes elite polarization, it is clear that both voter sorting and the polarization of the engaged electorate can reinforce if not exacerbate elite party divisions. Even if voters are merely sorted into parties, the incentives for parties to take positions that appeal to supporters of the other party will diminish—leading to greater partisan polarization and greater incentives for voters to sort.

2.6 Why is polarization bad?

Very few people use the word "polarization" to describe a healthy state of political affairs. It is almost always used as a near-synonym for dysfunctional conflict. But at the same time, we might imagine situations in which polarization were too low. If there is little polarization among the public, we might worry about the costs of conformity. Few citizens will challenge current practices and conventions, and there would be little impetus for social progress and reform. For example, the American electorate of the 1950s demonstrated a very high degree of consensus on the issues that were on the public agenda, but this consensus left issues related to the rights of African Americans, ethnic minorities, women, immigrants, and the LGBTQ community largely unaddressed.

Polarization among political elites and the parties is also not unambiguously bad. Indeed, the consensus among political scientists is that democracy works best when parties provide the voters with distinct menus of policy positions. Some degree of polarization is necessary for political representation and accountability. When the parties do not take distinctive positions, voters lack a clear choice with regard to policy. Moreover, heterodox parties reduce the usefulness of partisan cues as to which candidates to support. But when parties are distinct and coherent, voters can better register their views through their vote. Additionally, when parties push different policies, voters know who to hold accountable when a policy approach fails. These arguments, known as Responsible Party Theory, were summed up nicely in the American Political Science Association's report from its Committee on Political Parties in 1950:

> In a two-party system, when both parties are weakened or confused by internal divisions or ineffective organization it is the nation that suffers. When the parties are unable to reach and pursue responsible decisions, difficulties accumulate and cynicism about all democratic institutions grows. An effective party system requires, first, that the parties are able to bring forth programs to which they commit themselves and, second, that the parties possess sufficient internal cohesion to carry out these programs . . .
>
> On the other hand, . . . a coalition that cuts across party lines, as a regular thing, tends to deprive the public of a meaningful alternative. When such coalitions are formed after the elections are over, the public usually finds it difficult to understand the new situation and to reconcile it with the purpose of the ballot. Moreover, on that basis it is next to impossible to hold either party responsible for its political record. This is a serious source of public discontent. [21]

In sum, without some differentiation of the political parties, it would be almost impossible for the typical voter to have any influence over the direction of public policy. But as I discuss in chapter 7, there is considerable evidence that the level of polarization among the elites and the public is well to the warm side of the Goldilocks point.

2.7 What have we learned?

Polarization has become a catch-all word used to describe almost any form of political conflict and disagreement. But understanding the causes of political dissensus requires distinguishing polarization from many other sources of partisan conflict. While partisanship, partisan sorting, and ideological consistency may be closely related to polarization, it is important to identify them as distinct phenomena. For example, the extent to which conflict reflects polarization or sorting has implications for the extent to which conflict is bottom-up from the voters or top-down from the elites.

It is equally important to consider who is polarized—elites and elected officials or regular ordinary voters. It is entirely possible that one group but not the other is polarized. The question of the extent to which elites are polarized is taken up in the next chapter, while voter polarization is considered in chapter 4.

Finally, it is important to remember that polarization is not always a bad thing. If the parties did not offer distinctive public policy positions, voters could hardly be in a position to influence public policy through their votes. We might also be wary of those calls to reduce polarization in the public that would involve repressing certain viewpoints. To riff on Madison in Federalist 10, there are two methods of removing the causes of polarization: the one, by destroying the liberty which is essential to its existence; the other, by giving to every citizen the same opinions, the same passions, and the same interests. Clearly, the first is worse than the disease, and the second is unlikely to happen given the diversity of American public life. But unfortunately, as I discuss in chapter 7, Madison's constitution may not provide the needed relief in controlling polarization's effects.

3

ARE PARTISAN ELITES
POLARIZED?

One of the signature achievements of Barack Obama's presidency was the passage of the Affordable Care Act (ACA) in 2010. Because the bill received almost no Republican support, its passage required a very complicated set of parliamentary maneuvers to get through the House and the Senate and onto the president's desk. The Republicans did not accept this defeat lightly. They immediately began calling for the "root and branch" repeal of the ACA and supported challenges to its provisions in court. After taking control of the House in 2011, the GOP voted dozens of times for repeal despite the fact that the repeal could not pass the Senate and would have been vetoed by President Obama.

That the Affordable Care Act would become such an object of partisan division is somewhat ironic. Its most prominent provision was the so-called Individual Mandate, which required all citizens to buy insurance or pay a fine. This proposal, however, had originated at the Heritage Foundation, a right-of-center think tank. Moreover, it had been the centerpiece of GOP presidential candidate Mitt Romney's health insurance reforms in Massachusetts.

Following the Republican takeover of the Senate in 2014 and Donald Trump's election in 2016, the Republicans finally had an opportunity to repeal the ACA. But it was also an opportunity for the Democrats to withhold any support for reform and force the Republicans to push their legislation through the eye of a procedural needle. When GOP unity broke and Senator John McCain went famously "thumbs down" on the ACA repeal, the GOP had to settle for removing the mandate through its tax cut/reform legislation. This partial repeal was expected to lead to higher premiums and lower rates of coverage.[1]

The response to the demise of the individual mandate of many Democratic activists and officials has not been to campaign for the restoration, strengthening, and other improvements to the ACA. Instead, increasing numbers of progressives now want to replace the ACA with a single-payer health plan similar to Medicare—the so-called Medicare-for-All option.[2]

The saga of the ACA contains many of the elements that have marked the polarization of American political and policy elites: bitter partisan division, the willingness to play procedural hardball rather than negotiate, and the abandonment of centrist policy ideas such as the individual mandate. And the end result of this clash—like so many others—may be ineffectual and counterproductive policies.

Yet it is reasonable to question whether such conflicts are unique to our time and reflect anything other than the normal give-and-take of American politics. One can always point to some intense ideological or partisan struggle of the past to argue that American politics has always been rough and tumble and divisive. While these episodes undoubtedly show that there was never a time in our history that we were governed by cool, dispassionate deliberation among citizen-scholar-statesmen, argument by example is not very helpful in establishing broader historical patterns and developments. To capture those trends, we require much more systematic evidence.

Unlike voters who have been regularly asked questions about their policy views and partisanship, the lack of such information precludes direct assessment of the polarization of the views of elite partisan actors. Thus, scholars have had to use a wide variety of other data to learn about elite partisan conflict and its sources. One important source of information is legislative roll-call voting that has the advantage of covering thousands of legislators over large swaths of history. But the inferences from roll-call voting are not always direct, so some claims about elite polarization remain somewhat contested. Recent efforts, however, to measure elite polarization from other sources have been very helpful in clarifying some arguments and dispelling others.

Because the use of roll-call votes to measure polarization raises a wide variety of methodological issues, I dedicate a substantial part of this chapter to discussing the strengths and weakness of various measures. Because no measure of elite polarization is perfect, I highlight those results that hold up across a wide variety of measures. A slightly more technical discussion of some of the issues raised appears in Appendix A.

3.1 How do we measure elite polarization?

As previously noted in chapter 2, congressional roll-call voting has been a very important source of measuring elite polarization. Given that every member of the US House and Senate casts hundreds of public roll-call votes per year on a wide variety of public policy matters, the congressional voting record provides a window into how partisan and regional political conflicts have evolved over time.

One of the simplest ways in which roll-call votes can be used to measure polarization is to compute *party voting scores*. A legislator's party voting score is simply the percentage of votes she casts that agree with those of a majority of her party. At an aggregate level, a party vote is a roll call in which a majority of one party votes against a majority of the other party. Thus, a plausible measure of congressional polarization is the percentage of roll calls that can be classified as party votes.

Figure 3.1 shows the percentage of roll-call votes in each congressional term where one party voted against another.

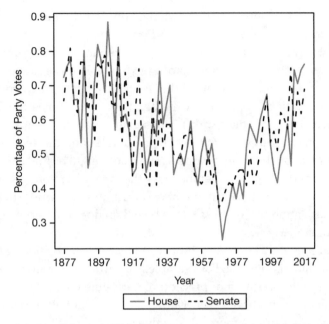

Figure 3.1: Party Voting in the US Congress Figure shows for each term and chamber the percentage of roll calls in which a majority of one party voted against a majority of the other.

These measures go back to 1877, the first congressional term after Reconstruction following the Civil War.[3] Although the party voting measures are noisy and bounce around from term to term, some clear patterns and trends are evident. First, levels of partisan voting are highly correlated across the House and the Senate. As party voting rises in one chamber, it also tends to rise in the other. Second, party voting rates were high in the late nineteenth century and then began falling through much of the twentieth century. But party voting turned sharply upward in the mid-to-late 1970s—the period in which political scientists generally agree that our contemporary polarized party system emerged.

While figure 3.1 reveals much about the history of polarization in Congress, a significant limitation of party voting measures is that they are hard to decompose into each individual legislator's contribution to polarization. Consider an example from recent years. The current Republican conference in the House has roughly three factions—a moderate one, a mainstream conservative one, and an extremely conservative Tea Party faction. Sometimes the moderates and mainstream conservatives vote against the Tea Party. Sometimes the Tea Party and the mainstream conservatives vote against the moderates, but we rarely see the moderates and the Tea Party gang up on the mainstreamers. The result might be that a moderate and a Tea Party member have the same party voting score. Yet clearly, the Tea Party member contributes much more to the polarization of Congress as a whole than does the Republican moderate. A second concern with party voting measures are that they may be heavily influenced by the composition of the roll-call vote agenda. For example, if a particular congressional term witnesses a lot of procedural party-line votes, it may appear more partisan, even if there is a substantial amount of bipartisanship on more substantive votes.

Given these concerns with party voting measures, political scientists have developed many other measures of roll-call voting behavior to assess polarization. The earliest alternative approach involved the use of interest group ratings. Interest group ratings of legislators have been compiled by a very diverse set of advocacy groups, most notably the Americans for Democratic Action, the American Conservative Union, and the League of Conservation Voters. Many of these ratings go back a long time. Though precise details differ across interest groups, these ratings are generally constructed in the following way:

1. An interest group identifies a set of roll calls that are important to the group's legislative agenda.
2. The group identifies the position on the roll call that supports the group's agenda.
3. A rating is computed by dividing the number of votes in support of the group's agenda by the total number of votes identified by the group.

For example, suppose an interest group chooses twenty votes. A legislator who votes favorably eighteen times gets a 90% rating, and one who supports the group five times gets a 25% rating. From these ratings, it is straightforward to compute polarization by comparing the average score of Democrats with the average score of Republicans.

Clearly, the use of interest group ratings has many advantages. First, the scores directly relate to the policy concerns of the groups that compile them. The League of Conservation Voters scores are based on environmental votes while the National Right to Life Committee chooses votes on abortion, euthanasia, and stem cell research. Second, groups often focus on substantively and politically important votes. By contrast, the party vote measures and the statistical models discussed next use all or almost all votes. Clearly, the expertise of the interest group in identifying key amendment or procedural votes adds considerable value to the measures. Third, interest group ratings can distinguish between party extremists and party moderates in a way that party vote scores cannot.[4] Finally, interest group ratings are easy to understand. A rating of p means that legislator x supported group y's position p percent of the time.

But the use of interest group ratings to measure legislative polarization has a number of drawbacks:

1. The ratings can be lumpy. Since relatively few votes are used, scores can only take on a relatively small number of values. For example, if a group only uses twenty votes, there are only twenty-one unique scores. So legislators with very different policy preferences may end up with the same score.

2. It is difficult to compare interest group ratings over time. The scales of any interest group rating depend on the exact votes chosen over any legislative session. Since the nature of the congressional agenda changes, we should

not confidently conclude that a score of 80% in one year is the same as a score of 80% in another year.[5]

3. Interest groups often choose votes to create the appearance of polarization.[6] The goal of many groups is to create interest group ratings that clearly distinguish between their friends and their enemies. Thus, they will not choose votes where those two groups agree. The result is an "artificial extremism" that amplifies any measure of polarization.

One of the first important studies of congressional polarization was conducted by Keith Poole and Howard Rosenthal. They used a statistical model designed to incorporate multiple interest group ratings and address some of the problems listed above.[7] Poole and Rosenthal found that beginning in the mid-1970s, American politics at the congressional level became much more divisive. More Democrats staked out consistently liberal positions, and more Republicans supported the menu of conservative ones. The primary evidence in that study, which focused exclusively on the Senate, were the ratings issued by interest groups such as the Americans for Democratic Action (ADA), the League of Conservation Voters (LCV), and the United States Chamber of Commerce.

To overcome some of the limitations of interest group ratings, political scientists have developed methods to estimate the positions of legislators on an ideological scale. These methods assume that legislators make their choices in accordance with the *spatial model of voting*. In the spatial model, each legislator is assumed to have a position on a liberal-conservative dimension. This position is termed the *ideal point*. The ideal point is directly analogous to a rating if the interest group is either more liberal or more conservative than all of the legislators.

Just as the 435 representatives and 100 senators are assumed to have ideal points, analysts allow each roll call to be represented by *yea* and *nay* positions on the liberal-conservative scale. For example, a proposal to move the minimum wage to fifteen dollars per hour from its current seven dollars and twenty-five cents would plot a liberal *yea* position against a conservative *nay* position. A proposal to unwind banking regulation would pit a conservative *yea* position against a liberal *nay*. The underlying assumption of the spatial model is that each legislator votes *yea* or *nay* depending on which outcome location is closer to his ideal point. Any legislator whose ideal point is closer to a $15 minimum wage than to a $7.25 one would vote *yea*. The legislators whose ideal points align better with the point representing the proposal for banking deregulation will support it.

Of course, the legislator may make "mistakes" and depart from the predicted vote. Such deviations may be the result of pressures from campaign contributors, constituents, convictions, or other factors. For example, a legislator who might have been expected to vote against banking deregulation might have been persuaded by a lobbyist just before the vote, resulting in support for the measure. Since the analyst cannot possibly observe all such encounters, we model them as "random errors." Using the assumptions of spatial voting with error, one can estimate the ideal points of the members of Congress directly from the hundreds or thousands of roll-call choices made by each legislator. Moreover, one can also estimate the positions of the *yea* and *nay* outcomes.

I discuss the logic of ideal point estimation in more detail in Appendix A, but its underlying intuition is straightforward. From the roll-call voting record, we can easily see who votes with whom and how often. Those who vote together with a very high frequency are assumed to have similar ideal points. As a pair of legislators vote together less frequently, the algorithm moves their ideal points further apart. This logic allows one to estimate ideal points on a left-right scale. Liberals are those who often vote with liberals against moderates and conservatives. Conservatives are those who frequently vote with other conservatives against moderates and liberals. Moderates vote with both liberals and conservatives on a regular basis. An iterative computer algorithm sorts all of this out. Although there are a large variety of approaches to ideal point estimation, I focus primarily on results of the DW-NOMINATE algorithm.[8] As I discuss later, other approaches reveal very similar findings with regard to polarization.

Once we estimate the ideal points on the liberal-conservative scale, measuring polarization is straightforward. One need only compute the differences in the typical position of Democratic and Republican legislators. While some scholars prefer to measure the difference in party medians, I focus on the difference in mean (average) party positions. There are a number of other options for measuring polarization such as the average difference between members of opposite parties or the axiomatic measures of Joan-Maria Esteban and Debraj Ray.[9] Two other common measures are the partisan overlap and the percentage of moderates. The partisan overlap is a measure that counts the number of members whose ideal point lies between the most liberal Republican member and the most conservative Democratic member. During the 1960s and 1970s, the partisan overlap was large as some of Congress's most liberal members were Republicans and some of its most conservative members were Democrats. Today the partisan overlap in the US House and Senate is zero as the most liberal Republican is positioned to the right of the most conservative Democrat. Similarly, the percentage of moderates is a count of the number of members who fall within a prespecified range of ideal points, say from -0.2 to 0.2. The percentages of moderates in the House and the Senate have fallen when measured across a wide variety of ranges. Ultimately, the use of these different metrics has very little impact on the basic story of legislative polarization in the United States. Figure 3.2 shows the levels of polarization as measured by the difference in party means on the DW-NOMINATE scale since the end of the Reconstruction era.

Let me note several important takeaways. First, polarization as measured by DW-NOMINATE shows the same broad patterns as the level of party voting illustrated in Figure 3.1.

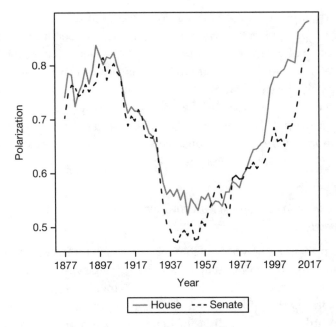

Figure 3.2: Polarization in the US Congress Figure shows the mean differences between Republicans and Democrats on the DW-NOMINATE scale.

There is considerably less short-term fluctuation in the yearly DW-NOMINATE measures, however. This is because the DW-NOMINATE measure is less influenced by year-to-year changes in the content of the congressional agenda. As we saw with party voting, polarization was high in the nineteenth century and then fell from the 1910s to the 1930s. It remained relatively low through the 1970s before growing to all-time highs by the 2000s. Second, given that there is less year-to-year fluctuation, it is easier to see that there are few true breakpoints in the polarization trends. Polarization tends to be either stable, continuously falling, or continuously rising. As I discuss later, this fact has important implications for evaluating plausible explanations for rising polarization.

Third, as we saw with party voting, there are no important differences in the trends of the House and the Senate. While currently the House is more polarized than the Senate, there is no general pattern. In earlier periods, the Senate was the more polarized. Most importantly, however, polarization in the House and the Senate turned sharply upward at approximately the same time in the middle of the 1970s. As I discuss later, polarization is also evident in state legislative bodies over the past twenty years. Thus, any explanations for polarization that depend on House versus Senate differences or federal versus state differences will not take us very far.

3.2 Why do you assume legislative voting occurs only on the liberal-conservative dimension?

In principle, the voting behavior of a legislator may vary dramatically from one issue to another. A legislator might take a pro-intervention position on environmental regulation and a pro-market position on financial regulation. There may be little or no correlation of her voting on abortion and her voting on agricultural subsidies. But empirically this is not the case. The liberal-conservative ideal point models previously discussed do a very good job explaining congressional voting. Legislators tend to exhibit what Philip Converse calls *belief constraint*.[10] In the context of contemporary congressional politics, examples of belief constraint abound. If we know a legislator's position of the minimum wage, we can be fairly confident about her views about income tax rates, financial regulation, and labor unions. We can also make reasonable predictions about her positions on gay marriage, abortion, defense policy, and affirmative action.

Roll-call analyses such as DW-NOMINATE can be very helpful in assessing the degree of belief constraint in Congress. If there is little or no constraint, we would need to estimate different ideal points for each distinct policy area. If abortion preferences and tax preferences were completely different, votes on abortion would have no explanatory power for votes on tax rates. Consequently, many issue dimensions would be required to explain congressional voting. But suppose constraint were high so that abortion views perfectly predict tax preferences. Then we would need to estimate only one set of ideal points. These ideal points would do an equally good job predicting votes on both issues. Politics would be "one dimensional."

Studies of congressional voting typically conclude that voting is very low dimensional. It can largely be explained by two or fewer dimensions of ideal points. As Keith Poole and Howard Rosenthal have documented, the bulk of congressional voting can be explained by a dimension that corresponds to the liberal to conservative continuum. The liberals on this dimension support higher minimum wages, more progressive taxation, tighter regulations, liberalized abortion policies, and gay marriage.[11] Conservatives support lower minimum wages, lower taxes and regulation, banning abortion, and oppose same-sex marriage. But Poole and Rosenthal also note that during specific historical periods, a second dimension helps explain voting patterns that are not well captured by the liberal-conservative scale. This second dimension generally explains regional conflicts, such as those centered on slavery and civil rights for African Americans.

One of the most prominent features of our current era is that polarization has gone hand-in-hand with a decline in the importance of this second dimension. In the 1950s and 1960s, the two dimensional version of DW-NOMINATE explained from 5% to 6% more roll-call voting decisions than the one-dimensional version. By the 2000s, the second dimension contributed less that 0.5% to the explanatory power of the model. The explanatory power of the one-dimensional model grew from about 80% to well over 90% over the same period.[12] Thus, almost every vote was one where a conservative coalition voted against a liberal coalition, and few individual legislators cast votes that defected from this pattern.

This change in the dimensionality of congressional voting is largely the result of changes in the politics of race. Racial issues that were once distinct from legislators' positions on the liberal-conservative dimension are now well explained by it. In other words, a legislator's position on civil rights in the 1960s was distinct from his position on taxes and government regulation. By the 1990s, the positions of legislators on affirmative action were highly correlated with their position on economic issues. Moreover, issues such as welfare and redistribution were highly racialized.[13]

In chapter 7, I consider the role of polarization in producing legislative gridlock. It is important to note that low dimensionality might also be an important constraint on the legislative process. Low dimensionality substantially limits the types of coalitions that we can expect to form, making it harder to construct a winning majority of legislators.

3.3 Are there other sources of data for measuring congressional polarization?

Indicators and measures of polarization based on information other than roll-call voting have also been developed. One example is the National Political Awareness Test (NPAT), a survey of state and federal legislative candidates, administered by Project Vote Smart, a non-partisan organization. The questions asked by Project Vote Smart cover a wide range of policy matters, including foreign policy, national security, international affairs, social issues, fiscal policy, environmentalism, criminal justice, and many more. Most of the survey questions are asked in a yes or no format so that the data have a form very similar to that of roll-call voting. Stephen Ansolobehere and his colleagues use these surveys to study candidate positioning in US House elections and to disentangle the effects of party and preferences in roll-call voting.[14] Most importantly, these studies observe considerably more polarization in member roll-call voting records than in their survey responses. They interpret this pattern as evidence that party leaders and party constituencies pressure members into more extreme positions than those based on their true preferences. But because the NPAT survey responses are disseminated to the media and voters, it is not clear a priori that the survey response is a better measure of true legislative preferences than the roll-call voting record. Moreover, Boris Shor and I do not find systematic evidence of greater polarization in roll calls than survey responses in our study of state legislatures.[15] While NPAT surveys have been very useful in the study of polarization, they have two limitations. The first is that they are only available back through the middle of the 1990s, so they do not provide the coverage needed to understand the first part of the current rise in polarization. Second, the response rates are modest and declining over time, so scholars have to worry about the possibility of response biases. If extreme members are less likely to answer surveys than moderate members, polarization would be underestimated.

Another valuable source of data on polarization comes from campaign contributions. Since the 1980s, all federal candidates have been required to report all contributions exceeding two hundred dollars to the Federal Elections Commissions. Many states and cities have similar reporting requirements for their elections. By examining which interest groups and which individuals give to which candidates, we can apply a logic similar to that of roll-call voting analysis to recover estimates of the candidates and those of the contributors. One of the earliest attempts to use campaign finance data for this purpose was my work with Keith Poole where we estimated the positions of House candidates and political action committees (PACs).[16] More recently, Adam Bonica has improved on these methods to estimate the ideological positions of candidates for all federal and state elections as well as the positions of PACs and individual contributors.[17] Bonica has dubbed these measures *CFscores* (short for "campaign finance scores"). Polarization measures based on the CFscores of US House members and senators have grown markedly since the 1980s, just as we find in the roll-call voting measures.

Legislative polarization may also be measured by examining the patterns of sponsorship and co-sponsorship of legislation. As part of the legislative process, legislators often add their names to pending pieces of legislation as indications of support. In general, patterns of co-sponsorship of legislation are considerably less partisan than roll-call voting. Laurel Harbridge reports that the percentage of bills with bipartisanship co-sponsorship coalitions fell only 20% from the early 1970s to 1995 as compared to the 50% increase in party voting on roll calls, while Nathan Canen and colleagues report that House members are only about 8–10% less likely to join a cosposorship network with a cross-partisan.[18] But there are a number of reasons why we might expect less partisanship on co-sponsorship coalitions than on roll calls, survey responses, or campaign contributions. First, successful legislation generally requires bipartisan coalitions because of the supermajority requirements associated with bicameralism, the filibuster, and the presidential veto.[19] James Curry and Frances Lee have documented that, despite polarization, some bipartisanship tends to be the norm on enacted legislation.[20] So co-sponsors from the other party will generally be helpful in building a successful coalition. Second, opposition partisans may be overrepresented in co-sponsorship coalitions relative to their party's support of the bill. Consider a Republican bill sponsor. If she understands that a modest amount of Democratic support is needed for the bill to pass, a Democratic co-sponsor may be more valuable than an additional Republican. So the sponsor may target those Democrats who might plausibly support the bill. Harbridge defines a bipartisan co-sponsorship coalition as one where 20% of the members are from the opposite party from the original sponsor. She also reports that in recent years the median bill with co-sponsors had around 10 co-sponsors. Thus, targeting two or three opposition party members would be sufficient to classify the median co-sponsored bill as bipartisan given her scheme.

In recent years, several scholars have been using the text from congressional speeches and bills to improve the estimation of ideal points. The logic of using text to estimate ideal points is very similar to that of using roll-call votes. In the roll-call setting, ideological allies are those who vote together. In text analysis, allies are those who talk alike. The ideological content of speeches is identifiable from the fact that liberals and conservatives tend to emphasize distinct phrases and arguments. Conservatives talk about "death taxes," while liberals refer to "estate taxes." Conservatives distinguish between "pro-life" and "pro-abortion," while liberals classify views as "pro-choice" and "anti-abortion."

While one can plausibly estimate ideal points based on text alone, many applications use roll calls and text together to improve upon estimates based on one source or the other. Sean Gerrish and David Blei use roll-call data to help orient and interpret preference estimates based on text, while In Song Kim and coauthors develop procedures to estimate ideal points using text and ideal points together.[21]

Another use of text analysis is to use the text of bills or expert descriptions to help identify the dimensionality of voting. Sean Gerrish and David Blei use a procedure known as topic modeling to estimate the probability that a given bill is related to a particular topic (e.g., foreign policy, regulation, and the like). They then estimate a model where every member has an overall liberal-conservative ideal point that may shift to the left or the right on a given topic.[22] They observe that the level of polarization in the baseline ideal points is greater than polarization from a model that ignores the topic-specific effects. They find, however, considerable variation in polarization and party overlap across topics.[23]

One advantage of incorporating text and speech into ideal point estimates is that ideal point and polarization measures can be extended to news organizations, think tanks, and policy intellectuals.[24] Given the network structure and ideological content of social media usage, data from platforms such as

Facebook and Twitter have emerged as useful sources of information about the preferences of politicians, voters, and other political actors. Pablo Barberá, for example, uses data from Twitter on who follows whom. His statistical model is similar to a roll-call model where "following" is the rough equivalent of "voting for." From the set of members of Congress with Twitter accounts, he is able to produce ideal point measures that correlate very highly with DW-NOMINATE estimates. Importantly, he observes a substantial partisan gap in the Twitter ideal points in the House and very minimal preference overlap in the Senate.[25]

In summary, with the possible exception of analyses of co-sponsorship networks, findings of high and growing polarization are borne out in a very large number of quantitative indicators. While any single measure is subject to many caveats and criticisms, the collection of evidence across a wide variety of data tells almost the same story about the increasing polarization of legislators over the past forty years.

3.4 Do roll-call ideal points really reflect congressional ideology?

A very important question about ideal points, whether measured by roll-call votes, campaign contributions, or speeches, is what exactly they measure. While we often use the shorthand of calling them ideology measures, it is hard to argue for the proposition that DW-NOMINATE or other ideal points are pure measures of legislator ideology. Clearly, partisanship, constituency interests, and regionalism impact the estimates of legislator positions on these scales. It is equally clear that even if the scores were purged of these other factors, the resulting ideological scales would not pass a political philosophy seminar. But this is also true of the "ideologies" that constitute much of the public discourse, or at least the part that goes on outside of elite political magazines.

Nevertheless, I contend that DW-NOMINATE scores largely reflect an ideology-like substance. Let's call this substance *ideo-lite*. Ideo-lite shares two features with ideology. First, ideo-lite shares the ability to link choices across different issues together. Unlike full-strength, political-theory-seminar ideology this requires that the linkage be born of logical deductions from first principles, the issue linkages in ideo-lite may be largely politically and socially constructed. Second, ideo-lite generates consistency across legislative behavior over time, just as we would expect of the full-strength version. Finally, ideo-lite is not reducible to party or constituency. Like ideology, we would expect to see correlations due to the selection effects related to the processes of party affiliation and elections, but ideo-lite has explanatory power even when those factors are accounted for.

There is a substantial amount of evidence that DW-NOMINATE ideal points contain ideo-lite. First, DW-NOMINATE idea points clearly have significant explanatory power for votes across a wide variety of substantive issues. That DW-NOMINATE is also very successful in capturing intra-party divisions suggests that the issue linkages that it uncovers do not simply reflect partisan agendas. Second, ideal point estimates are quite stable for politicians throughout their career. Of course, there are a few prominent examples of politicians whose positions did change, such as John McCain and Kirsten Gillibrand. But for the most part, legislators' ideal points only move significantly if they switch parties (and, of course, party switching is quite rare).[26] Even a member whose constituency changes quite dramatically, either by elevation to the Senate or through major redistricting, rarely changes positions in a significant way. In a very careful study, Keith Poole shows that the assumption that legislators maintain the same ideological position throughout their careers performs just as well statistically as the assumption that legislators are able to change positions in each biennial term.[27]

The second piece of evidence in favor of ideo-lite is that the behavior of legislators deviates in large and systematic ways from the preferences of their average or median constituent. This conclusion persists even when the mismeasurement of constituency interests or preferences is not a concern. For example, senators from the same state rarely vote identically. Most obviously, senators from the same state but different parties, such as Sherrod Brown and Rob Portman of Ohio, vote very differently, and the difference is picked up in their polarized ideal point estimates.

If the two senators are from the same party, they are, of course, more similar. Even here, however, there are differences. Consider California Democrats Diane Feinstein and Barbara Boxer. They not only represented the same state but were first elected by exactly the same electorate on the same day in 1992. In the 113th Senate term, Boxer has a DW-NOMINATE score of -0.486 making her the fifteenth most liberal member of the US Senate. Conversely, Dianne Feinstein's ideal point is just -0.351 making her the thirty-third most liberal.[28] Moreover, there is nothing unusual about this California duo. Seven other states have pairs of senators from the same party whose NOMINATE scores differ at least as much.[29]

House districts, being single-member, do not allow the same natural experiment that is possible for the Senate. It is possible, however, to compare the voting behavior of a member to his or her successor. The same-party replacements of House members can have ideal points that are very different from those of their predecessors. True, a relatively liberal Democrat is likely to be replaced by another liberal Democrat, but the variation in the scores of the same-party replacements is very large. It is about half as large as the total variation of positions within the party.[30] In other words, the ideal point of the outgoing incumbent is at best a crude predictor of the position of the new member even if they are in the same party.

The evidence that ideo-lite is not simply partisanship is also fairly well established. DW-NOMINATE has become widely applied in large part because it has considerable explanatory power beyond simple party indicators. It also does a very good job of explaining internal divisions within the parties. This feature is hard to reconcile with the notion that the DW-NOMINATE dimension reflects "party-ness." Indeed if that were the case, Bernie Sanders would be the pillar of Democratness while Rand Paul and Mike Lee would anchor Republicanness. But in reality, the reason that these senators have extreme DW-NOMINATE scores is that they vote quite often against their partisan colleagues.

3.5 What issues divide Congress the most?

One of the advantages of measuring polarization with DW-NOMINATE as in Figure 3.2 is that the measures provide a summary of the average ideological divisions across all issues. But, of course, this is a bug as well. There is little reason to believe that partisan and ideological differences are equally strong across all issues. Differences in the political context, interest group environment, and the technical details of policy might promote more or less partisan cooperation.

To assess the extent to which polarization has varied over time across issues, John Lapinski undertakes a massive effort to code each roll call from the House for 1877–2010 according to its policy content.[31] He codes bills according to a three-tiered scheme where each top-tier category is divided into subcategories. His top-tier categories and major subcategories were:

1. Sovereignty: immigration, naturalization, civil rights
2. Organization and scope of federal government: government organization, constitutional amendments
3. International affairs: defense, international political economy
4. Domestic affairs: agriculture and food, social policy, planning and resources
5. Miscellaneous

To assess how polarization has varied across these categories, he estimates issue-specific ideal points for all House members serving between 1877 and 2010. From these estimates, he is able to calculate the issue-specific level of polarization for each congressional term.[32]

Across all of his major issues categories, Lapinski reproduces the "U-shape" evident in Figure 3.2. But there is considerable variation in the levels of polarization as well as the magnitude of the recent upward trends. He observes the most pronounced variation in polarization in two of his categories: sovereignty and international affairs. Each of these issue clusters were either bipartisan or organized by cross-partisan coalitions in the middle of the twentieth century, but have become more partisan at a rapid rate since the 1960s. The pattern for domestic affairs is somewhat different. That issue cluster has long been the most partisan and party-defining. So the gaps between the parties were already substantial when they started growing even larger in the 1970s. Because the base level of polarization was already so high, the growth rate has been slower than that in the other areas. As of 2010, Lapinski reports very little difference in the level of polarization across his four non-miscellaneous top-tier categories.

So the answer to what divides Congress seems to be "all of the above."

3.6 Are both parties responsible for polarization?

Figure 3.3 presents a third historical fact about polarization that is important to keep in mind when discussing reform. Rather than a case of both parties moving toward the extremes, polarization over the past forty years has been very asymmetric. It is overwhelmingly associated with the increased movement of Republican legislators to the right. Each new Republican cohort has compiled a more conservative record than the returning cohort. Importantly this has been the case since the

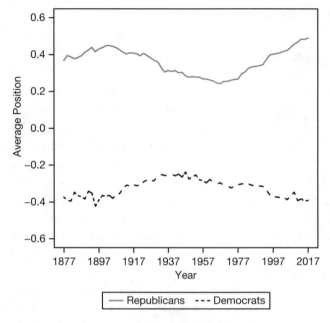

Figure 3.3: Party Positions in the US House 1877–2014 Figure shows average DW-NOMINATE scores by party.

1970s; it is not a reflection of the emergence of the "Tea Party" movement.[33]

The Democratic party has not followed a similar pattern. While some new cohorts are more liberal than the caucus on average, many are more moderate. The slight movement of the Democratic party to the left can be accounted for by the increase of African American, Latino/a, and female legislators in its caucus. From 1971 to 2018, the number of African American Democrats in the House has increased from thirteen to forty-three, the Democratic Latino/a members have grown from four to twenty-nine, and the number of Democratic women went from ten to sixty-two.[34] The liberalism of the representatives of these groups has pushed the average position of the Democrats to the left.[35] The relative position of white, male Democratic party legislators has changed very little.[36]

3.7 Are state legislatures polarized?

The methods cited above can easily be used to estimate the ideal points of state legislators within a specific state.[37] But measurement of polarization in state legislatures has been limited by two important factors. The first is the lack of roll-call voting data across all fifty states for an extended period of time. The second is that ideal point estimates are not generally comparable across states or even chambers within a state. The source of this incomparability follows directly from the discussion of ideal point estimation above.[38] We can determine the relative ideal points of two legislators only to the extent to which we see them voting on the same bills. We identify a legislator as a conservative because he is observed voting with other conservatives more frequently than he is observed voting with moderates, which he does more often than he votes with liberals. But when two legislators serve in different bodies, we cannot make such comparisons. A conservative in the Alabama House is quite different from a conservative in the Massachusetts Senate.

Recently, Boris Shor and I tackled both of these problems to produce measures of state legislative polarization.[39] First, we used a combination of state legislative journals and online records to acquire the roll-call voting record from every state from the 1990s to the present. But because of the incomparability problem, these data are useful only in tracking polarization within particular states, but not its variation across states. To make cross-state comparisons, we use the NPAT.[40] While the NPAT survey could have been used to estimate the ideal points of all respondents, the response rate of the survey is fairly low and thus provides ideal points for only a fraction of state legislators. Consequently, we combine the NPAT data with roll-call voting data. Under the assumption that each legislator's survey responses and roll-call voting reflect the same underlying political preferences, we are able to estimate a common ideological scale for almost all state legislators serving since the 1990s. Since members of Congress also answer the NPAT, our scores can also be compared with those of federal legislators.

Although the Shor-McCarty measures only cover the past twenty-five years, the trajectory of polarization at the state and national levels has been remarkably consistent over that period. Aggregate trends and patterns of polarization at the state level tend to match those of the US House and Senate. Figure 3.4 shows the average difference between Republican and Democratic state legislators for each year on the NPAT scale. The first takeaway is that just like in the US Congress, partisan differences have been growing steadily. Second, the patterns for members of state lower chambers are essentially identical to those of state senators. That state senators have

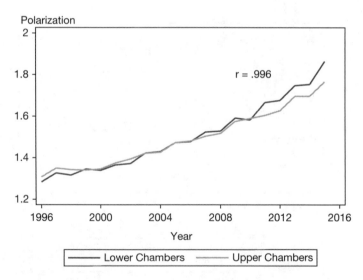

Figure 3.4: Polarization in the US States 1996–2015 Computed from NPAT Common Space Scores scores (Shor and McCarty 2011). The polarization measure is the difference in the mean score for Republicans and the mean score for Democrats for all state legislators by chamber.

larger and presumably more heterogeneous constituencies does not seem to lead to a measurable diminution in the polarization in those bodies.

But importantly, there is significant variation in the levels and trends in polarization across states and regions. Figure 3.5 plots polarization of lower chamber legislators across the four US census regions for the 1996–2015 period. The figure indicates that polarization tends to be lowest in the South (due to more moderate Democratic parties) and the Northeast (due to more moderate Republicans parties). The West and North Central regions have the most polarized parties. Until very recently, the Northeast and the North Central region have witnessed more modest increases in polarization than the South and West.

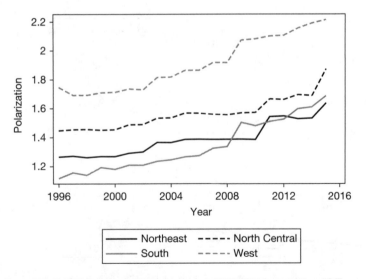

Figure 3.5: Polarization across US Census Regions 1996–2015 Computed from NPAT Common Space Scores scores (Shor and McCarty 2011). The polarization measure is the difference in the mean score for Republicans and the mean score for Democrats for all state legislators serving in lower chambers.

3.8 Are the courts polarized?

Tom Clark applies a polarization measure developed by Joan-Maria Esteban and Debraj Ray to the *judicial common space* Supreme Court justices' ideal points from 1953 to 2004.[41] These scores shows a rise in polarization during the 1950s before falling in the 1960s. There was a dramatic rise in the Nixon Administration following the appointments of Warren Burger, William Rehnquist, and Lewis Powell. Polarization was relatively stable during the 1980s with the appointments of "swing justices" Sandra Day O'Connor and Anthony Kennedy. But polarization returned in the late 1980s and 1990s when Antonin Scalia replaced Burger and Clarence Thomas replaced Thurgood Marshall.[42] These measures show a slight decline in the 2000s.[43]

Other scholars have utilized different metrics for evaluating polarization on the Supreme Court. Brandon Bartels considers trends in margins on disposition votes. Consistent with polarization, his data show an increase in the number of five to four decisions on the court. Yet at the same time, he notes an increase in the number of unanimous votes, indicating what he calls the "polarization paradox."[44] It is this increase in unanimous votes that accounts for the slight decline in Clark's polarization measure. Bartels also provides evidence that fewer justices split votes evenly between liberal and conservative dispositions when they happen to be the swing justice on a case, suggesting an increase in ideological consistency.

Importantly, Supreme Court polarization is both a cause and a consequence of more general polarization. Congressional polarization has resulted in much more ideological conflict over Supreme Court nominations and increased the incentive to appoint ideologically consistent judges. The resulting increased judicial polarization raises the stakes for ideological conflicts over open seats. I take up questions related to these consequences in chapter 7.

3.9 And the media?

In recent years, social scientists have paid substantial attention to measuring so-called media bias. The study of media bias is conceptually tricky as none has yet proposed an objective, workable definition of "unbiased" media. As a result most work has centered on the measurement of the partisan or ideological *slant* of various media outlets. In an early study, Jeff Milyo and Tim Groseclose exploit the fact that both members of Congress and journalists cite the research of think tank scholars.[45] Their key finding is that most media organizations have citation patterns that look much more like those of Democratic legislators than those of Republican legislators. Indeed, only two media outlets had citation patterns that were reflective of legislators that were more conservative than the median, *Fox News Special Report* and the *Washington Times*. Alternatively, *CBS News* and the *New York Times* had citations close to the average Democrat.

Similarly, Matthew Gentzkow and Jesse Shapiro use newspaper articles and congressional speeches to measure the partisan positioning of newspapers.[46] Their estimates come from an analysis of the propensity of newspapers and legislators to use partisan words or phrases such as the use of "death tax" as a description of the estate tax. By assuming that a legislator and newspaper who use the same set of partisan phrases share an ideology, Gentzkow and Shapiro measure the ideology of newspapers on the same scale as legislators. The authors use the 2004 Bush presidential vote in each district as a measure of legislator ideology.[47] Thus, their newspaper ideology ratings are denominated in 2004 Bush vote shares as well. Among large newspapers, these scores range from around 0.38 for the *Atlanta Constitution* to 0.52 for the *Daily Oklahoman*. In terms of the 2004 Bush vote, this is the difference between Vermont's at-large congressional district and Peter King's Long Island congressional district. So there are clear differences across newspapers, but the ideological range is small compared to that of Congress. It is tempting of course to interpret Gentzkow and Shapiro's estimates as evidence that newspapers lean to the left. The fact that a newspaper article reads more like a Democratic speech than a Republican speech does not need imply that such a slant arises through some sort of bias. If Republicans were to use more ideologically loaded terms in their speech, a news outlet that used neutral terminology would appear left wing.

3.10 What have we learned?

The evidence that the political parties have polarized over the past forty years is quite strong. Whether one considers measures related to roll-call voting, campaign contributions, the discourse of congressional speeches, or social media usage, there is strong evidence of greater and greater distinctiveness of the parties. Moreover, these divisions seem to have permeated political elites at all levels. We find considerable evidence of polarization in state legislatures, courts, and the media.

A second important finding is that polarization has coincided with a large drop in the dimensionality of voting in Congress. At one time, different public policy issues could produce very different support coalitions in Congress. Now almost all political conflicts pit liberals versus conservatives with moderates playing the pivotal role of determining which side is bigger.

Finally, the evidence suggests that polarization has been asymmetric with the Republicans shifting to the right at a rate greater than the Democrats moving to the left.

4

IS THE PUBLIC POLARIZED?

Given the widespread belief that the American public is deeply divided into Red and Blue camps who view each other with disdain and distrust, many readers may be surprised to learn that there is still a vigorous academic debate as to whether the public is nearly as polarized as the political elites.

At the heart of this continuing debate is how best to interpret two very well-established facts about the American electorate. The first fact is that the frequency at which Americans express extreme public policy positions on surveys has not budged over the past four decades. In fact, most Americans still indicate moderate or centrist positions, even on very divisive issues such as abortion and sexuality.[1] In other words, there is very little survey evidence of overall voter polarization as it was defined in chapter 2.

The second fact, however, is that the expressed policy preferences of voters are increasingly associated with their partisan identifications (PID). If we know the PID of a voter today, we can much better predict her positions on economic policy, abortion, guns, and a whole host of other issues. A generation ago this would not have been the case. As a consequence of this high association between party identification and policy positions, the average position of a Democratic voter increasingly diverges from that of a Republican on most issue areas. But as Morris Fiorina has stressed, such changes may not be driven primarily through polarization but simply be the response of the voters to polarized parties. As voters observe increasingly polarized parties, they may adjust their partisan loyalties (or their issue positions) to be better *sorted* in partisan terms.

This interpretation is not without its critics, most notably Alan Abramowitz.[2] Abramowitz concedes that many voters still choose moderate positions on surveys but stresses that such voters are typically not very informed about or engaged in politics. Those voters who are more engaged in politics tend increasingly to choose relatively extreme positions and to identify with the party that supports those views. This polarization of the politically active contributes to the polarization of the elites.

The distinctions between the Fiorina and Abramowitz accounts can be a little subtle at times. Fiorina's sorting story is not inconsistent with the observation that those voters who express moderate views are disengaged from politics. He would argue that this disengagement is itself another voter reaction to elite polarization. When moderate voters see that no party is representing their views, disengagement may be a reasonable response. Abramowitz's argument is more consistent with the view that disengaged voters give moderate responses because they are disengaged. So, as we will see, the proper resolution of the debate revolves around how we interpret "moderate" survey responses.[3]

4.1 How is it even plausible that the public is not polarized?

In one of the first systematic studies of the polarization of public opinion, the sociologist Paul DiMaggio and his collaborators examine responses to regularly repeated policy and attitude questions from the American National Election Study and the General Social Survey.[4] These data allow the researchers to assess whether public opinions and attitudes have become more polarized in the sense of increasing the variance or bimodality of responses. The study considers a number of policy and social attitudes as well as feeling thermometers toward groups such as blacks, the poor, liberals, and conservatives. They observe very little evidence for polarization within the general population. Indeed on general measures of ideology, they find a downward trend in the variation and no trend in the bimodality of responses. When they examined issues separately, they found few examples of polarization. In fact, they find that Americans have become more united on issues related to the role of women, racial integration, and views on crime and justice. The only issues that had become more divisive were abortion and feelings toward the poor.

The authors also examined whether opinion differences across groups were growing. They encountered no such evidence. They report that attitudes were converging across age groups, education levels, racial groups, and religious affiliations. The only groups that were clearly diverging were the adherents of the two parties.[5]

Morris Fiorina also provides a number of important pieces of evidence that run counter to the mass polarization narrative.[6] First, he notes that public opinion and cultural values do not differ greatly between Red and Blue states. He also notes that the level of issue disagreements between Republican and Democratic voters, while growing, is quite small.

In one of his more compelling demonstrations, he shows that even abortion views have been very stable for many decades. Since 1972, the General Social Survey (GSS) has asked respondents about the situations under which they would find an abortion morally acceptable.[7] Voters have long been supportive of abortion when the health of the women is seriously jeopardized. Approximately 90% of respondents have supported it in every GSS survey since 1972. Support for more controversial exceptions, such as those based on the marital status or income of the mother, have garnered a consistent 40–50% support since the 1970s. Were attitudes polarizing we would have expected more support for the extreme positions—a total ban or unrestricted access—to increase. That has not happened.

A recent study by Seth Hill and Chris Tausanovitch bolsters Fiorina's main claim. Using methods similar to those used to calculate legislative ideal points to compute voter ideal points based on data from the American National Election Study (ANES), Hill and Tausanovitch produce very little evidence that variance in voter ideology increased substantially from 1956 to 2012. In fact, they find that the standard deviation of voter ideal points was lower in the 2000s than it was in the late 1960s and early 1970s.[8]

Scholars have also explored other phenomena related to polarization in the general public. One such manifestation is Philip Converse's notion of belief constraint.[9] Recall that beliefs are considered constrained to the extent that holding a position on one issue is correlated with holding positions on other issues. Delia Baldassarri and Andrew Gelman argue that increased belief constraint can produce a form of polarization.[10] Assume there are two issues: taxes and guns. Suppose that on each issue there is little polarization: most voters prefer a moderate position while a smaller number support more extreme policies. As long as preferences on taxes and guns are not correlated, the overall polarization across issues is quite low in that the number of citizens that are extreme on both issues is very low. Now assume that issue positions are more constrained so that positions on taxes and guns are highly correlated. Now a tax extremist is likely to be a gun extremist and vice versa. So the increase in constraint increases the percentage of consistent extremists, which Baldassari and Gelman argue is a form of polarization.

The authors use the data from the ANES to assess changes in the measured constraint in individual issue positions. They measure constraint as the correlation of issue positions with other issue positions and with party and ideological identification. They find little evidence that correlations of positions across pairs of issues have grown.[11]

As previously noted, this evidence and its interpretations have been challenged by Alan Abramowitz.[12] He emphasizes that while the overall public appears moderate, those citizens most engaged in politics are quite polarized. He presents considerable evidence that when one focuses on the most engaged voters—those who vote and are interested in politics, the responses to many policy questions and ideological scales are more bimodal. He does not, however, demonstrate that the bimodality of engaged voters has increased.[13] Abramowitz also observes considerably higher levels of issue constraint among more engaged voters. Not surprisingly, these more sophisticated voters have a better understanding of what issue positions go together. Evidence of trends is provided in the work of Baldassari and Gelman who show that the issue consistency of highly engaged voters has increased substantially more than that of those who are disengaged. Clearly, that the voters most likely to vote and to contribute to campaigns are polarized can be an important source of the polarization of elected officials.

But Abramowitz's main focus is on the increasingly divergent policy views of partisan voters. He notes the large increase in the correlation of party identification (party ID) and ideological self-placement, which almost doubled between 1972 and 2004.[14] Correlations between party ID and positions on several individual issues grew as well. But as I previously noted, increases in such an association may not reflect voter polarization but rather be a response of voters to increasingly polarized parties. So it is necessary to drill down into the data much deeper to determine whether these patterns reflect polarization or partisan sorting.

4.2 Is the public moderate?

One of the arguments against voter polarization is based on the fact that the number of people responding "moderate or middle of the road" on the ANES has not declined over time. If you interpret such voters to be true political centrists, it would be hard to conclude that voters have polarized very much.

But there are reasons to be suspicious of whether these self-identified moderates are committed centrists. Donald Kinder and Nathan Kalmoe analyze the responses to the 1965 and 1973 waves of the Youth-Parent Socialization Panel Study that asks a battery of questions designed to measure political information in addition to the standard ideology self-placement question.[15] Kinder and Kalmoe classify voters into three groups based on their responses to the ideological identification scale. The three categories included (1) those who considered themselves liberals or conservatives, (2) moderates, and (3) those who did not think of themselves in these terms. They find that in terms of political information, political involvement, and education, moderates are not statistically distinguishable from the non-ideological group. The most straightforward interpretation of these observations is that most if not all moderate respondents are non-ideological rather than committed devotees of the middle way. As Kinder and Kalmoe put it, "all things considered, the 'moderate' categories seems less an ideological destination than a refuge for the innocent and confused." If this interpretation is correct, we should take far less comfort in findings such as Fiorina's showing high and persistent support for moderate positions.

4.3 What is the evidence in favor of increased voter sorting?

Unfortunately, there is no simple way of settling the polarization versus sorting argument definitively. But many scholars have tackled the question in a variety of ways. Recall that there are two possible ways in which voters can become better sorted into the parties. First, there is ideology-driven sorting in which voters choose a new party affiliation that better aligns with their issues preferences. Second, there is party-driven sorting where voters switch their issue positions to correspond with those of their party. In a prominent study,

Matthew Levendusky uses panel data to identify both types of sorting.[16] In his data, the same voters are interviewed in 1992, 1994, and 1996. He isolates those voters who became sorted between 1992 and 1996 and assess whether it was ideology-driven or party-driven. For example, a Democratic voter with a conservative opinion can become sorted either by becoming a Republican or by changing the opinion to a liberal one. With the exception of abortion attitudes, he finds considerably more evidence for party-driven than ideology-driven sorting. Another exception to this pattern is white southerners who did overwhelmingly abandon the Democratic party for a Republican party more consonant with their views. These observations may, however, underestimate the role of ideology-driven sorting. Since the study was based on people who were already eligible to vote in 1992, it cannot capture the ideology-driven sorting of new voters. Second, it does not address the issue of salience. Voters are likely to switch parties only when it will bring them into better alignment with their party on very important issues.

Levendusky also uses the 1992–1994–1996 ANES panel study to assess polarization.[17] In a panel study, polarization would be observed when Democrats became more liberal from one election to another while Republicans became more conservative. He finds very limited evidence of such effects. Between 1992 and 1996, only 7% of Democrats became more liberal than could be accounted for by measurement error. But 4% became more conservative. More Republicans moved in a measurably liberal direction (4%) than moved in a conservative direction (3%).

Thomas Carsey and Geoffrey Layman use the same panel study to better understand the conditions under which voters engage in party-driven or ideology-driven sorting.[18] They argue that ideology- or issue-driven sorting should occur when voters are aware that the party diverges from their position on some issue that the individual finds important. Conversely, party-driven sorting can occur when voters are aware of partisan differences on an issue but do not attach much importance to them. In such cases, voters will be more inclined to bring their issue preferences in line with their partisan commitments.

In support of this argument, Carsey and Layman estimate a statistical model where issue positions in 1994 are associated with issue positions and partisanship in 1992. Similarly, partisanship in 1994 is assumed to also be related to past issue positions and partisanship. Consistent with their expectations, they conclude that voters who are unaware of partisan issue differences exhibit stable partisanship but less stable issue preferences. Moreover, they show no signs of party- or issue-driven sorting. Those who are aware of non-salient differences have greater stability in issue preferences than the unaware but are somewhat more likely to move their positions to be better aligned with their party. The final group, those aware of salient difference, engage in party- and issue-driven sorting at roughly equal rates.

Other scholars have addressed the question of sorting by examining trends in issue consistency and constraint. Baldassarri and Gelman argue that an increase in pair-wise issue position correlations unrelated to party ID would be evidence of a polarization effect.[19] On the other hand, if issue positions were to become correlated only because individual positions were increasingly tied to partisanship, sorting would be implicated. Consistent with the sorting hypothesis, they estimate that the average correlations of issue positions and party ID have grown substantially since the 1970s. This is also true of the correlations between issues and ideological self-placement. They interpret the growing correlations as evidence that the changes in issue constraint should be "interpreted as an illusory adjustment of citizens to the rejuvenated partisanship of the political elite" (p. 441).

Recall that Hill and Tausanovitch found little evidence of overall voter polarization between the 1950s and today. But consistent with sorting, they did find that partisan attachments explain an increasing amount of the variance in their voter ideal point measures.[20]

4.4 Why does it matter whether voters are sorted but not polarized?

In many ways it doesn't. Later when I discuss some of the implications of sorting, we will see that the effects may be exactly what we would expect from polarization. But the differences matter for two very important reasons. Recall that a key distinction between sorting and polarization involves the direction of causality between elite and mass behavior. One claim is that mass polarization is a very important cause for the increased conflict at the elite level. But sorting suggests that voters are responding somewhat predictably given the polarized set of choices that the parties have placed before them.

4.5 Is sorting a good thing or a bad thing?

Yes.

Clearly, some level of voter sorting is a precondition for political parties to play their representative function. A true Big Tent party cannot put firm programmatic commitments before the voter. At best it can promise, "elect us and we'll sort it out among our factions." Thus, a party that represents all viewpoints represents none.

But too much sorting can be problematic. In a sorted electorate, there are fewer issue positions that can gain bipartisan support. Consequently, partisan politicians will find it much harder to form cross-party coalitions. Second, while sorting and polarization are different, sorting can clearly contribute to elite polarization. Politicians who must garner support from a partisan constituency for nomination will struggle to maintain moderate or heterodox positions. Finally, to the extent to which partisanship has become a salient social identity, social and policy sorting can induce higher levels of partisan animus.[21]

4.6 What issues are the public sorted on?

In a study using the ANES, Geoffrey Layman and Thomas Carsey use a technique called factor analysis to generate estimates of voter conservatism on distinctive clusters of issues.[22] They identify three clusters of issues:

- Social welfare issues: support for government spending, government health insurance, tax rates, and the like.
- Racial issues: Support for civil rights, racial equality, integration, fair housing, affirmative action
- Cultural issues: Abortion, sexuality, gender roles, drug legalization

With estimates of voter positions on these three scales, Layman and Carsey are able to assess distinctive trends in partisan ideological divergence from 1972 to 2000. The difference in the conservatism of partisans on social welfare issues was much higher than that for the other two issue groups. But there was no trend toward greater divergence on that issue. On cultural issues, there was no divergence in the 1970s but substantial divergence by the 2000s. Racial issues represent a middle case. Republicans were more conservative on these issues in 1972 and that gap has grown.

Consistent with the studies previously discussed, Layman and Carsey observe that the correlation between individual positions on these scales grew rapidly among strong partisans. Thus, they argue that the macro changes in partisan divergence are best captured by a model of "conflict extension," where the parties stake out distinctive positions on a larger number of issues rather than seeking to replace old issue cleavages with new ones.

4.7 Is it the economy, stupid?

Devin Caughey, James Dunham, and Christopher Warshaw use responses to almost all national survey questions on economic issues. They use a statistical procedure to estimate the ideological positions of defined subpopulations of voters.[23] In their study, these groups are defined by party and state of residence. Thus, they generate estimates of the liberalism of Texas Democrats, California Republicans, New York independents, and so on in each year since 1946. With proper weighting, these estimates can be aggregated up to a measure of the liberalism of national Democrats, Republicans, and independents. They find that sorting has produced a party ideological gap that is now four times larger than the one observed in 1946. Consistent with other studies, however, they encounter little evidence of a clear trend toward polarization. Their estimated variance of ideology in the mass public is lower in 2012 than it was in the late 1970s and early 1980s.

4.8 Does polarization reflect a "culture war"?

It is hard not to notice the sharp partisan divisions over issues such as abortion, homosexuality, and gun rights. The intensity of these conflicts has led many to speculate that they represent the primary axis of conflict in American politics as well as the drivers of polarization. Stephen Ansolabehere, Jonathan Rodden, and James Snyder assess the claims that moral and cultural issues have come to define the partisan cleavage.[24] They use the ANES and the GSS to measure issue scales for voters from 1977 to 2004. Echoing findings of Fiorina, they observe little polarization on either of these issues. The distribution of economic preferences is bell-shaped while the moral issues dimension is somewhat more bimodal, indicating a slight overrepresentation of extreme views.

To measure the relative salience of the two issues, these authors conduct a regression model to determine which issue scale is most closely associated with voting for a Republican candidate or identifying with the Republican party. Based on this analysis, they conclude that voters place more than twice as much weight on economic issues as moral and cultural issues when casting their ballots and identifying with a party. While the importance of moral issues has clearly been growing over time, they do not come close to supplanting economic issues as the primary consideration. Perhaps more surprising is that the relative weight of economic and social issues does not vary across social groups. All voters, even religious and rural voters, place more weight on economic issues than moral ones. Similarly, Larry Bartels concludes that voter preferences on government spending are much more predictive of presidential votes between 1984 and 2004 than are preferences on abortion or on women's role in society.[25] Importantly, he observes that this is true of both college-educated voters and voters without such degrees. This evidence stand against a commonly-held view that downscale voters are especially driven by cultural issues. In a detailed analysis of the 2004 election, he finds that it is college-educated voters that place approximately equal weight on economic and cultural issues.

While the role of the "hot button" issues in policy polarization of the voters may be modest, there is evidence of a much greater role of these concerns in the affective polarization of voters that I discuss next. Not surprisingly, when voters perceive the out-party as having morally repugnant views or overrepresenting out-social groups, partisan animosity increases.[26] Furthermore, as Dan Hopkins has argued, preferences on social issues tend to exhibit more geographical variation, which may in turn heighten their electoral salience given our reliance on geographically based first-past-the-post elections.[27]

4.9 What is affective polarization?

While much of the debate about mass polarization has focused on whether voters' policy preferences and ideological orientations have become more extreme, another group of scholars have focused on whether parties and partisanship have become more salient markers of social identity and whether this has resulted in greater levels of partisan conflict. These scholars have stressed that "affect, not ideology" is responsible for high levels of party conflict.

The literature on affective polarization has generally drawn on the Social Identity Theory (SIT) developed by Henri Tajfel.[28] SIT is based on the following precepts:

1. Individuals want to maintain or enhance their self-esteem.
2. Social groups are associated with negative or positive connotations.
3. The evaluation of one's own group is determined by comparisons with reference groups. Positive discrepancy in the comparisons between the in-group and the out-group generate high self-esteem; negative ones lower self-esteem.

From these principles, SIT predicts that "pressures to evaluate one's own group positively through in-group/out-group comparisons lead groups to attempt to differentiate themselves from one another."[29] In the application to political parties, scholars have postulated that political parties are salient social identities and that citizens derive self-esteem and satisfaction from the relative success and status of their party compared to that of the other. It is further postulated that voters will be biased in the process of political information focusing on interpretations that favor their own party and disfavor the out-party. The combination of these strong identities and formation of biased beliefs is hypothesized to generate affective polarization between the parties.[30]

In an influential study, Shanto Iyengar, Gaurav Sood, and Yphtach Lelkes empirically examine the implications of SIT on affective polarization and suggest that affective polarization is a more proximate source of partisan conflict in the United States than policy or ideological polarization.[31] They argue that "partisan affect is inconsistently related to policy preferences and that the relationship between partisan affect and policy attitudes hasn't notably strengthened over time."

Among their most memorable findings is that support of partisans for inter-party marriages of their offspring have fallen dramatically over the past several decades. In 2008, almost 50% of Republicans and over 30% of Democrats reported that they would be upset if their children married some one from the other party. These numbers were negligible in 1960.

The primary analysis of Iyengar et al. focuses on partisan feeling thermometers as measures of partisan affect.[32] Using these thermometer scores for each party from the American National Election Study, they show that the average rating for the respondents' own party hovered from seventy to seventy-five since the 1970s. The Democrats have viewed their party slightly more warmly than have Republicans. The major change over time is how partisans evaluate members of the other party. In the 1970s, the average evaluation of opposite party members was in the high forties. By 2008, these numbers had dropped to the mid-thirties. There is very little difference across parties. Democrats rate Republicans as coolly as Republicans rate Democrats. To support their argument of increasing affective polarization, Iyengar et al. estimate a statistical model that predicts the net (own party minus out-party) thermometer rating on a set of variables related to partisanship and issue preferences. After controlling for a set of other variables, they show that the correlation between an individual's strength of party identification and the net thermometer rating increased modestly between 1988 and 2004. But the percentage of strong partisans did not budge over this time. The percentage of strong Democrats was 18% in 1988 and 17% in 2004. For Republicans those numbers were 14% and 16% respectively.[33] So strong partisan ID can only account for a relatively small part of the trend in affective polarization.

They also estimate correlations between the net thermometer rating and issue scales they constructed for voters' preferences on economic and cultural issues. The economic scales include questions about spending on social security and other government services, government-provided health insurance, and the government's role in guaranteeing jobs and living standards. The cultural scales cover abortion, gay rights, and gender equality. Surprisingly, Iyengar et al. observe almost no correlation between the cultural scale and affective polarization. They do find, however, that economic policy preferences correlated with the net thermometer ratings. In 1988, the most economically liberal Democrats rated the Democratic party twenty points better against the Republican party than the most conservative Democrats. The equivalent gap between economically conservative and liberal Republicans was twelve points. In 2004, both of the predicted effects were nineteen thermometer points. Iyengar et al. downplay the role of ideology in the increase in affective polarization since the correlations did not increase as significantly as those for strong party identification. But they do not account for any trends in economic policy preferences that might account for increased affective polarization. While they do not report the trend in their economic conservatism measure, their scales are similar to those used by Layman and Carsey who document a very large increase in economic conservatism among Republican voters.[34] Thus, it is plausible that a substantial share of the increase in affective party polarization among Republicans can be attributed to an increase in economic conservatism.[35]

In follow-up work with Sean Westwood, Iyengar demonstrates that the effects of affective polarization are not simply attitudinal.[36] Partisans exhibit discriminatory behavior against opposing partisans at levels exceeding discrimination based on race. Moreover, this discrimination is manifest on nonpolitical behaviors. For example, the authors report the results of an experiment where respondents were asked to rate job candidates based on their resume. In the experiment, the partisanship, race, and qualifications of the applicant were randomized.[37] Partisanship played a very decisive role in which job candidate was preferred. Partisan subjects chose a co-partisan candidate 80% of the time. But partisanship was not simply a tiebreaker. Subjects chose the co-partisan at very high rates even when he was the less qualified candidate. Race played a much smaller role in the resume evaluations. Both white and African American subjects chose the black candidates more often than the white candidate, with African Americans choosing the in-group candidate 18 percentage points more often.[38]

Not all the evidence about affective polarization is consistent with accounts based solely on partisan identification. Yphtach Lelkes conducted a survey experiment where respondents were randomly assigned to learn about a political candidate's ideology (and its extremity) or partisanship or both.[39] Importantly, the information about ideology was communicated through the policy positions of the candidate rather than ideological labels. Lelkes finds that a respondent's evaluations are much more affected by the candidate's ideology than her party affiliation. Information on party affiliation changed the thermometer evaluations about nine points on a hundred-point scale. But learning that a candidate was an ideological extremist moved the thermometers twenty-three points.

Respondents tended to reward extremists and punish moderate candidates of their own party. But the biggest negative affect was against extremists of the other party. Interestingly, learning that an out-party was a moderate had no effect on the thermometer ratings. Finally, the effects of policy positions are not reduced when respondents are also provided information about party. So respondents appear not to be using ideology as a proxy for party.

Lelkes's findings are consistent with several other studies. For example, using the ANES, Steven Webster and Alan Abramowitz show that opinions on social welfare issues have polarized, and opinions on those issues are increasingly predictive of affective evaluations of each party and its presidential candidates.[40] Preferences about abortion and gay rights had considerably less effect on these evaluations. Their own survey experiments show that ideological distance influences feelings of the out-party and its candidates. Respondents were shown to prefer an out-party moderate over an out-party candidate with unknown ideology, who in turn was preferred to an out-party extremist. The Webster and Abramowitz experiment differs from that of Lelkes in that they randomize ideological labels in addition to policy positions. Jon Rogowski and Joseph Sutherland get similar results from an experiment that uses only ideological labels.[41] These authors also provide non-experimental evidence that ideology is related to affective polarization from data on evaluations of US senators. There are considerably larger differences in the thermometer rating of opposite party senators when they have large differences in their DW-NOMINATE scores. Taken together these results seem to suggest that affective partisan polarization is largely driven by evaluations of the ideologies associated with the parties rather than *partisan* social identification.

Of course, these results do not necessarily rule out a role for other social identities in driving affective polarization. Lilliana Mason embraces the notion that affective polarization is driven by both social and ideological factors.[42] The primary dynamic in her story is the process of party sorting. As partisans become more sorted, the social and ideological differentiation of the parties is heightened, inducing greater levels of inter-party dislike. She tests this argument by demonstrating that partisans who are correctly sorted in ideological terms (i.e., conservative Republicans and liberal Democrats) report higher net thermometer ratings. She also observes that sorted partisans report greater numbers of likes and fewer numbers of dislikes for their own party relative to the out-party, engage in more political activism, and feel more anger toward the out-party presidential candidate. In a subsequent study with Julie Wronski, Mason shows that partisans who identify strongly with the constituent groups (e.g., racial and ethnic minorities and liberals for Democrats, and whites, Christians, and conservatives for Republicans) of their party exhibit higher levels of partisanship and report higher own-party thermometer ratings.[43]

4.10 What have we learned?

While it may come as a surprise to many readers, there is no strong consensus on whether there has been any meaningful polarization among ordinary voters. Moderate responses to survey questions continue to be quite common as does self-identification as an ideological moderate. But these optimistic findings are somewhat undercut by the research that questions whether these "moderate" voters are centrist in any principled sense, or are just simply confused and disengaged. When one looks at the more engaged and sophisticated electorate, there is considerably more evidence of polarizing trends.

While debates over polarization continue, there is little doubt about the extent to which voters have become much better sorted along ideological and social identity lines. Conservatives are increasingly identified as Republicans and liberals identified as Democrats. Groups such as African Americans, Latinos, evangelicals, and working-class men are increasingly aligned with parties. As a result, both parties' constituencies are more homogeneous.

While there is a tendency to view sorting as far less pernicious than polarization, it has been associated with a number of detrimental changes to American politics. No longer do elected officials face the diverse partisan constituencies that might give them leeway to make important cross-party concessions and compromises. Ideologically sorted partisan activists, donors, and primary voters stand ready to sanction any such transgressions. Second, while early research stressed partisanship as the fundamental identity underlying affective partisanship, more recent work by Llekes, Mason,

Abramowitz, and others suggests that social and ideological sorting is the proximate cause of cross-partisan hostility. While partisanship may be emerging as an important social identity, it is one built upon a large number of other group and ideological conflicts.

5

WHAT ARE THE CAUSES
OF POLARIZATION?

Much of the academic interest in polarization focuses on trying to uncover its *causes*. Since the underlying idea of causation is so important for these arguments, it is worth stopping to address the question of what it means to cause polarization.

It has become customary for social scientists to think about causation in terms of counterfactuals. We say event X causes outcome Y if and only if Y would not have occurred absent X. With respect to polarization, we would say that an economic, social, or political factor caused polarization if and only if polarization would not have occurred without it. Clearly it is hard to sustain such claims since we do not get to observe the counterfactual scenarios in order to determine whether polarization occurs or not. So there will be a fair amount of uncertainty associated with any claim like "the Southern Realignment," "gerrymandering," or "immigration" caused polarization.

Clearly, we can think about different aspects of causation. We can say X caused polarization if the ideological gap between the parties would not have grown if X had not occurred. But we might also claim Z caused polarization if polarization would not have been as severe in the absence of Z. We might rephrase this second claim, however, as "Z contributed to polarization." As we will learn over the next couple of chapters, social scientists have been far better at identifying such contributing factors than we have been at identifying the ultimate causes of polarization.

In the next few questions, I lay out some patterns in the data that I believe any argument about "causes" of polarization needs to take into account.

5.1 Why was polarization so low from the 1930s to the 1960s?

The simple answer is that many of the factors that we associate with our contemporary polarized politics were not present in the middle of the twentieth century. Perhaps most importantly, in the aftermath of the Great Depression and World War II, a bipartisan consensus in favor of an expanded role of the federal government took hold. For sure, the Republican party was less supportive of many features of the new American welfare state than were Democrats, but the growing popularity of the safety net precluded wholesale opposition of the sort we have observed in recent years. For example, while there were many very partisan disagreements over the details of the Medicare program when it was debated in 1965, a slight majority of Republicans supported the bill on final passage in the House while fourteen out of thirty-two GOP senators voted for it. Contrast that outcome with the voting on the Affordable Care Act (ObamaCare) in 2010. On final passage, the bill received no support from Republican legislators.

Other social and political factors may also have contributed to bipartisan coalitions. The postwar era was one of rapid growth at all levels of the income distribution. Thus, income inequality and economic stagnation were not issues that shaped politics in the same way they do today.

But there are obviously less salutatory features of the middle twentieth century that limited partisan polarization. First, the New Deal Democratic coalition of northern liberals and southern conservatives straddled the issue of civil rights for African Americans and worked to keep the issue largely off of the public agenda. Second, because non-European immigration to the United States was severely limited in the 1920s, the nation became much more ethically homogeneous, which limited the potential for ethnic conflict.

5.2 Can the polarization of the late nineteenth century be compared to what we see today?

Recall Figure 3.2, which shows that Congress was very polarized from the end of Reconstruction to the 1920s. Thus, it is natural to ask what we might learn about our contemporary era from the earlier one. In terms of broader social and economic trends, the two eras had some important similarities. First, both eras were marked by dramatic rises in economic and wealth inequality. Both eras have been called Gilded Ages. In general, the different parties represented constituencies on opposing sides of this divide. The Republicans tended to be the party of business and the middle classes while Democrats represented industrial labor and agrarian interests. Of course, then as now, there were exceptions to this pattern—most notably wealthy backers of the Democratic party.

Both eras were marked by intense party competition where both parties were positioned to win control of either branch of the federal government.[1] The similarities are striking. Between 1872 and 1920, partisan control of the House switched seven times while the Senate switched three times. The GOP has a modest advantage in presidential elections (9 to 4). Over a similar stretch of time from 1968 to 2016, House control switched only three times but the Senate switched eight times. The GOP won eight of the thirteen presidential elections.

The nature of the ideological conflict is quite different across the eras. Whereas today, the pro-business orientation of the GOP leads them to oppose expansions of federal power, the post-Reconstruction Republicans were proponents of centralization in order to promote greater economic development. Whereas the modern GOP tends toward free trade, nineteenth-century Republicans were unified in their support for high protective tariffs to insulate industry from foreign competition. Only on issues where federal power threatened industrial expansion, such as railroad regulation, did the GOP adopt the anti-statist position. Finally, the post-bellum Republicans were the strongest supporters of civil rights for African Americans.

Frances Lee argues, however, that the policy differences between the two parties during the post-bellum era were not very substantial and therefore the divisions between the parties evidenced on roll-call votes primarily reflect partisan conflict over patronage rather than ideological polarization.[2] In addition to a review of the historical work on the era, Lee shows that roll calls on several non-ideological partisan issues such as patronage and contested elections were as common and fit the DW-NOMINATE model as well as the supposed ideological ones related to the tariff and public works.

In my rejoinder to her arguments, however, I note that the structure of roll-call voting during this period was remarkably stable, especially the intra-party cleavages. A right-leaning Republican in one term tends to be a right-leaning one in the next.[3] A leftist Democratic tends to continue to be a leftist throughout his career. And moderates tend to stay in the middle. To demonstrate, I correlate static NOMINATE scores of members across pairs of congressional terms. Over the entire period, the correlation for the House is consistently above 0.9. More importantly I show that the within-party correlations are quite substantial. For Democrats, the correlation often exceeds 0.8. The Republican correlation is a little lower—around 0.5.[4] If "party" and "partisanship" were the only issues that mattered, it would be hard to understand why internal party coalitions were so stable.

5.3 What is the Southern Realignment and why did it happen?

When V.O. Key penned his classic *Southern Politics in State and Nation*, the Democratic party was monolithic in its control of southern local politics and was the only relevant intermediary between southerners and national politics.[5] The southern Republican party was, ironically, a more liberal alternative, but one available only to voters in the mountainous, impoverished regions of Virginia, Kentucky, and Tennessee. The Democratic dominance of the South combined with the congressional seniority system and the party's presidential nomination rule requiring a two-thirds majority (in force until 1936) guaranteed that national Democrats would be responsive to the interests of its southern wing and be cautious about upsetting the cross-regional coalition.

With the possible exception of partisan polarization, no other change to the American polity is as important as the transformation of the southern United States from the core of the Democratic party to the reddest of Republican strongholds. This national realignment began with a shift in presidential voting, starting with the strong southern support of the Goldwater candidacy in 1964. By 1972, the South was solidly Republican. The only time after 1964 that a Democratic presidential candidate performed better in the South than in the North was 1976, when Jimmy Carter, a governor from the Deep South, defeated Gerald Ford. Bill Clinton, another southern governor, did relatively well in the South, but he won his two elections on the basis of northern votes. By 2000, Al Gore, another southern Democratic presidential nominee, even lost his home state.

The realignment moved slowly down the ballot. Southern Republicans gradually increased their numbers in Congress, but they did not obtain a majority of southern seats in both the House and Senate until the 1994 elections. State and local politics long seemed immune to the Republican advance. Nevertheless, by 2017, the Democratic party had lost control of all twenty-six southern state legislatures.

There is an extensive literature in political science devoted to uncovering the primary causes of this major shift in the partisan loyalties of southern whites and the resulting partisan cleavage on issues related to race. The conventional narrative is that of Edward Carmines and James Stimson.[6] These authors note that prior to the 1960s, the national parties did not take clear and distinctive positions on issues related to the civil rights of African Americans. From the origins of the party and the Civil War, Republicans had traditionally been the more progressive party on race relations, but they rarely prioritized those issues especially after African American voters moved their support toward the Democratic party during the New Deal. National Democratic leaders were hamstrung by the need to maintain the coalition with the segregationist South. As a result of the lack of clear partisan differentiation, Carmines and Stimson argue that the racial policy preferences of white voters did not align very well with their partisan identities.

This partisan configuration on the issue was upset in the late 1950s when racially liberal northern Democrats won enough congressional seats to overturn the bisectional bargain and to push for stronger civil rights legislation. When Republican conservatives such as Barry Goldwater opposed civil rights legislation as an unwarranted federal intrusion on local affairs, Republican prospects among southern whites improved. As the party elites realigned on racial issues, the public eventually followed, leading to the defection of conservative southern whites from the Democratic to Republican party.

Recently, however, Eric Schickler provides a wealth of new evidence that calls into question the timing and structure of the traditional account.[7] He argues that the racial realignment began much earlier in the 1930s and 1940s as African Americans and their labor allies in the Congress of Industrial Organizations worked with state parties outside of the South to address policies related to racial inequality. To support these claims, Schickler shows that the correlations between economic liberalism, racial liberalism, and Democratic party identification began to appear in the 1930s and grew stronger through the 1960s. It was during that decade that the pressure from these state and local parties and activists forced the national Democratic party to take a stronger stand on Jim Crow, which ultimately triggered the defection of conservative white southerners into the Republican party.

5.4 Why did southern whites move to the GOP?

There is also an extensive literature in political science and economics trying to explain how and why southern whites switched their allegiances to the GOP. There are several contending explanations.

First, the realignment could have been a simple normalization of southern politics. Once the old rationale of the solid Democratic South (maintenance of segregation) ceased to be relevant, southern whites aligned their partisanship in ways that were similar to the alignments in the non-South. So economic and social groups that supported the GOP outside the South moved toward the party in the South. An obvious concern about the normalization argument is that it would not necessarily predict that the South would become a GOP bastion. In particular, because of the economic underdevelopment of the region, several of the groups that leaned toward the GOP nationally were much smaller in the South—for example, the college-educated and high-income voters.

But it is important to note that the South underwent very dramatic economic growth in the latter half of the twentieth century. Real per capita income in the South grew 200% between 1959 and 1999, compared to 140% for the country. The eight fastest growing states over the period were all former members of the Confederacy. So it is plausible that some part of the realignment might reflect demographic shifts, which generated larger natural constituencies for the GOP.

While not completely ruling out the politics of race, Byron Shafer and Richard Johnston stress economic changes in the postwar South as the key shaper of the partisan realignment.[8] They observe that family income and preferences over welfare policy became the key correlates of Republican voting in US presidential, Senate, and House elections after the 1960s.

Moreover, early GOP success was considerably higher in areas with large numbers of white-collar voters. Similarly, they find Republicans did better earlier on in those areas of the South that had few blacks, suggesting that GOP did not emerge primarily as a vehicle to resist the demands of newly enfranchised African Americans. Finally, while they do conclude that racial attitudes and racial policy preferences do correlate with Republican voting, they find those relationships to be much smaller than those related to income and redistributive preferences.

While Shafer and Johnston do not compare southern whites with those from the rest of the country, Keith Poole, Howard Rosenthal, and I estimate that, after controlling for a variety of other variables, the correlation of income and Republican ID among southern whites trailed that of non-southern whites until the 1980s, when it became much larger.[9] Combined with the region's large number of low-income blacks who uniformly support the Democrats, the South is the region of the country where partisanship is most linked to income and economics.[10]

A second line of argument focuses on the legacy of racism and racially conservative attitudes in the South. Nicolas Valentino and David Sears argue that "symbolic" (belief that blacks violate basic American values) rather than "Jim Crow" (explicit support for segregation) racism played a crucial role in the advance of the Republican party in the South.[11] They observe that southern whites score higher on a measure of symbolic racism and this measure correlates more strongly with Republican vote choice in the South.[12] However, the gap between southern and non-southern whites on the scale is fairly modest until the year 2000, and the higher correlation of symbolic racism and Republican vote choice and ID among southern whites is not apparent until the 1990s. Thus, the authors' explanation is less satisfying for understanding the earlier period of realignment. They also do not consider economic and class arguments.

In more recent work, Ilyana Kuziemko and Ebonya Washington utilize Gallup surveys going back to 1958 that ask respondents whether they would vote for a black president.[13] They use responses to this question to measure the racial conservatism of voters. To capture the effects of racial attitudes on realignment, they correlate Democratic party ID with racial conservatism in the South and non-South before and after President Kennedy introduced civil rights legislation in 1963. They find that racially liberal voters (those who would vote for a qualified black candidate) in the South were just as Democratic as voters in the rest of the country, both before and after the introductions of the Civil Rights Act. But racially conservative southerners were 16 percentage points more Democratic than non-southern whites before Civil Rights. But after Kennedy's move, racially conservative voters were no more Democratic than any other group of whites during the period of 1963 to 1980. These findings imply that the entire defection of southern whites from the Democratic party can be accounted for by the movement of those who had racially conservative attitudes.

It is worth noting a couple of limitations of this study. Ideally, one would want a panel of voters that measures partisanship and racial attitudes before and after the introduction of civil rights legislation. But Kuziemko and Washington must rely on a series of cross-sectional surveys. Second, their results focus of voter dealignment with the Democratic party, not the alignment with the Republican party. They find a much smaller and less precise effect for post–Civil Rights racial conservatism with Republican party ID. This suggests that much of the early reaction of southern racial conservatives was to move toward political independence. Kuziemko and Washington report that their results are robust to the inclusion of variables related to income and economic growth.

Unfortunately, there has been little work synthesizing the economic and racial arguments. For example, we should expect both income and animus toward lower-income racial and ethnic groups to be correlated with opposition to welfare and redistribution. Thus, the interaction of these factors could produce exceptionally high Republican support among southern whites. There has been even less work exploring the interactions of race, economics, and distinctively southern social attitudes.

5.5 Why is congressional voting on racial issues no longer distinctive?

In Poole and Rosenthal's original work on ideal point estimation, they argued that a single left-right dimension was sufficient to explain most legislative roll-call decisions for much of American history. But they noted that there were distinct periods where sectional and regional difference divided legislators in ways not captured by a single dimension. During these periods, a two-dimensional model was necessary to represent many voting coalitions.

The 1950s and 1960s were one such era of two-dimensional politics where a second dimension was necessary to capture the differences between northern and southern Democrats on issues related to segregation and civil rights for African Americans. For example, in the congressional term spanning 1963 to 1964, a two-dimensional model increases the predictive power by 8.5 percentage points in the Senate and 3.5 percentage points in the House over a one-dimensional model.[14] In 2013 and 2014, these equivalent increases were less than one-half of a percentage point. Thus the coalitions on votes related to race are identical to those on other policy issues.

5.6 Does economic inequality cause polarization?

While changes in electoral competition, especially those presumed to be influenced by legislative districting, have limited power to explain trends and patterns in polarization, there is considerable evidence that polarization may be affected by long-term changes in the American economy and society.

Keith Poole, Howard Rosenthal, and I have demonstrated that there is a very strong historical correlation between the level of polarization in the US Congress and the degree of economic inequality.[15] Figure 5.1 demonstrates this connection. First, our measure of polarization in the House (solid line) is juxtaposed against the Gini index of family income (dotted line). The Gini index is a measure of income inequality where higher values represent more unequal incomes. Note that both the polarization measure and the Gini index remain at quite low levels before both series turned sharply upward at about the same time in the late 1970s.

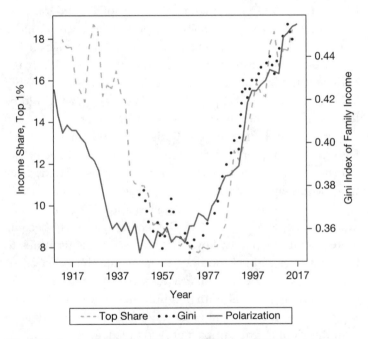

Figure 5.1: Congressional Polarization and Economic Inequality The figure plots the McCarty, Poole, and Rosenthal (2016) measure of polarization in the US House against the Gini index of family income and the Piketty and Saez (2003) (updated) measure of the income share of the top 1% of taxpayers. The Gini index is a measure of inequality that ranges from 0 (pure equality) to 1 (complete concentration of income).

Unfortunately, the Gini index is available only back to the 1940s, so Figure 5.1 also illustrates a different measure of inequality, the share of income going to the top 1% of taxpayers as computed by Thomas Piketty and Emmanuel Saez and subsequently updated (dashed line).[16] The use of this extended measure shows that high polarization and high inequality tend to move roughly in tandem going back at least as far as the introduction of the income tax.

Despite this suggestive evidence, scholars have not been able to precisely assess the extent to which income inequality causes polarization. First, the relationship might be the other way around so that polarization causes inequality through its impact on the policymaking capacity of the federal government. Indeed there is some suggestion of such an effect in Figure 5.1 as polarization appears to lead to changes in the top income share especially during the first part of the twentieth century. Second, it is also possible that the relationship between inequality and polarization is spurious, as would be the case if both were caused by some third factor.

But recently John Voorheis, Boris Shor, and I use our state legislative ideal point data to test for a causal relationship between inequality and polarization in the states.[17] We observe that income inequality has a large, positive, and statistically significant effect on political polarization. Economic inequality appears to cause state Democratic parties to become more liberal. Inequality, however, moves state legislatures to the right overall. Such findings suggest that the effect of income inequality impacts polarization by replacing moderate Democratic legislators with Republicans. We provide some suggestive evidence linking unregulated campaign finance with this right-shifting impact of rising inequality.

These findings about the link between polarization and inequality suggest that our political divisions are to a large degree related to deeper social and economic changes. So tackling political polarization may require policies designed to target economic inequality and economic growth for the middle and working classes. Yet polarization negatively impacts the capacity of policymakers to deal with those problems.

5.7 Do party leaders engineer polarization?

Journalists and academics alike have focused on the role of legislative leaders in contributing to congressional polarization. Some accounts focus on the role of particular leaders such as Newt Gingrich or Nancy Pelosi while others note general trends toward the elevation of extreme leaders and strategies.[18]

Most scholarship on the role of congressional leadership does not posit extreme leadership as the original cause of polarization. Rather the argument is that choosing extreme leaders is an outgrowth of polarization and, in turn, has the ability to enhance it. This argument has been made most explicitly by John Aldrich and David Rohde.[19] According to their account, legislative parties that are heterogeneous and undistinctive have very little incentive to endow their leaders with strong powers. But as the ideological preferences of members and their constituencies increase, the incentives to centralize control of the party increases. Empowered leaders will in turn help to define the party's image by working to promote a partisan agenda and distinguish it from the opposition. Thus, strong leadership may serve as an accelerant to polarization.

If the leadership story were true, we would expect to observe a couple of other trends. The first is that we would expect to see an increasing tendency of legislative parties to elevate extreme members into important leadership positions. Eric Heberlig and his coauthors do observe that the polarization of top House leaders has been greater than that of the House in general since the 1990s. But the ideological differences between leaders and the rank-and-file are not large.[20] Stephen Jessee and Neil Malhotra find that elected leaders are actually closer to their party's median member than one would expect if the leaders were selected randomly from their caucus/conference.[21] They do conclude, however, that they skew slightly to the extremes with Democratic leaders more liberal on average than a randomly selected leader and Republican leaders more conservative. In the 113th House, the differences were equivalent to those between Nancy Pelosi (ironically the median Democrat) and Jerrold Nadler (NY). The Republican difference is roughly that between Eric Cantor (just left of the Republican median) and Cory Gardner (CO).

The second pattern that we would expect is an increase in polarizing leadership behavior. Here there are two possibilities. First, we might expect strong leaders to increasingly use the "whip" to discipline wayward members. If this were the case, we might expect to see increases in both party voting and measures of ideological polarization. The question of whether we have observed greater levels of party discipline in roll-call voting is the subject of a great deal of scholarly debate.

James Snyder and Tim Groseclose present a methodology for distinguishing party pressure from member ideology as a determinant of roll-call voting.[22] They estimate considerably larger partisan differences on close roll calls for which party whips are likely to be active than on lopsided votes that are assumed to be "free" votes for members. But Poole, Rosenthal, and I raise several methodological concerns and propose an alternative.[23] We argue that while legislative partisanship has a big impact on roll-call voting, there is not much evidence consistent with the discretionary use of the whip across votes. If anything, we conclude that that form of party discipline has been declining.

But Gary Cox and Keith Poole propose yet another test that shows substantial variation in party voting that cannot be accounted for by the ideal points of the legislators. They interpret this variation as party influence.[24] Nevertheless, Cox and Poole do not find a pattern of increasing party effects that would contribute to polarization. They find that the proportion of party-inflected roll calls drops by about half between 1977 and 1997.

Another aspect of leadership that might contribute to polarization (or at least the appearance of polarization) is agenda setting. In American legislatures, the leaders of the majority party have substantial influence over what gets voted on and when. If these powers are used to promote partisan goals, the level of partisanship in observed roll-call behavior would increase. Logically, there are two forms of agenda control: positive and negative. Positive agenda control is the ability of leaders to put their own initiatives to a vote. Party leaders might therefore use positive agenda control to promote party legislative priorities. As a consequence, we would observe more partisan voting behavior because the majority party would be very likely to support those bills, while the minority party would oppose them. Relatedly, party leaders might use positive agenda control to schedule "message" votes, such as the repeated votes by the GOP during the Obama Administration to repeal the Affordable Care Act.[25] By the nature of these issues, the votes are likely to be very partisan (though they sometimes afford members of the minority the opportunity to signal moderation or bipartisanship).

Negative agenda control is the ability of leaders to prevent votes on specific bills. Typically, party leaders will use this power to suppress issues that divide the majority party. Leaders have therefore often invoked the so-called Hastert Rule to justify blocking any legislation that does not have the support of a majority of the majority party.[26] Adherence to the Hastert Rule will tend to make roll-call voting more partisan. Few issues will reach the floor that divide the majority party, increasing the likelihood that a majority of the majority votes against a majority of the minority party. As Gary Cox and Mathew McCubbins have argued, negative agenda control and the Hastert Rule imply that the majority party will often "roll" the minority party by passing legislation opposed by the majority of the minority party.[27] Conversely, the minority party will not have the opportunity to roll the majority party by passing legislation opposed by the majority of the majority.[28]

There are many reasons to be skeptical that partisan agenda control by itself can explain the polarization of American legislatures. First, as Cox and McCubbins have argued, the practice of using negative agenda control to avoid party splitting legislation predates the Hastert speakership by over a century.[29] Thus, a constant feature of the legislative process is unlikely to produce the dramatic changes in polarization we have witnessed since the 1970s. Second, the effects of agenda setting on the measurement of polarization are not as large as one would expect. Clearly, positive and negative agenda control will inflate measures of party voting such as shown in Figure 3.1. But polarization as measured by DW-NOMINATE is less affected. First, because it uses information about each legislator's career, it leverages information both from when she was in the majority and when she was in the minority. Second, by using all the votes in a given term, it can exploit information from the votes that are not purely partisan to measure intra-party divisions. As an empirical demonstration of this claim, Poole, Rosenthal, and I re-estimate DW-NOMINATE under the assumption that the distributions of the roll calls was held fixed.[30] Thus, any effects that leaders have to create partisan coalitions or to avoid party splits are held constant. The resulting measure of polarization assuming the fixed agenda of roll calls is slightly higher than the actual DW-NOMINATE polarization measure. But the trends in the simulated and actual measures are identical. A plausible interpretation is that party leadership strategies have raised the level of measured polarization, but they cannot account for its rise over time.

5.8 Is the rising competition for congressional majorities to blame?

In a recent book, Frances Lee argues that the increasingly intense partisan battles over the control of the House and the Senate are largely responsible for the rise in partisan behavior in Congress.[31] She notes that the era of bipartisanship and low polarization in the middle of the twentieth century was also a period of Democratic party dominance where the Republicans had little opportunity to win legislative majorities in either chamber. Indeed, between 1933 and 1980, the GOP held House and Senate majorities for just four years. The election outcomes were rarely even close. Over this period, the Democrats averaged 59 Senate seats and 261 House seats. That all began to change in the 1980s. The Republicans won the Senate in 1980 (only to relinquish it in 1986). While the Republicans would not win the House until 1994, they cut into the Democratic majority substantially in 1980 and have held the Democrats below their 1933–1980 average in all but two elections since. Thus, the era of rising polarization has also been a period of intense competition for control of Congress.

Lee argues that this rise of competition has infused Congress with partisanship in a variety of ways. It has nearly eliminated the incentives of the minority party to work with the majority party on legislation. When the Republicans were in a permanent minority, the only influence a GOP member might have on legislation was in collaboration with a member of the majority party. In today's environment, the incentives of a minority party member are to work to defeat the majority party in the next election in order to influence policy as a member of the majority. Second, the majority party has little incentive to cooperate as they want to use their power, not just for policy, but to keep the minority party at bay. In general, Lee argues that these changes have led Congress to shift its emphasis from legislating to messaging. This phenomenon, she argues, is manifest in the large number of roll calls whose only purpose appears to be partisan differentiation for electoral purposes. It has also resulted in a huge proliferation of communications staff in Congress, often at the expense of policy staff.

These trends clearly contribute to the intensely partisan environment in Congress and are reflected in the levels of party voting.[32] Lee also presents evidence of a correlation between party competition and polarization in state legislatures.

Moreover, Lee's account can also help explain the high levels of polarization at the end of the nineteenth century, another era of intense battles over the control of Congress.[33]

But the association between party competition and polarization leaves several questions unanswered. The first relates to causation. Does the causal arrow move from competition to polarization or polarization to competition? It might also be possible that both phenomena are related to other factors. For example, at the national level and in many states (especially those in the South), increases in the competition for legislative control are a function of the growth in the electoral success of the Republican party. But the findings of asymmetric polarization imply that changes in polarization are also directly related to Republican seat share. So the rise of the modern conservative Republican party may provide an alternative explanation. Second, there is still relatively little evidence that party branding and messaging provides substantial benefits to most legislators. The evidence we do have seems to suggest that members are hurt electorally for extremely ideological or partisan voting records.[34] Moreover, recent work by John Henderson demonstrates that individual members tend to stress moderate or "party-blurring" issues and themes in their campaign advertisements.[35]

5.9 Why don't more moderates run for Congress?

That legislators have polarized much more than voters raises the question as to why more moderate candidates do not run for office. The conventional wisdom, of course, is that given high levels of partisan sorting, few moderates can win their party's primary even if they would have an advantage by appealing to moderate and independent voters in a general election.

Certainly, these electoral calculations are a deterrent to moderates. But their role may be overstated given the largely null findings about the effects of primary electoral systems.[36]

Even studies that observe an electoral value of extremism in primaries estimate it to be small in magnitude. For example, David Brady, Hahrie Han, and Jeremy Pope find that the primary election reward for extremism is only about 1–2 percentage points per one standard deviation increase in extremism on the NOMINATE scale.[37] So there may be other non-electoral factors at play. In recent work, both Danielle Thomsen and Andrew Hall argue that moderates have dropped out of electoral office because polarization has reduced their policy impact and otherwise reduced the utility of service.[38]

Thomsen reports that in recent years fewer than 5% of each party's candidates are moderates. However, she notes that there are many more moderates in the pool of *potential* candidates. She calculates that 30% of the state legislators in each party are moderates by her definition.[39] Of course, this gap between actual and potential candidates may be driven by the expectations about the success of moderates in primaries, but there is a variety of evidence pointing in other directions.

1. When moderates do run, they fare quite well in primaries.
2. Surveys of state legislators indicate that moderates are less likely than ideologues to desire House seats. This effect is concentrated on Republican state legislators suggesting a source of asymmetric polarization.[40]
3. While moderate Republican state legislators do express more concerns about losing House primary elections, they report an even greater relative fear of being ineffective in the House.
4. Since the 1990s, each cohort of retiring House members has been more moderate than the returning cohort. There is little evidence that the fear of not being renominated plays a significant factor in these retirement choices.[41]

While the evidence presented by Thomsen and Hall does not show that the attrition of moderates is the original cause of polarization, that process has clearly been a contributing factor. In fact, it appears to be part of a feedback loop where polarization causes moderates to drop out, which leads to greater polarization, which makes public office even less attractive to moderates.

The decline of moderate candidates may have other representational consequences as well. As Thomsen points out, the United States lags behind almost all other countries in the proportion of women who serve in the national legislature. The underrepresentation of women in Congress is particularly acute on the GOP side. Thomsen argues that a likely source of this problem is that the pool of female Republican candidates is overwhelmingly moderate. Thus, the decision of moderates to eschew running for Congress has a large impact on female representation.

5.10 Is the media responsible for polarization?

With the emergence of the Fox News Channel, MSNBC, and a variety of other partisan and ideologically slanted outlets on the Internet, it has become quite common to blame the media for much of the polarized preferences and behavior of the public. There are three general ways in which individual media outlets and the overall media environment can contribute to polarization and partisan sorting among voters. The first is *selective exposure*. The argument is that increasingly ideologically diverse media outlets allow voters to self-select into ideologically comfortable and self-confirmatory audiences. Liberal voters primarily consume the output of liberal outlets while conservatives watch and read only conservative journalism. As a result of selective exposure, partisan voters are likely to have different understandings of politics and interpret events through an ideological and partisan lens. The second mechanism is that of persuasion. Ideological outlets persuade voters to accept more extreme positions or to adopt positions on specific issues that are more ideologically consistent. Finally, a third channel comes through the disengagement of less partisan voters as they take advantage of other media options, such as entertainment and soft news, to avoid hard news and politics.

Partisan selection exposure has been documented in a number of studies. Natalie Stroud uses the 2004 National Annenberg Election Survey to determine how the media consumption of respondents evolves over the course of a political campaign.[42] If selective exposure captures media consumption decisions, Stroud argues that we would expect to see the correlation between political preferences and the slant of the media consumed increase over the course of a campaign as voters learn about the dispositions of various media outlets. Stroud found this pattern of increasingly selective exposure over the election across media platforms (newspaper, cable television, and talk radio). The effects, however, are somewhat modest. Over ninety days, an extreme conservative's probability of naming CNN or MSNBC as the most watched cable station was estimated to drop from 45% to just over 30%. The changes for other ideological profiles are considerably smaller. The pattern for liberals and Fox was almost the mirror image.

Given the limitations of observational research on media choices and exposure, many scholars have employed survey experiments. For example, Shanto Iyengar and Kyu Hahn present online experimental subjects with the choice of news reports from Fox News, CNN, NPR, or the BBC.[43] Conservatives overwhelmingly chose to read the Fox News report while liberals divided between CNN and NPR. These patterns were not only evident for hard political news but softer news. Selective exposure was found to be highest among the most sophisticated citizens.

In interpreting results of studies on selective exposure, it is important to note that mechanisms other than selective exposure can lead to a statistical association between the ideology of a consumer and the slant of an outlet. Either a media outlet may slant its coverage to match the preferences of its audience or voters might find information from ideologically compatible outlets more credible.[44]

A number of other studies have probed the effects of persuasion of voter behavior and polarization. The major challenge of detecting persuasion is to distinguish it from selective exposure. In an ideal study, the researcher would expose a treatment group to some news content and measure whether the behavior was different than that of a control group that was not exposed. But outside of laboratory and survey experiments, that ideal is hard to implement. But researchers have made important strides in overcoming these problems.

For example, Alan Gerber and colleagues conduct a field experiment associated with the 2005 Virginia gubernatorial election. Voters were randomly assigned to receive a free subscription to the *Washington Post* (a liberal paper), the *Washington Times* (a conservative paper), and to a control group that did not receive any subscriptions.[45] The study was designed to see whether exposing voters to the different ideological slants of the papers would influence their voting behavior. The results, however, did not confirm this expectation. It turned out that those voters who received either subscription were more likely to support the Democratic candidate. The results suggest that the level of information mattered more than its slant.[46]

Another strand of research on persuasion has exploited the fact that Fox News Channel (FNC) was rolled out gradually between 1996 and 2000. Therefore, some voters were exposed to FNC's conservative take on the news well before others were. Stefano DellaVigna and Ethan Kaplan compile data on 9,256 towns across 28 states.[47] Of these towns, 1807 had FNC by the 2000 election. This allows them to compare the change in Republican vote shares between 1996 and 2000 in the FNC towns and the non-FNC towns. They estimate that the availability of FNC raised aggregate support for GOP presidential candidates by 0.4 to 0.7 percentage points. Because FNC viewership was relatively low, these estimates suggest a rather large persuasion rate of voters not already voting Republican.

The effects appeared to be largest in Democratic towns, also implying a substantial persuasion effect. Of course, given the use of aggregate data, the results are also consistent with a larger effect on Republicans living in Democratic towns.[48]

Daniel Hopkins and Jonathan Ladd replicate DellaVigna and Kaplan's findings using individual survey data. However, this also allows them to assess whether the effects of FNC are persuasive or reinforcing.[49] Consistent with reinforcement, they observe that the effects are most pronounced among GOP identifiers and independents. FNC did not appear to lead Democratic identifiers to vote for George W. Bush in 2000. Finally, Joshua Clinton and Ted Enamorado find that members of Congress representing districts where FNC was introduced in the late 1990s provided less roll-call voting support for Democratic president Bill Clinton's legislative agenda.[50] In an earlier version of the paper,[51] the authors also show that the ideal points of members of Congress shift modestly to the right upon introduction of FNC in their district. The effect, however, is largest among Democratic representatives. They do not encounter any evidence that FNC exposure affected which representatives were elected.

A limitation of these studies, however, is that they focus on exposure to FNC during a relatively early period of its existence when it was less overtly partisan than today and had a much lower viewership. To get a better estimate of the contemporary effect of FNC exposure, Greg Martin and Ali Yurukoglu use the positioning of the Fox News channel on each cable system as a source of variation in viewership unrelated to partisanship or policy preferences.[52] In systems where Fox is lower on the cable dial, viewership is larger than those where it is higher.[53] They find that for every two-and-a-half minutes of Fox viewing induced by the variation in channel ordering, the propensity to vote for a Republican presidential candidate goes up by 0.3 percentage points. By 2008, the effect of eliminating FNC would have been a 6 percentage-point reduction of John McCain's vote share. Unlike the Hopkins and

Ladd results, Martin and Yurukoglu find the largest effects of FNC exposure are on independents and Democrats. Finally, the authors demonstrate how the combination of a persuasion effect and a taste for like-minded news can create a polarizing dynamic among voters.

Markus Prior provides evidence of the third mechanism— the disengagement effect of media choice.[54] Prior argues that the emergence of cable television had two important effects. First, cable TV created many new opportunities for the consumption of political news. Therefore, those citizens most interested in politics were both able to increase their total news consumption and tailor it to their political dispositions. This increased availability and choice led these voters to become more engaged in politics. The second effect of cable TV, however, was to increase the opportunities for non-news entertainment programming. During the broadcast era, the early evening TV programming was dominated by national and local news. So the introduction of cable allowed millions of Americans to completely turn off the news. The implications for polarization are clear. The most engaged voters, those who tend to have the strongest and most consistent ideological views and partisan commitments, became even more engaged. The disengaged citizens could totally check out and watch Seinfeld reruns. The result was a more polarized distribution of voter preferences even if the distribution of citizen preferences remained moderate.

Media effects on polarization need not only arise through the persuasion and mobilization of voters. Changes to the economics of journalism that have reduced the coverage of certain aspects of politics may also be to blame. James Snyder and David Strömberg exploit the fact that some congressional districts align with local media markets better than others to estimate the effects of media coverage on congressional behavior. They define *congruence* as a measure of the extent to which media markets and districts overlap.[55] Members representing congressional districts that are congruent with local media markets tend to receive much more local press coverage than those that do not. This variation allows the authors to assess the casual impact of coverage on various aspects of congressional representation. They observe that members who receive more coverage perform better in a wide variety of domains. They do more constituency service, participate in more hearings of the Appropriations (spending) and Ways and Means (tax) committees, and bring more spending to their districts. But most importantly for polarization, press coverage tends to lead members to vote in a less partisan way.[56] These results suggest that the decline of local news coverage of Congress may have been a contributor to the increase in polarization. Two long-term forces made important contributions to the decline in local coverage of politics. The first is obviously the expansion of television. Matthew Gentzkow finds that the introduction of television into a news market led to a drop in consumption of newspapers and radio, which in turn reduced levels of political knowledge. The second is the expanded reach of national papers.[57] Similarly, Lisa George and Joel Waldfogel find evidence that the expanded national circulation of the *New York Times* led to a substantial drop in local newspaper readership among highly educated readers and an increase in local readership of less educated voters.[58] As a result, local papers covered much less national and international news. Clearly, the shift to the Internet should present similar issues.

Finally, it may be the case historically that developments in the media had a de-polarizing effect. Filipe Campante and Daniel Hojman provide evidence that the introduction of TV contributed to a decrease in polarization.[59] They hypothesize that the mechanism is that nationalized (and centrist) coverage of politics reduced the variation in voter preferences.

5.11 What about the emergence of the Internet and social media?

Since the advent of the digital age, many concerns have been expressed about the way in which the Internet and (later) social media might impact politics. While many commentators have lauded the potential of these technologies to promote civic engagement and foster collective action, concerns about their potential to divide and polarize have been prominent, especially in light of the experiences of the 2016 presidential election.

In many ways, the concerns are similar to those raised about the advent of cable news. The proliferation of media consumption choices allows citizens to engage in greater levels of selective exposure and hive themselves off from any information that does not conform to their preexisting views.[60] But modern social media adds an additional wrinkle. With the development of powerful machine learning algorithms, social media platforms curate information in ways tailored to each individual user. So even users who are not actively seeking ideologically conforming information may end up with news slanted toward their preexisting political beliefs.

Legal scholar and behavioral scientist Cass Sunstein has drawn specific attention to the role of platforms such as Facebook and Twitter in creating the "Daily Me."[61] In the Daily Me, social media users engage almost exclusively with networks of like-minded friends who share news stories and information. The creation of these "filter bubbles" and "echo chambers" in turn creates and exacerbates group polarization.

While the research on the impact of the Internet and social media is relatively nascent and faces an ever-evolving target, the existing evidence does not point toward the worst-case scenarios. To be sure, the social networks on platforms such as Facebook and Twitter show a substantial degree of partisan and ideological homogeneity.[62] But the appropriate question is the extent to which social media's chambers actually echo any more than those of other social arenas. To address this crucial question, Matthew Gentzkow and Jesse Shapiro examine the ideological segregation of citizens in news consumption and daily interactions with neighbors, friends, and co-workers.[63] They measure ideological segregation as the difference in the exposure of conservative citizens to conservative media outlets or individuals, minus the exposure of liberal citizens to conservative outlets or individuals. They conclude that ideological segregation of online news consumption is low in absolute terms. The average conservative's conservative Internet media exposure was 60.6%, approximately the same that would be obtained by exclusively reading USAToday.com. For liberals, the conservative exposure was 53.1%, the result that would be obtained by an exclusive reader of CNN.com. They also find that few citizens have extreme exposure to conservative media. Almost all consumers had Internet news diets that ranged between those associated with exclusively reading FoxNews.com and exclusively reading NYTimes.com.

Although Gentzkow and Shapiro do observe that ideological segregation on the Internet is higher than most non-Internet media outlets, with the exception of national newspapers, eliminating the Internet would only result in a trivial reduction in the overall segregation in news consumption. Internet news consumption is considerably less ideologically segregated than voluntary association, the workplace, or families. They posit two reasons why Internet news consumption is not as highly segregated as is often believed. First, while there are a wide array of politically extreme blogs, content aggregators, and news sites, they account for a very small share of online consumption. Most consumers get their news from the large mainstream sites. Second, most online consumers get news from a variety of outlets. In fact, those who frequent extreme sites are more likely to also view content on the mainstream sites.

While Gentzkow and Shapiro identify no trend toward greater ideological segregation on the Internet between 2004 and 2008, one might be concerned that these relatively benign patterns of ideological segregation have reversed themselves in the past decade. But recent work by Andrew Guess shows that this is probably not the case.[64] By combining an individual-level survey with respondents' Internet browsing history, he finds that most Americans have moderate online media diets and obtain most of their news through large mainstream portals.

Even in the final days of the 2016 campaign, he finds a large degree of overlap in the media consumption of Democrats and Republicans. This moderation is due less to citizens seeking ideological balance than to the fact that most citizens get their online news through moderate mainstream sites. He detects, however, a very small group of citizens whose media consumption is over-represented by ideologically slanted websites. This is almost exclusively a phenomenon of the political right. Overall, however, Guess finds that relatively few Americans live in ideological echo chambers. Guess does find, however, that when news of Hilary Clinton's private email server broke, conservative news consumers overwhelmingly sought out conservative coverage.[65] So there may be much greater levels of ideological segregation for certain types of highly partisan news.

Some evidence points to the possibility that social media usage may be depolarizing. In a study of the Twitter users in Spain, Germany, and United States, Pablo Barberá found that most users are located in networks that are relatively ideologically heterogeneous.[66] He argues that users in these heterogeneous networks are likely to encounter much more incidental information that does not conform with their prior ideological beliefs. Such information, he argues, should moderate their political beliefs. Consistent with this argument, he observes that those users with heterogeneous networks in 2013 were more likely to begin following political accounts (parties, politicians, interest groups, and journalists) with opposing ideological orientations between 2013 and 2015.[67] Moreover, using election surveys, he concludes that self-identified social media users moderated over the course of political campaigns in Spain and the United States. German social media users were estimated to depolarize by a small amount, but the effect of social media was not statistically significant.

Another strain of research on the Internet and polarization focuses on how the polarization of Internet users compares to that of those less inclined to go online. Levi Boxell and his collaborators find that political polarization has grown the most among demographic groups that are least likely to use the Internet.[68] Specifically, affective polarization and partisan sorting among older Americans has grown substantially despite relatively low usage of the Internet or social media. The authors also use demographic information such as age, education, race, and gender to predict Internet usage in 1996. They find that individuals with demographic profiles consistent with low propensities to use the Internet polarized much more than those who were predicted to be high users.

Yphtach Lelkes, Gaurav Sood, and Shanto Iyengar, however, use variation in broadband right-of-way regulations, geographical terrain and weather to capture broadband access at the county level.[69] States that allow greater municipal regulation of Internet right-of-ways increase the costs to providers, leading to less access. High flooding risk, high summer temperatures, and steep terrains increase the cost of building and maintaining broadband infrastructure. Thus, these regulatory and geographic factors shape the availability of access of broadband in ways that are not correlated with the political preferences of citizens.[70] Using the 2004 and 2008 National Annenberg Election study, they find that respondents who live in counties with more broadband access exhibit higher levels of affective polarization. Comparing a resident from the county with the fewest number of providers to the county with the highest number of providers increases affective polarization by 7% of the scale. The authors provide some evidence that citizens with broadband visit more partisan websites than those who only have dial-up.

In summary, the evidence of the polarizing effect of the Internet and social media appears mixed. While some studies do find modest polarizing effects, the stronger versions of the "echo chambers" hypothesis gets rather little support.

5.12 Is the United States unique?

Direct comparisons of the level of polarization in the United States and those in other democracies are not straightforward. Some of the key data used to study the United States, especially legislative roll-call votes, are either not available or are generated in a very different context in other countries. For example, in many parliamentary democracies, party discipline at the voting stage is so strong, all we observe are party line votes. Such outcomes make it impossible to use tools like DW-NOMINATE to measure polarization.

Scholars have made efforts at comparing polarization using data on policy positions of party supporters and surveys of experts. For example, Philipp Rehm and Timothy Reilly develop a measure of polarization that reflects a combination of the average differences across parties and their internal homogeneity.[71] They consider trends in polarization across nine OECD[72] countries. The measures of party positions are drawn from mass and elite surveys. Party positions are estimated in three different ways. First they are estimated as the average positioning on a left-right scale from the responses of an expert survey. In such surveys, experts are requested to use their judgment to place party positions and platforms on a set of scales. Second, the authors estimate party positions based on the perceptions of voters from a mass survey. Third, positions are computed using the average individual placement of partisan respondents to a mass survey. Using the UK as an example, this measure of party positions would be the average self-placement of Labour voters on a left-right scale, the average placement of Conservative voters on that scale, as well as the average placement of Liberal Democratic voters. With these data, Rehm and Reilly are able to compute three measures of polarization: elite perceptions, mass perceptions, and constituency placement. In each of the measures heterogeneity is measured by the standard deviation of the placements of supporters.

The current US polarization is the highest among the nine countries when polarization is measured using elite or mass perceptions. But when the polarization of party constituencies is measured, the level of polarization in the United States does not stand out. Notably all three measures have trended up in the United States since the 1980s. This is true of no other country in their sample. In fact the modal pattern is one of depolarization where the parties have become less distinct and more heterogeneous. Thus, their evidence shows that at least with regard to polarization, America is exceptional.

To this point research has not uncovered what may account for these differences. One likely suspect is the electoral system. There may be something polarizing about the use of single-member, first-past-the-post electoral systems. But Rehm and Reilly show clear depolarization for the UK and a very mixed pattern for Canada, the two other countries in their sample that use first-past-the-post elections. Another common observation is that depolarization in Europe has been associated with the rise of far-right anti-system parties. But as Morris Fiorina notes, that empirical relationship is not well established.[73]

5.13 What have we learned?

The polarization of the American political parties is a complex phenomenon with many plausible causes and is influenced by an even larger set of contributing factors. For ultimate causes, it seems logical to focus on those economic, political, and social changes that appear roughly contemporaneously with the emergence of party polarization in the 1970s and 1980s. Thus, strong cases can be made for a wide variety of causes ranging from the Southern Realignment to increasing economic inequality and racial/ethnic diversity to the reemergence of strong party competition for the control of the federal government.

But whatever the sparks, certain accelerants have played important roles. Polarized politics produces a vicious cycle when it drives moderates from public life or encounters new media technologies that can serve to reinforce ideological messaging and partisanship.

6

HOW DOES ELECTORAL LAW AFFECT LEGISLATIVE POLARIZATION?

In recent years, journalists and activists have also become interested in reforms that might reduce the level of polarization in Congress.[1] The most common prescriptions for reducing polarization tend to fall into one of three areas. Perhaps the most frequent suggestion is that gerrymandered legislative districts are a significant source of polarization and that turning redistricting decisions over to nonpartisan bodies can reduce legislative conflict. A second argument centers on the use of partisan primaries to nominate legislative candidates. If primaries were more open to moderate and independent voters, so the theory goes, those elections would be considerably less likely to produce extreme nominees. Finally, many observers blame the legislators' reliance on campaign contributions from groups and citizens with extreme preferences. Accordingly, public financing of campaigns, limits on large donors, and subsidies for small donors have been proposed to battle polarization.

In this chapter, I try to answer many of the relevant questions raised by this reform agenda.

6.1 How much does polarization reflect geographic sorting?

There are two logical ways in which a legislative body can be polarized.[2] The first is what we call geographic *sorting*.[3] Polarization due to sorting occurs when liberal Democrats become increasingly likely to win elections in liberal districts while conservative Republicans increasingly likely to represent conservative districts. Such sorting can produce polarization even when the parties differ very little in how they represent moderate districts. Such a hypothetical pattern is shown in the left panel of Figure 6.1. In the figure, the x-axis represents the conservatism of the district while the y-axis represents the conservatism of the representative. The Democrats (token D) represent almost all of the liberal districts and the Republicans (token R) represent almost all of the conservative districts. But Democrats and Republicans represent the moderate districts very similarly.

The second pattern is what I call *divergence*. Divergence occurs when Democratic and Republican legislators represent otherwise identical districts in increasingly extreme ways. Such a pattern is also consistent with what Joseph Bafumi and Michael Herron call "leapfrog" representation, where liberal and conservative legislators rotate in office with the same constituency.[4] Divergence may lead to polarization even if there is a low correlation between the party of the representative

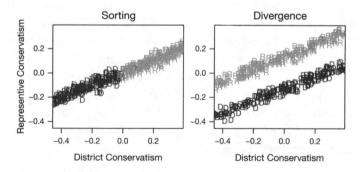

Figure 6.1: Polarization from Sorting and Divergence The panels show the relationship between voter preferences and legislative positions for two hypothetical legislatures. In panel a, the legislature is polarized due to the sorting of Republicans legislators into conservative districts and Democratic legislators into liberal districts. In panel b, the legislature is polarized because Democrats and Republicans represent districts in divergent ways. "D" represents Democratic members and "R" represents Republican members.

and the preferences of the median voter of her constituency. Panel B of Figure 6.1 illustrates polarization due to divergence. In this panel, both Democrats and Republicans represent liberal and conservative districts, but there is a gap between the parties at each level of district conservatism.

These two different forms of polarization have distinct implications for thinking about the causes of polarization and the potential for reform. If polarization is caused by sorting, then polarization may be addressed by reducing the number of extreme districts. But if polarization is primarily a reflection of within-district divergence, engineering moderate districts may be ineffectual or even counter-productive.[5]

The available evidence shows that the contemporary trend is mostly a process of divergence. This pattern is demonstrated by comparing the two panels of Figure 6.2. This figure plots the conservatism score for each House member against the Republican presidential vote (a measure of district conservatism) for two different elections—1972 and 2012. A simple comparison reveals how the gap between the parties in moderate districts has grown since the 1970s. Figure 6.2 also shows sorting.

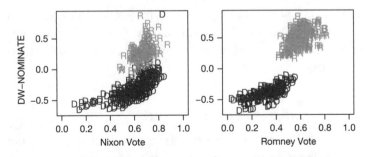

Figure 6.2: Sorting and Divergence 1975 and 2015 The figure plots DW-NOMINATE scores against Republican presidential vote for two congressional terms. The widening gap between the parties at each level of presidential vote indicates greater divergence. The declining overlap of the parties on presidential vote indicates greater sorting.

Poole, Rosenthal, and I developed a procedure to decompose measures of polarization into the components related to divergence and sorting.[6] Using these measures, we find that from the 1970s to the mid-2000s divergence accounted for 80% or more of the level of polarization in any congressional term. Moreover, almost two-thirds of the increase in polarization between 1972 and 2004 can be accounted for by divergence.

These findings are echoed in state legislatures. Boris Shor and I apply this technique to state legislatures.[7] We find that divergence, rather than sorting, is the dominant pattern in state legislatures. In all but four states, divergence accounts for more than 80% of the level of polarization.

In sum, any proposed reform for tackling polarization must account for the fact that Democrats and Republicans represent nearly identical districts in very distinctive ways. As Poole, Rosenthal, and I argue, a focus on gerrymandering is hard to square with divergence-based polarization.[8] The underlying hypothesis linking gerrymandering to polarization is that politicians draw maps that minimize electoral competition. Thus, if gerrymandering were the cause of polarization, the mechanism should be through greater sorting. Not only do we show that the rise of polarization is caused primarily by divergence, we find little evidence of a consistent pattern of increased sorting following the decennial reapportionment. Conversely, the argument that gerrymandering is the cause of polarization provides little explanation as to why Republicans and Democrats would represent moderate districts in increasingly divergent ways.

6.2 Does gerrymandering cause polarization?

One of the most common beliefs about polarization is that gerrymandering is a significant contributor if not the primary cause. The logic of this argument is straightforward. When politicians draw district boundaries for themselves and their parties, they design districts that minimize inter-party electoral competition. Without inter-party competition, legislators are both free to push their own ideological objectives and pander to their bases. To the extent to which they face any electoral risk, it comes from primary opponents from the more extreme wing of their parties. Consequentially, gerrymandered congressional districts produce more partisan and extreme legislators. There are, however, a number of conceptual and empirical reasons to doubt this story.

First, it is not clear why we would expect gerrymanderers to produce safe electoral districts. Consider the case of a majority party in a state legislature that would like to gerrymander to maximize its seat share. The standard approach to partisan gerrymandering is the "packing and cracking" of the constituencies of the minority party. First, the majority party would pack minority party voters by putting them into a small number of districts. Second, the majority party would crack the remaining opposite party members by spreading them over a large number of districts that would be won by the majority party. The result of these strategies is a small number of very partisan districts controlled by the minority party and a larger number of somewhat less partisan districts that lean toward the majority party. So a minority of districts will be very safe, but the majority will have some semblance of partisan balance. So even if electoral safety contributed to legislative extremity, the effects of partisan gerrymanders would be ambiguous, as there would be a small number of extreme minority party legislators posed against a larger number of more moderate majority party legislators. The sort of gerrymander that might unambiguously produce safe seats is one in which the mapmakers went out of their way to protect the incumbents of both parties. Thus, it is the bipartisan "incumbency-protection" gerrymander rather than the partisan gerrymander that we might expect to exacerbate polarization. But since polarization itself makes these sorts of bipartisan compromises less common, we should expect to see them primarily when control of redistricting is divided between the parties.

The empirical support for the argument that gerrymandering causes polarization is not solid either. First, gerrymandering as an explanation for polarization is hard to reconcile with the fact that the Senate has polarized in an almost parallel fashion.[9] Obviously, there has been no partisan gerrymandering of the Senate since the Dakota Territory was split into two in the 1890s to enhance the number of Republican senators.[10] Relatedly, gerrymandering cannot explain why House members from states with one or two districts have also compiled more extreme voting records. For many years, Bernie Sanders who represented Vermont's single congressional district, compiled one of the most progressive voting records in the House. Similarly, Wyoming and other small states of the West often provide some of the most conservative members of the House. In the 1970s, the average partisan difference in DW-NOMINATE scores for members representing states with one or two districts was around 0.6. Today it is just below 0.8. These levels generally reflect those of the chamber overall, as indicated in Figure 3.2.

There are several other patterns that gerrymandering cannot explain. First, the distribution of partisanship (as measured by presidential voting) across congressional districts is very similar to the distribution across counties, which are not gerrymandered.[11] If gerrymandering were creating safer districts, we would expect the distribution of partisanship across districts to be bimodal or at least have fatter tails than the distribution across counties.

Second, there does not seem to be any unusual increase in the level of polarization following the elections subsequent to redistricting. Consider the data underlying Figure 3.2. The average biennial increase in the polarization measure was 0.015. The changes associated with the reapportionment following the 1980, 1990, 2000, and 2010 censuses were 0.021, 0.045, 0.006, and 0.007, respectively.[12] So only two out of the four rounds of redistricting led to an above-average increase in polarization.

And importantly, it was the two earlier rounds that experienced the larger increases, and these occurred well before the concerns about gerrymandering's effects on polarization became widespread.[13]

Third, recall the discussion in section 6.1 where I distinguish between polarization related to divergence and that related to sorting. This distinction has a direct bearing on the gerrymandering argument. The argument holds that polarization has increased because the numbers of safe partisan seats has increased and because members therefore hew more closely to the extreme preferences of their partisan constituencies. In other words, the gerrymandering hypothesis predicts that sorting, not divergence, is the primary source of polarization. But Poole, Rosenthal, and I find that almost two-thirds of the increase in polarization between 1972 and 2004 can be accounted for by divergence alone.[14] But more importantly, we find that polarization attributed to sorting did not rise especially fast following redistricting.

Finally, Poole, Rosenthal, and I conduct a number of simulations to determine how large an effect gerrymandering might have on levels of polarization. The logic of these simulations is straightforward. They involve randomly creating congressional districts, using the partisanship and demographics of those simulated districts to predict the party of the representative and her NOMINATE score, and computing polarization based on these simulated scores. The most striking finding is that simulated districts created to randomly assign citizens to districts within their own states account for almost the entire level of polarization. Simulations that impose further constraints based on geography come even closer to predicting the observed level of polarization. These simulation results suggest that the upper-bound effect of gerrymandering on polarization is quite small, only around 10–15% of the polarization between the 1970s and 2008.

6.3 Isn't it possible that the effects of gerrymandering on the House carried over to the Senate?

Some scholars have argued that the close connection in the levels of polarization of the House and Senate does not rule out an effect of gerrymandering, especially if the polarization in the House causes polarization in the Senate. Perhaps extreme House members who benefit from gerrymandered districts are likely to be elevated to the Senate where they continue in their hyper-partisan ways.[15]

Such an argument suggests that we should expect that changes in the polarization of the Senate should be strongly related to *past* changes in the polarization of the House. For example, if an especially polarized cohort of House members is elected, we should expect to see a rise in polarization in the Senate at some future date as some of those members elevate to the Senate. But such a pattern is not found in the data. In the postwar era, *contemporaneous* changes in House polarization correlate with changes in Senate polarization. But the correlations between the change in Senate polarization and previous changes in House polarization are not statistically different from zero.[16]

6.4 But isn't gerrymandering responsible for a decline in electoral competitiveness?

A common belief is that polarization is strongly associated with declining inter-party electoral competition within districts. Despite the widespread belief in declining competition, however, the evidence that legislative elections have become less competitive or that noncompetitive elections caused polarization is not very strong.

One of the most common ways of measuring the competitiveness of legislative elections is to examine the distribution of presidential vote shares across districts.[17] The underlying premise is that presidential vote share is a good measure of district partisanship. Districts that vote heavily Democratic in presidential elections are unlikely to elect Republican representatives, and vice versa. But districts that split their presidential votes are more likely to see competitive legislative elections. Thus, scholars have used the presidential vote as a measure of district competitiveness on the premise that it is uncontaminated by legislative campaigns.[18]

If legislative elections were becoming less competitive, we would expect to see average district presidential vote share margins growing or see fewer districts at parity in presidential voting.

Figure 6.3 shows the average absolute mean-deviated vote share for congressional districts for all elections since 1992. For example, a district with a 56% Democratic vote when the average district has a 48% share has an absolute

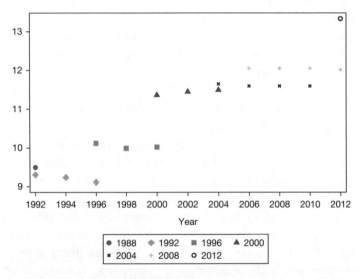

Figure 6.3: Average Absolute Mean-Deviated Presidential Vote Margin across Districts
The figure is based on mean-deviated presidential vote share for each district and for each presidential election. Each marker shows the average absolute margin for each combination of congressional term and presidential election.

mean-deviated vote of 8. Under the same scenario, a district with a 38% Democratic vote has a score of 10 while the average district has a score of 0.[19] So this statistic measures the overall level of competitiveness, where higher scores mean less competitive.

Figure 6.3 does appear to indicate declining competition as the average vote margins have increased. But it is important to note that the increase has little or nothing to do with redistricting. Figure 6.3 plots the vote-share variable for multiple presidential elections for the same congressional districts. Thus, we can determine how much the measure changes based on redistricting and how much is just the peculiarities of each presidential election.

Note that redistricting in 2002 and 2012 had no impact on the measure when the results of the same presidential election are compared. When the 2000 election results are applied to the pre-reapportionment districts, the average mean-deviated vote margin is about 11.4 points and rises only to 11.5 points under the districts drawn in 2002. Similarly, when the 2008 election returns are applied to the 2010 congressional districts, the average margin is 12 points, the same margin under the post-reapportionment districts. The apparent decline in competition following the latest reapportionment is an artifact of using the 2012 presidential election.

The use of the average margin may be misleading if what one wants to know is how many districts are in play in any given election year. Using the percentage of districts where the absolute mean-deviated presidential vote margin is less than 10 points, I find a slight decline in competitiveness following the reapportionment in 2000—roughly the equivalent of eight seats. But there is no similar decline following the 2010 reapportionment.[20] These findings are consistent, however, with a decline in electoral competition unrelated to redistricting. The most likely culprit is the long-term regional realignment in presidential voting. Such a realignment is unlikely to be reversed through electoral engineering.

Measures of electoral competitiveness based on presidential votes have certain conceptual limitations. Ultimately, interparty competition should be measured as the *ex ante* likelihood that a seat could switch partisan hands. Such *ex ante* measures are difficult to develop, but we can look at the *ex post* likelihood by examining the magnitude of partisan swings over time. Figure 6.4 plots the absolute swing in party seat share for every election since the 1930s, as well as the associated three-election moving average. It is hard to see any trend that matches up with the polarization trend. The magnitude of the swings declines from the the 1930s to the 1970s when polarization was low. There is no obvious trend following the 1970s. It appears that there may be a new upward trend beginning in 2006. Every swing from 2006 to 2014 exceeds every swing from 1996 to 2004. So inter-party electoral competition is far from dead.

A second related question is whether inter-party electoral competition affects the level of polarization in a legislature.

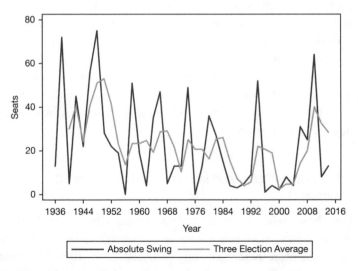

Figure 6.4: Partisan Swings in the US House The figure shows the absolute swing in the partisan seat shares for each election from 1936 to 2014.

To address this question, I used data on polarization in state legislatures.[21] First, I consider whether the number of state lower house districts that are competitive at the presidential level correlate with the level of polarization observed in the lower house. If low levels of inter-party competition at the district level produced higher levels of legislative polarization, we would expect to see a negative and statistically significant correlation for each election. In analyzing returns for the 2000, 2004, and 2008 presidential elections, I find a negative correlation for only one election. But the magnitude is very small and I can not reject the null hypothesis of no relationship between inter-party district-level competition and polarization. The only statistically significant correlation I find was for 2008 where the correlation is positive. In sum, my data do not suggest that district-level electoral competitiveness affects polarization at the state legislative level.[22]

In summary, the evidence does not support the widely held notion that polarization has resulted from a lack of inter-party competition at the constituency level associated with redistricting. Standard measures of competitiveness based on presidential vote appear to be driven by the particularities of the presidential elections rather than aspects of the allocation of voters across districts while competitiveness, measured by seat swings, does not appear to have declined. Evidence from state legislatures finds no impact of district-level competitiveness on polarization.

6.5 Are there other ways in which redistricting can impact polarization?

For those who contend that declining district-level inter-party competition is a cause of polarization, the answer is to create more heterogeneous districts. Such districts would be more likely to swing back and forth between Democratic and Republican representatives and would therefore induce competition that would reduce the chances of electing an extreme legislator.

Existing political science research, however, questions the wisdom of heterogeneous legislative districts. Tom Brunell argues that heterogeneous districts maximize the average preference divergence between citizens and their representative.[23] To support this argument, he shows that citizens in competitive legislative districts report less satisfaction with Congress. Elisabeth Gerber and Jeffrey Lewis show that legislators from heterogeneous districts compile voting records less congruent with the median voters of their district.[24] Similarly, Matthew Levendusky and Jeremy Pope find that House members representing districts with heterogeneous voter preferences compile more extreme voting records.[25]

Recently, my collaborators and I have added to the evidence against heterogeneous districts by demonstrating how such districts produce *greater* levels of partisan divergence.[26] Our argument is that heterogeneity creates greater levels of electoral uncertainty. Such uncertainty weakens the centripetal incentives toward convergence and allows policy-motivated candidates to pursue policy goals that diverge from the preferences of the median voter.[27]

To provide support for this argument, we supplement the Shor-McCarty data on the ideal points of state senators with data on the distribution of preferences within each state senate district. The data on citizen preferences are drawn from the work of Christopher Tausanovitch and Christopher Warshaw.[28] The Tausanovitch-Warshaw data are computed by linking the responses on policy questions across a number of large surveys to produce estimates of the liberal-conservative position of over 350,000 respondents. With such a large sample, we are able to estimate the heterogeneity of each senate district as the standard deviation of the respondent ideal points.[29]

First, we find that polarization in a state senate is strongly related to the average preference heterogeneity of its districts. There is a strong positive correlation between the average district heterogeneity and the polarization of the state senate. This correlation is just as large as the correlation between polarization and the variation of median ideal points across districts. Thus, the variation of voter preferences within districts matters as much as the variation across districts.

Unlike many arguments about polarization, which are predicated on ideological sorting across districts, our argument explicitly predicts that the link between polarization and district heterogeneity operates through divergence. Thus, our primary empirical finding is that Republicans and Democrats represent heterogeneous districts in divergent ways. Figure 6.5 demonstrates this point. The sample of state senate districts is divided into three groups based on the standard deviation of citizen preferences. For each group, the Shor-McCarty ideal points are plotted against the mean voter preference. Clearly, as one moves from the least heterogeneous districts to the most heterogeneous districts, the gap between Democratic and Republican legislators grows at each level of citizen preference.

The results of Figure 6.5 are robust while controlling for a number of factors that might confound the relationship

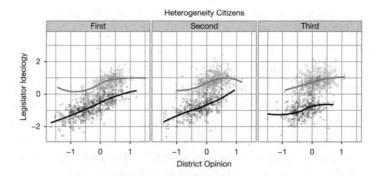

Figure 6.5: Voter Heterogeneity and Divergence Each panel represents a tercile of state senate districts based on the heterogeneity of citizens' preferences. The x-axis of each panel plots the mean citizen preference. All preference measures are derived from Tausanovitch and Warshaw (2013). The y-axis shows the ideal points of state senators from Shor and McCarty (2011).

between district heterogeneity and partisan divergence.[30] The regression results indicate that Democrats and Republicans representing districts at the 75th percentile of district heterogeneity diverge 0.1 units on the Shor-McCarty scale more than those representing districts at the 25th percentile. The magnitude of this effect is about 25% of the inter-quartile range of polarization measures across states.

Inducing political competition by striving for more heterogeneous districts runs into additional problems. Given the strong residential clustering of citizens with similar social, economic, and political profiles, the creation of heterogeneous districts also certainly requires creating what legal scholar Nicholas Stephanopoulos calls "spatially diverse" districts.[31] Spatial diversity refers to the variation of individual attributes (e.g., income, race, education) across geographic space. For example, a spatially diverse district might be one where conservative, wealthy white neighborhoods are combined with low income, liberal, minority neighborhoods. Stephanopoulos argues that spatially diverse districts tend to perform poorly on many indicators including voter engagement, participation, and representation. But most importantly for this discussion, he finds a greater degree of ideological polarization among members of the House of Representatives who represent spatially heterogeneous districts than those representing other types of districts.

6.6 Do partisan primaries cause polarization?

A conventional argument about the sources of polarization is based on the use of primaries to select each party's nominee for legislative elections. The argument focuses on the fact that primary electorates tend to be much smaller and more partisan than general electorates. Such partisan voters, it is argued, tend to select extreme nominees turning general elections into choices among extremists. A related argument is that legislators fear primary challengers much more than their general election opponents and therefore are forced to maintain extreme positions. In response to these concerns, reformers have advocated a series of changes to the structure of primary elections. The first reform is to eliminate the so-called closed primary where only party members can vote on their party's nominees. The idea is that if each party's primary is open to participation by independents and members of the other party, more moderate candidates have a better chance of getting nominated. The second proposed reform is to nominate candidates through mechanisms such as the nonpartisan blanket or "top-two" primary used in California and Washington, or the "jungle" primary used for many years in Louisiana. Under both these systems, candidates of both parties compete in a single primary and the top-two vote-getters face off again in the general election.[32]

As compelling as these arguments are, they have not found robust support in the academic literature. If one looks historically at the introduction of primaries, there seems to be no evidence that they contributed to an increase in extreme candidates. In a detailed study of the history of Senate primaries, Shigeo Hirano and his colleagues found that the introduction of a primary had no effect on polarization in the Senate.[33] They also refute a common corollary argument that primaries have become polarizing because turnout has fallen— it turns out primary turnout has always been low. Second, the timing of primary reforms is hard to reconcile with the trends in polarization. Primaries have become more open to participation by independents and cross-partisans as polarization has increased. In a study based on state-legislative elections, Eric McGhee and his coauthors estimate the effects of changing primary election participation rules on the polarization of winning state legislative candidates.[34] This study considers the effects of transitions to and from the following rules:

- Closed: only registered party members may participate
- Semi-closed: independent voters may vote in a party's primary

- Semi-open: independent voters may participate, and cross-party registrants can participate by declaring a new party
- Open: Cross-partisans and independents can participate in either primary
- Nonpartisan: all candidates are listed on a single ballot open to all voters

The expectations of reformers are that the closed primaries should be associated with much more polarization than the open and nonpartisan primaries with the semi-closed and semi-open versions falling somewhere in the middle.[35] But this was not the pattern that McGhee and his colleagues found. For the most part, they found that the different types of primary election law had very little impact on the polarization of state legislatures. Open primary systems were consistent with electing more moderate Democrats than were closed primary systems, but there was no effect of open primaries on Republicans. It turns out that the primary system that produced the most polarization was the semi-closed. Those primaries produced consistently more liberal Democratic and more conservative Republican legislators than closed primaries.[36] It is not clear, however, why the participation of independent voters should have this effect.

An important reason that primary electoral institutions do not have large effects on polarization is that the widespread belief that primary voters are more extreme than general election voters may be wrong. In a recent study, John Sides and his colleagues compare the policy preferences of each party's primary voters and its general election followers.[37] They find that Democratic primary voters are only slightly more liberal than the Democratic general electorate and the Republican primary voters are slightly more conservative than the GOP's general election voters.[38] But the differences are quite small and could not plausibly account for a substantial impact on congressional polarization.

6.7 Hasn't California's "Top-Two" system reduced polarization there?

Perhaps the most popular reform proposal is to do away with partisan primaries altogether and nominate general election candidates via the nonpartisan "top-two" system recently adopted by California. Under the top-two system, a nonpartisan primary is held where the top two vote-getters (regardless of party) move to the general election ballot. Reformers generally argue that moderate candidates would be advantaged by such a system because some supporters of the minority party will support the more moderate candidate of the majority party, which will lead to the nomination and victory of moderates. Because the top-two reform is relatively recent, there are not a lot of data, but the early returns are decidedly mixed. Will Bullock and Joshua Clinton investigated California's short-lived move from a closed primary to a blanket primary in which any registered voter can vote for candidates of either party.[39] They found that the change led to more moderate candidates in competitive districts, but not in districts where one party had a clear majority. Thus, their study provides little reassurance that blanket or top-two primaries are a solution to the problem of a lack of inter-party competition. In a more recent study, Douglas Ahler and his collaborators conduct an experiment in which voters are randomly provided either a top-two style nonpartisan ballot or a closed partisan ballot. They find that moderate candidates fared no better on the top-two ballot.[40] Finally, Thad Kousser and his team find that the top-two primary actually made things worse as representatives became less tied to the median voter of their district.[41] Because California implemented its Citizens Redistricting Commission at the same time as the top-two primary, it is not clear which reform generated this perverse outcome. Christian Grose does find moderating effects of California's redistricting and primary reform by comparing legislative voting in short windows just before and after the reforms were implemented.[42] It is not clear however whether those patterns will persist over the long run. No moderating effects are apparent in updates to the Shor-McCarty data on state legislative ideology.

6.8 What role does campaign finance play in polarization?

Following the Supreme Court's controversial decision on *Citizen's United*, concerns about an influx of corporate and labor union independent expenditures into American elections has topped the list of concerns for reformers. While the decision and the new campaign finance regulatory regime that it represents raise many valid worries, political scientists have been very dubious of any direct link between corporate and labor union election financing and polarization. Although labor unions do tend to concentrate their funding on liberal and pro-labor Democrats, corporations are not nearly as ideological. While some corporations concentrate their money on conservative, pro-business Republicans, "access-oriented" corporations spread their largess across the ideological spectrum. As a result, Poole, Rosenthal, and I demonstrate that extreme legislators obtain no fundraising advantages from corporate political action committees (PACs).[43]

But recent research has found much more promising evidence for a different channel through which campaign finance may affect polarization—increased contribution activity by ideological individuals. While the growth in contributions by PACs has been relatively flat, contributions from individual citizens have been growing dramatically. Candidates have become correspondingly more reliant on individual contributions. Michael Barber reports that the median federal candidate now obtains 80% of her funds from individual donors, up from only 20% two decades ago.[44] Moreover, Barber and Adam Bonica have shown that individual contributors are far more ideological than are PACs.[45] Consequently, candidates for federal and state office are now far more reliant on ideologically motivated contributions than was the case in the 1990s.

Barber provides two important pieces of evidence that suggest that this rise in money from ideological individuals contributes substantially to polarization in legislatures. First, he finds that there is a significant correlation between the extremity of a legislator (where extremity is measured as the absolute value of the DW-NOMINATE score for federal legislators, and by the absolute value of the Shor-McCarty scores for state legislators) and the percentage of campaign funds raised from individuals.[46] Although such a correlation is consistent with an impact of individual contributions on polarization, it is difficult to know which way to direct the causal arrow. Rather than ideological contributors forcing candidates to extreme positions, it might be the case that legislators that hold extreme positions for other reasons are simply better at raising money from individuals or that they are punished by organizational donors. But even if the donors are not causing the polarization, the success of extreme legislators in tapping into individual money can help sustain it.

The second piece of evidence is more plausibly interpreted as indicating a causal relationship between the reliance on individual contributors and polarization. To establish such a link, Barber uses within-state variation in contribution limits on individuals and PACs.[47] Such laws provide plausibly exogenous variation in the reliance of legislators on individual contributors. If a state has tight limits on individual contributors, Barber argues that candidates will be forced to seek funds from corporations, labor unions, and PACs, and vice versa.

Barber shows that the fundraising portfolios of legislators are responsive to contribution limits—as individual limits are lowered, incumbents raise less money from individuals.[48] But the most important finding is that legislators from states with high or no legal limits tend to have more extreme ideological positions, ceters paribus. In a state that switches from unlimited individual contributions to one with limits, legislators will moderate by about a third of a standard deviation of the absolute values of the Shor-McCarty scores. The effect is considerably larger in the more professionalized state legislatures.

But while Barber's results lend considerable support to arguments for tighter regulation of individual contributions, his findings about regulations on political action committees are almost the mirror image of those for individual contributions. Legislators are least polarized in states that have high or no limits on PAC contributions. Thus, the reform implications may be unsettling to some—clamp down on individuals but deregulate PACs.[49] Barber's findings are reinforced by Andrew Hall's study of the effects of states adopting "clean election" laws that provide public financing to those candidates who opt to forgo private contributions.[50] He finds that the adoption of these laws led to greater polarization in state legislatures.[51] Moreover, he demonstrates that this effect is driven almost exclusively by the declining contributions from access-oriented interest groups.

Tackling polarization through campaign finance reform involves a significant dilemma. As Adam Bonica shows, small donors are considerably more ideological and extreme than larger donors. While some large donors such as Charles Koch or George Soros have very clear ideological agendas, many wealthy contributors are more centrist and pragmatic and employ strategies similar to corporations. Smaller contributors, however, are more likely to allocate their donations according to ideological criteria.[52]

Yet at the same time, wealthy individuals have come to play an increasingly outsized role in campaign finance. Figure 6.6 (drawn from Bonica et al. (2013)) shows how campaign contributions have increasingly been concentrated at the top of the income distribution. The figure presents the proportion of contributions made by the top 0.01% of American citizens in each election since the 1980s. In the 1980s, the top 0.01% accounted for only 10–15% of the total contributions in federal

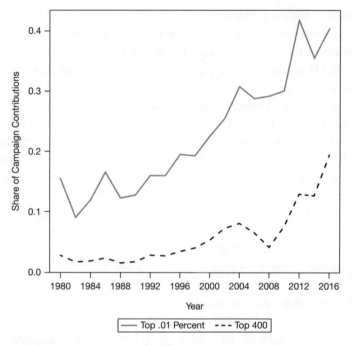

Figure 6.6: Contribution and Shares of the Top 0.01% and Top 400 Donors Contribution data updated from Bonica (2013). The solid line tracks the share of campaign contributions in all federal elections donated by the top 0.01% of the voting age population. The dashed line tracks the share of contributions from the top 400 largest donors. The figure includes individual contributions to Super PACs and 527 organizations but excludes contributions to nondisclosing 501c(4) organizations, which are recorded to have spent approximately $143 million in 2010 and $318 million in 2012, much of which was raised from wealthy individuals. Were it possible to include contributions to nondisclosing 501c(4)'s, the trend line would likely be 1–2 percentage points higher in 2010 and 2012.

elections. In 2012, more than four out of every ten dollars in contributions came from one of these top donors.

6.9 Would stronger parties reduce polarization?

As I have described in earlier chapters, a central confusion in both the academic literature and public discussions of legislative polarization in the United States is the conflation of polarization and partisanship. This confusion arises naturally because the two phenomena are hard to distinguish empirically. For example, using roll-call votes and derived indices, political scientists have noted the increasingly divergent positions of the parties. But it is very difficult to discern whether those increased differences reflect true ideological changes or simply increased intra-party cooperation and inter-party conflict. In light of our inability to distinguish between these explanations, scholars often use the terms polarization and partisanship almost interchangeably.

This conflation of polarization and partisanship is relevant for discussions of political reform. Many popular prescriptions for reducing polarization call for decreasing the role of political parties. But if polarization in the United States is the consequence of relatively weak parties rather than strong parties, as I argue may be the case, then such reforms may be ineffectual if not counterproductive.

Over the past few years, I and several other scholars have argued that polarization may in fact be a reflection of party weakness rather than strength.[53] At the core of these arguments is the idea that party leaders and internal party organizations may weigh winning elections and maximizing seat share much more highly than the ideological purity favored by outside interests. To the extent to which party leaders have sway over individual legislators, they may push for more moderation and compromise than outside interests groups. Consequently, the argument implies that if party leaders were strengthened, perhaps by obtaining greater control of renomination or of campaign finances, the more extreme legislators within each party could be better disciplined or replaced.

This perspective is helpful in explaining some empirical findings and observations about contemporary politics:

- The "weak party" hypothesis is consistent with the persistent conflict between the Republican leadership and its more conservative wing represented by the Tea Party and the House Freedom Caucus. This conflict has been blamed for the ouster of John Boehner as House speaker in 2015. That the Democratic party, so far, has not encountered similar conflicts suggests that the "weak party" hypothesis may explain the asymmetric polarization of the Republicans. Although the success of many progressives against establishment Democrats in the 2018 primaries may soon present similar problems for the Democrats.

- The fear of being "primaried" appears to be stronger among Republican legislators. That party leaders cannot protect members from primary challenges funded by outside groups limits their ability to craft bipartisan compromises.

- Ray LaRaja and Brian Schaffner examine how variations in state laws regulating campaign contributions to political parties affect the financial role of formal party organizations relative to outside groups in funding campaigns.[54] They argue that state parties, which have faced fewer legal constraints raise more money and then target it in pragmatic ways designed to maximize the party's legislative seat share. They contrast this behavior with that of individuals and outside groups who tend to focus on ideologically extreme candidates. In support of this argument, they find evidence that legislative polarization is considerably smaller in states where state party fundraising is less regulated.

- In separate work, Katherine Krimmel and I find that states identified by David Mayhew as having strong "traditional party organizations" (TPO) have less polarized state legislators than states with weaker party systems.[55]

There is no consensus for the "weak parties, more polarization" argument, however. The hypothesis does not square with recent theorizing about the nature of political parties.

The "UCLA School" of political parties, developed by a set of scholars associated with that institution, have argued that parties are coalitions of policy-demanding interest groups who exert strong control not just on elected politicians but also on the formal party leaders.[56] Thus, from that perspective, it would make little sense to empower party leaders to insulate rank-and-file legislators from the influences of outside groups—the outside groups are the leaders.

These debates took on a practical significance following the Supreme Court's decision in McCutcheon.[57] This decision struck down federal aggregate contribution limits on individuals. Prior to the decision, individual contributors were limited to a total of $46,200 to federal candidates and $70,800 to party organizations. Since limits on contributions to individual candidates were retained, the expected beneficiaries of the elimination on aggregate caps were the national party committees and the joint fundraising committees that are allowed to raise money for multiple candidate and party committees.[58]

6.10 Would a different electoral system reduce polarization?

Some scholars have come to argue that much of our polarized politics originates in the way in which we conduct elections for public office.[59] With few exceptions, federal, state, and local elections are conducted under the first-past-the-post principle. Under such an electoral system, also known as plurality voting, the office or the legislative seat is allocated to the candidate who receives the most votes. Our system contrasts with much of the rest of the world that uses some form of proportional representation to allocate seats roughly corresponding to each party's share of the vote.

Relative to proportional representation, plurality voting systems are believed to have certain deficiencies, many of which bear on polarization. First, plurality systems tend to support only two-parties.[60] This problem arises because votes cast for the third-place candidate or party are "wasted" in the sense of not having any impact on election outcomes. Supporters of the likely third-place candidate would be much better off to "strategically" cast their votes for its preferred candidate among the top two. This issue does not arise in proportional representation systems. The supporters of the third-place party have strong incentives to continue to vote for that party to increase its vote share, which translates into a higher seat share.

The association of plurality voting and the two-party system has important implications for representation. Voters are generally forced into a binary choice of candidates and their positions. Voters who prefer other alternatives will not be able to register their views through the vote. For example, suppose that there are four types of voters: those who are economically and socially liberal, those who are socially and economically conservative, those who are economically liberal and socially conservative, and those who are economically conservative and socially liberal. The first two groups are very well represented by the current Democratic and Republican parties, but the other two groups do not have a champion of their views. Thus, when they vote they have to compromise on either their economic or their social ideology. But under proportional representation, we would expect that there would be four parties—one catering to each type of voter. The parties would be represented in government roughly proportionate to the share of citizens that share their ideology. So clearly plurality voting does a worse job of representing the ideological diversity in society. The same argument might be made for other forms of diversity. Because ethic, racial, and religious minorities can form their own parties in a proportional system, the representative body is more likely to reflect the underlying society. Plurality voting, on the other hand, tends to underrepresent minorities and overrepresent majorities.

Plurality electoral systems also tend to produce lower levels of voter turnout relative to proportional systems. Part of this is due to the fact that there might be very little incentive to vote in a noncompetitive race. Supporting either the winner or the loser is a "wasted vote." Proportional systems do not suffer from such wasted votes, as boosting the vote share for any party increases its seat share. Second, plurality elections may have lower turnout because voters who do not share the views of either of the major parties may not feel inclined to participate. Because proportional systems have more parties, more voters have an opportunity to vote for a party that shares its positions.

The direct connection to polarization is less clear, however. Indeed it was once conventional wisdom that a plurality election with two candidates should produce platforms in the political center. If one party took an extreme position, the other party could gain vote share and increase its probability of victory by moving toward a moderate stance. In a unidimensional electorate, both parties would converge on the position favored by the median voter.[61] Proportional representation systems, on the other hand, may foster polarization through the proliferation of extreme parties.

Of course, since we do have polarization in our plurality system, it is possible that moving to proportional representation would be an improvement. Perhaps new parties would proliferate in the center or the formation of extreme parties might push the major parties to the middle. Of course, we can only speculate as to the actual outcomes as neither theory nor data provide much guidance.[62]

Despite these uncertainties, one reform idea that has gained traction over the past several years is that of ranked choice voting (RCV). In such systems, voters are asked to rank a set of candidates and those rankings are then used to determine the election winners. In elections for a single office or single-member legislative districts, such systems are also known as instant runoff voting (IRV). An IRV system works as follows:

1. Voters are asked to rank the candidates. In some systems, they can rank all the candidates while others

ask only that the voters rank up to a certain number of candidates.

2. The first rank votes are counted. If any candidate receives a majority of the first rank votes, she is declared the winner. If there is no majority winner, the last place candidate is dropped.

3. The votes are recounted using the first ranked votes of the remaining candidates and the second-ranked votes of those who supported one of the eliminated candidates.

4. If a candidate obtains a majority on this round, she is the winner. If not, the process continues until there is a winner.

In the case of multiple offices or multi-member districts, the process is often called the single transferable vote (STV). It works under the same principles as IRV. In the case of m seats, the last place candidate is eliminated each round and the votes of its supporters are reallocated to their next ranked choice. This process continues until there are only m candidates left.[63]

The proponents of RCV tout several advantages over plurality voting in single winner elections. In the case of single member districts, IRV is expected to advantage moderate candidates over extreme candidates. The argument is that successful candidates do not just want to maximize the number of first-rank votes but also want to secure a large number of second-rank votes for the later tabulation rounds. Consider a race between a leftist, a moderate, and a conservative. If voters rank the candidates based on ideology, the moderate candidate receives the first rank's votes from moderates and the second-ranked votes from everyone else. As long as the moderate has enough support to survive the first round, she wins the second round for sure. Thus, the moderate only loses under two scenarios. She loses if one of the extreme parties commands an absolute majority, and she loses if the number of moderate voters is lower than both the number of leftist voters and the number of rightist voters. But under the same assumptions, the moderate only wins in plurality voting if the moderate bloc of voters is bigger than both of the other blocs.[64] Indeed, the moderate might lose in a plurality election even though a majority prefers her to the leftist candidate and a majority of voters prefers her to the rightist. A clear advantage of IRV is that this scenario is unlikely.

Advocates also make similar arguments to suggest that IRV voting would reduce negative campaigning and attack ads. The argument is that candidates will refrain from attacking opponents if they expect to need high rankings from that opponent's supporters. Such a dynamic was clearly on display during the 2016 Republican presidential nomination. During the early part of the campaign, most Republican candidates thought that Donald Trump would eventually drop out. Thus, they refrained from attacking him in the hopes of positioning themselves to attract the support of Trump voters when he left the race. To the extent to which campaigns became less negative, one might expect reductions in affective polarization.

Finally, IRV is seen as a way of boosting America's endemically low turnout rates. There are several reasons why this might be the case. First, under IRV, elections would generally involve more than two candidates. So a much wider variety of voter interests and views would be represented by actual candidates. Thus, expanded choice would be an inducement for voters to participate. Second, as discussed, campaigns could become less negative and would re-engage voters who are turned off by campaign conflict.

Because a number of municipalities, and most recently the state of Maine, have adopted the IRV system, scholars are beginning to evaluate its effects. Unfortunately, most of the IRV elections held in the United States are nonpartisan municipal elections. Thus, the lessons for partisan elections are not quite clear.

Even in the context of nonpartisan elections the evidence in favor of IRV is somewhat mixed. The clearest finding is that IRV may indeed reduce the negativity of campaigns and increase voter satisfaction with the voting experience. In a survey of voters in three cities where IRV is matched with demographically and politically similar cities using plurality voting, Todd Donovan, Caroline Tolbert, and Kellen Gracey report that voters in RCV cities are 10 percentage points more likely to be very satisfied by the conduct of the campaign, 30 percentage points less likely to complain about the time candidates spend criticizing each other, and 12 percentage points more likely to say the campaign was a lot less negative than previous contests.[65]

The findings related to turnout are both mixed and nuanced. Jason McDaniel finds that turnout dropped in San Francisco mayoral elections following the adoption of IRV.[66] Moreover, these drops have been concentrated among African American voters, increasing racial disparities in the electorate. He argues that this drop was caused by the complexity of the IRV process and the obscuring of racial group interests. Similarly, in a second study with Francis Neely, McDaniel finds an increase in the number of disqualified ballots in San Francisco elections using the IRV system.[67] In a study of several IRV cities matched against comparable plurality cities, David Kimball and Joseph Anthony find a 4 percentage point drop in turnout associated with RCV, but the estimate is not statistically significant.[68] The study does find that RCV boosts turnout relative to primary or runoff elections. Thus, more voters appear to be involved in the candidate winnowing process. But this effect is offset by the decline in the number of voters who participate in the final round of balloting. Due to the limitations on the number of candidates a voter can rank, all of a voter's ranked candidates may be eliminated before the final round of vote tabulation. There is a rough 24 percentage point increase in the number of voters who are eliminated between the first and last tabulation rounds compared to the change between general election and primary/runoff participation in non-RCV cities.[69]

As previously mentioned, how IRV or STV would affect the outcomes of partisan elections is not clear. First of all, if parties were to continue to use primaries or adopt other mechanisms to winnow down the number of candidates, the results would differ little from the current system.[70] One might also question the extent to which partisan voters would ever rank candidates of the other party very highly. Thus, party moderates would not be able to defeat partisan extremists by counting on votes of the out-party. Therefore, achieving the moderating effects of RCV would require the creation of new parties or the reduction of the influence of parties on candidate selection.

Australian elections can provide some limited insight into these issues. Since the early 1900s, Australia has used IRV with single member districts for its lower chamber of parliament. Those elections have traditionally been dominated by two blocs—the Labor Party and a coalition of center-right parties (the Liberal and National parties and some affiliated state parties.) The coalition generally avoids running candidates against each other in lower house elections. In 2016, the major parties won 146 of 150 seats. Moreover, the candidate who was first in the first round of voting was the ultimate winner in all but sixteen constituencies. In fourteen of the sixteen cases, a first-round winner from the center-right coalition lost to a Labor party candidate.[71] Overwhelmingly these elections were ones where the Greens received a large number of first-round votes that were then transferred to the Labor candidate. A reasonable interpretation of these patterns is that IRV simply allows for expressive first-round votes and that the final allocation produces something similar to first-past-the-post. Given the heavy success rate of first-round winners and the partisan patterns in second and lower-ranked votes, it does not seem that there is a large bloc of "swing" voters whose second and lower ranks are up for grabs.[72] And the system does not seem to have undermined the dominance of the two major party blocs.

The Australian Senate, however, uses multi-member districts and STV. This has led to a proliferation of the number of parties that hold Senate seats. After 2016, twenty of seventy-six seats were held by seven parties outside of the major party groups. As a result, no party obtained a majority in the Senate. The comparison of the Australian House and Senate outcomes suggests, in terms of broadening representation, it is the multi-member districts that are key.

In evaluating any reforms, it is important to consider any potential side effects or unintended consequences. If ranked choice voting were to work as advertised, the likely outcome would be a proliferation of parties or at least an increase in clearly defined factions within parties. While this would improve the representation of voter interests, it might not interact well with our separation of powers system. The experience of multiparty systems and presidents has not always been encouraging.[73]

6.11 What have we learned?

The idea that we can reform our way out of the partisan polarization of elected officials is an idea that has a tremendous amount of currency among political commentators and activists. But to date, social science research has failed to bolster many of the claims of the reform community. Based on substantial evidence across many studies, it is hard to see reforms targeted at redistricting or primary elections fundamentally altering partisan and ideological conflict in the United States. Campaign finance does remain one area of possibility, but the history of campaign finance reform is one paved with unintended consequences. Any reforms to that system need to carefully weigh the effects on the balance of power between party organization and outside groups, as well as the balance between pragmatic corporations and ideological individuals.

Bipartisan redistricting commissions, nonpartisan primaries, and curbs on corporate spending may be good ideas independent of any effect on polarization. Undoubtedly, there are good non-polarization arguments in favor of these and many other reforms. Those are the arguments that should be made. Marketing ideas on undeliverable benefits is surely the best way to undermine otherwise important reforms.

7

WHAT ARE
THE CONSEQUENCES
OF POLARIZATION FOR PUBLIC
POLICY AND GOVERNANCE?

While partisan polarization is almost universally decried as a source of government dysfunction, it might have some tangible benefits. The differentiation of political leaders into two distinct groups may help facilitate within-party cooperation that might be both conducive to governing by the majority party and effective opposition by the out-party. In the terminology of political theory, polarization might produce the "Responsible Party" system that we often associate with the traditional Westminster democracies of the United Kingdom and the Commonwealth.

But unfortunately, the American constitutional system is not well designed to reap the benefits of polarized parties. First, bicameralism and other supermajoritarian institutions make the formation of winning coalitions very difficult even in the best of circumstances.[1] Now that polarization has increased the difficulty of building them across party lines, legislating only becomes harder. Second, compounding the problems of legislative partisanship is that each party is heavily ideologically factionalized. Unlike legislative leaders in parliamentary systems who generally have powers of confidence and dissolution as well as control of the renomination of legislators, American party leaders are often unable to manage conflicts within their own ranks.[2] These conflicts further narrow the needle's eye that legislation must thread. Finally, as legislative partisanship has increased, legislators of the president's party are often forced to act as advocates of the administration rather than as defenders of the prerogatives of a co-equal branch.[3] Thus, executive incursions on legislative prerogatives are likely to remain unchecked.

7.1 Why does polarization impact congressional policymaking capacity?

How does polarization affect the capacity of Congress to fulfill its constitutional functions? A variety of theories of policymaking suggest that polarization reduces the ability of Congress to act. At the core of these arguments is the fact that Congress is far from a majoritarian institution. Constitutional structures such as bicameralism and the separation of powers, as well as internal rules such as the Senate's cloture procedures, make it difficult for a legislative majority to act.

Indeed, if Congress were governed by pure majority rule, legislative outcomes would reflect the preferences of the median legislator.[4] If outcomes were governed by the preferences of the median legislator, increasing the number of extreme legislators would have no impact on policy outcomes. Moreover, there would be no policy gridlock. If the preferences of the median legislator changed, there would be a swift policy response, moving policy to the new median legislator's preferred outcome. In fact, in a purely majoritarian institution, the primary policy problem would be policy instability rather than stasis.

If legislative politics were dominated by the majority party as in Westminster parliamentary systems, polarization would not necessarily imply dysfunction and gridlock.[5] In such a parliamentary system, the winning party enacts its preferences rather than those of the median voter. Again there would be no gridlock. Polarization should simply lead to wider policy swings upon a partisan change in power.

Thus, any connection between polarization and congressional gridlock should be due to our "Madisonian Constitution" of checks and balances as well as the other non-majoritarian procedures that Congress has adopted. The next two questions explore those arguments that help to explain why Congress's capacity to govern has been reduced by polarization.

7.2 How do legislative parties turn polarization into gridlock?

Many legislative scholars argue that legislators have strong electoral incentives to delegate substantial powers to partisan leaders to shape the legislative agenda and to discipline wayward members.[6] To the extent that parties can successfully pursue such strategies, policymaking becomes the interaction of parties.

If control of the House, Senate, and presidency were concentrated in the hands of a single party, the impact of polarization would approximate that of the Westminster model previously described. But unfortunately, political polarization has occurred in an era where the control of the federal government is divided between the parties. In situations of divided government with cohesive parties, party theories predict that policymaking represents bilateral bargaining between the parties. Polarization, however, may affect whether a bargain can be struck. Just as a house cannot be sold when the buyer values it less than the seller's reservation price, increased policy differences shrink the set of compromises that both parties are willing to entertain. The increased policy differences have a second effect on bargaining that endangers even feasible compromises. Returning to the analogy of a homebuyer, consider the case when the buyer is willing to pay slightly more than the seller is willing to accept. Under such a circumstance, the buyer may be more willing to make a "low-ball" offer as her only risk is losing out on a transaction in which she stands to gain little. Returning to the political context, increased policy differences exacerbate the incentives to engage in brinksmanship, so that even feasible policy compromises might not be reached. Thus, this perspective predicts that polarization should lead to more gridlock and less policy innovation during periods of divided government.

More sophisticated partisan theories suggest that the legislature may be gridlocked even under unified party governments. Gary Cox and Mathew McCubbins argue that the majority party has strong incentives to prevent consideration of issues that divide the party.[7] Thus, they argue that the majority party will invoke a version of the so-called Hastert Rule, which requires a majority vote of the majority party before a bill may be considered by the chamber. This form of *negative agenda control* has important implications for legislative gridlock. If we were to assume that legislator preferences were arrayed along a single dimension, any new legislation would require the support of both the median legislator and the median of the majority party. But polarization may reduce this source of gridlock. The preference gap between the party median and the chamber median mainly reflects the lack of homogeneity in the majority party. When the two parties have no ideological overlap, as in recent years, both the majority party median and the House median must be members of the majority party. In this case, minority party preferences have no influence on the gap. This suggests that other features of our political system may be more consequential for linking polarization to gridlock.

Another mechanism related to partisanship that transforms polarization into legislative paralysis is the increased incentives of politicians to engage in strategic disagreement. Strategic disagreement occurs when a president, party, or other political actor refuses to compromise with the other side in an attempt to gain an electoral advantage by transferring blame for the stalemate to the other side.[8] Classical instances include attempts to bring up controversial legislation near an election in the hopes that a president will cast an unpopular veto, such as was done with the Family and Medical Leave Act in 1992 and the so-called partial-birth abortion bill before the 1996 election. Such electoral grandstanding not only lowers legislative capacity by diverting resources into an unproductive endeavor but also makes both sides less willing to engage in the compromises required for successful legislation.[9]

7.3 What about the filibuster and the presidential veto?

Perhaps the largest deviation from the majoritarian ideal is the institution of cloture in the Senate. Ostensibly to protect its tradition of unfettered and unlimited debate, the Senate requires that three-fifths (i.e., sixty) of its members vote for a cloture resolution before debate can be terminated and votes taken on the measure in question. Because opponents of legislation always have the option to keep talking until cloture is successfully invoked, sixty votes has become the de facto threshold for passing legislation through the Senate.

Cloture rules are particularly important determinants of legislative productivity.[10] Again assume that the ideal points of senators can be arrayed from left to right. Given the rules for cloture, we can characterize what a successful coalition must look like. Because sixty votes are required for passage, the senator with the sixtieth most liberal ideal point must support cloture. Let's call her Senator Sixty. Suppose the alternative for consideration is too liberal for Senator Sixty. Then it is also too liberal for the forty senators with ideal points to her right. These forty senators and Senator Sixty would vote against cloture and the bill would fail. In a world of liberal-conservative voting, Senator Sixty is pivotal for policy change. If a policy is too liberal for this senator, it is too liberal for forty more conservative senators and no change will occur. But if the policy change appeals to the senator, he can push through the policy by voting with the five-nine senators who are more liberal. In this sense, Senator Sixty is pivotal. Just knowing the vote of this senator allows us to know if a new policy that is more liberal will pass. Senator Forty-One (the forty-first most liberal) is similarly pivotal. If the bill is too conservative for him, it will also be too conservative for the forty senators to his left and cloture cannot be obtained. For this reason, we refer to Senators Forty-One and Sixty as the filibuster pivots.

Since the consent of both pivots is necessary for cloture, the new bill cannot be too liberal for Senator Sixty-One or too conservative for Senator Forty. So it is easy to see that no bill altering a status quo policy located between the pivots can be successfully revised. Thus, the ideological distance between Senator Forty-One and Senator Sixty's ideal points is a rough gauge of the Senate's propensity to stalemate due to the cloture rule. Because the majority party in the Senate rarely controls sixty seats, the link between polarization and filibuster-induced gridlock is almost immediate.

Internal roadblocks such as bicameralism and the filibuster are not the only impediments to legislative policy change. Bills that survive the legislative process face the presidential veto. Certainly, presidents can from time to time use the bully pulpit to force bills through the barriers posed by partisan agenda control and filibusters. But for the most part, the president's legislative powers are negative.[11]

The veto is a tool for blocking change rather than propagating it. A successful bill requires the presidential signature or a two-thirds vote on an override motion. Using logic exactly similar to that for the filibuster, Senator Thirty-Four becomes pivotal on the override motion for a leftist president's veto and Senator Sixty-Six becomes pivotal on a rightist veto. But because the override motion must carry both chambers, Representatives 148 and 287 are similarly empowered. The most extreme of these two legislators on the president's side of the spectrum is known as the veto pivot. Since adding new pivotal actors can never increase the number of status quo policies that can be successfully overturned, the propensity for gridlock expands.

Combing the effects of the filibuster and veto pivots, we can compute the gridlock interval. This interval is the policy gap between the leftmost pivot and the rightmost pivot. One or the other of these senators could block the change of any status quo in this interval. Therefore, the longer this interval, the more likely that policy change can be blocked. Again, the link between the gridlock interval and polarization is quite direct. As the parties' positions diverge, the distance between the pivotal legislative actors generally moves in tandem. Statistics based on DW-NOMINATE scores show that a very substantial fraction of the variance in the width of the gridlock interval is due to party polarization.[12]

7.4 Does polarization make Congress less productive?

The approaches to the study of lawmaking previously described predict that polarization should make it more difficult for Congress to pass important new legislation. David Mayhew's data on landmark legislative enactments have been used to demonstrate polarization's effects on the legislative process.[13] Congress enacted the vast majority of Mayhew's landmark measures during the least polarized period.[14] The ten least polarized congressional terms produced almost sixteen significant enactments per term, whereas the ten most polarized terms produced slightly more than ten.[15]

To control for other factors that might explain these differences, I developed a multivariate model of legislative output.[16] I attempt to isolate the effect of polarization by controlling for unified party control of government, split party control of Congress, the election cycle, changes in party control of the presidency and Congress, and secular trends. This work shows that there are substantively large and statistically significant negative effects of polarization. Based on the estimates, the least polarized congressional term produces 111% more legislation than the most polarized.

7.5 How has polarization affected the executive branch and the bureaucracy?

Recent scholarship has stressed how declining congressional capacity to override presidential and agency decisions allows the executive branch to become relatively more powerful.[17] Consider the conventional models of lawmaking such as pivotal politics[18] or majority party agenda control.[19] Each predicts a "gridlock interval" of policies that cannot be overturned by a statutory override. As discussed, these gridlock intervals tend to be larger when congressional parties are more polarized. Therefore, agencies have considerably more leeway to set policy without fear of congressional override when polarization is high.[20]

But this policy-setting autonomy may represent a relative gain in power rather than an absolute one. First, many tools of executive policymaking depend on legislative delegation to at least some degree. A less active Congress gives the president much less to work with. Moreover, a more partisan and ideological judiciary may read legislative grants of authority more restrictively. Such constraints are apparent in the judicial responses to recent executive actions on immigration.[21] Second, presidents may be charged with implementing and enforcing poorly drafted laws. When sending the bill back to a polarized Congress for technical corrections may not be an option, the administration is opened up to even more judicial scrutiny, such as in the recent *King v. Burwell* case over Obamacare subsidies.[22] Third, congressional delays in confirming presidential appointments and appropriating funds clearly reduce the policymaking capacities of the executive branch. For example, Anne Joseph O'Connell reports that, due in large part to greater confirmation delays, the initial vacancy period at the start of a new administration for all sub-cabinet officials increased substantially between the Reagan and Bush II administrations.[23] These vacancies, she argues, foster agency inaction and confusion while undermining agency accountability.

A common presumption is that the executive branch should be less internally affected by polarization in that it is headed by a single individual elected by a national constituency. There are many reasons to be skeptical that polarization will not undermine the inner-workings of the administration. First, polarization tends to increase the preference differences between political appointees and career civil servants in ways that would undermine the political control and performance of agencies.[24] Second, there is considerable ideological heterogeneity across agencies within a single administration.[25] Finally, legal restrictions on removal combined with the sluggish confirmation process dramatically limit the ability of presidents to shift the ideological nature of key agencies.[26]

But even if presidents were able to overcome all of these internal obstacles and govern as a unitary actor with few legislative constraints, executive power would be diminished by polarization in that the outputs of executive policymaking, such as orders, memoranda, and rules, are far less durable than statutes as they can easily be undone by the next administration.

7.6 Has the American judiciary and legal system changed as a result of polarization?

Political scientists have long stressed the role of ideology and personal preferences in judicial decision-making. Indeed, one school of thought subscribes to the *attitudinal* model, which predicts that the policy preferences of judges are paramount in their rulings.[27] For attitudinalists, the main implication of polarization is how it affects the preferences of sitting judges.

A second approach known as the "separation of powers" (SOP) model of judicial decision making also assumes judges have policy preferences, but their autonomy may be constrained by other actors, such as Congress and the president. If the Supreme Court were to interpret statutes in ways counter to current legislative majorities, it risks having those decisions overturned by new statutes. Courts may also be constrained by the other branches on constitutional cases over concerns that the decisions will not be vigorously enforced or that Congress and the president might directly challenge the court.[28]

As I discussed in chapter 3, there is considerable evidence that the Supreme Court and the federal judiciary have polarized along ideological lines. Both the attitudinal model and the SOP model predict significant consequences. That legal decisions depend in large part on the ideological and partisan composition of a given court lies uneasily with the notion that judges are impartial interpreters of the law. The natural result is the politicization of the courts and a loss of their legitimacy.

The most natural implication of a polarized court is that the partisan stakes of federal court nominations have risen. There is ample evidence of these effects. Charles Cameron and collaborators estimate that polarization can account for an average increase of ten negative votes on Supreme Court confirmations.[29] Moreover, Sarah Binder shows that the support coalitions for federal court nominees have gotten markedly more extreme over time.

Turning to the lower courts, Sarah Binder and Forrest Maltzman find that confirmation rates of federal judges have fallen.[30] From the 1940s to the 1980s, more than 80% of a president's federal court nominees were confirmed in a given congressional term. Since then the confirmation rate has fallen below 60%. Even among successful nominees, the length of time between nomination and confirmation has increased almost twofold over the same period. This change has been exacerbated by the fact that presidents leave judicial positions vacant for much longer periods. Statistical estimates show that each of these patterns is related to increased levels of partisan polarization.

In a novel study, Adam Bonica and Maya Sen are able to assess the extent to which the judiciary has been politicized along partisan and ideological lines at different levels.[31] They use Bonica's CFscores to compare the ideological distributions of lawyers and judges in each state and in the country as a whole. Overall they note that the distribution of lawyers is further to the left than the distribution of judges. This indicates that the judicial selection process tends to overrepresent conservatives. In general, they argue, that the leftward skew of the legal profession gives Republican politicians greater incentives to politicize judicial selection, whether it be presidential nominations and Senate confirmations at the federal level or elections at the state level. Democrats on the other hand can obtain ideologically-compatible judges with more neutral procedures that produce judges who are more representative of the population of lawyers.[32]

Importantly, Bonica and Sen note that politicization may not necessarily increase polarization among judges. The relationship depends on the underlying polarization of attorneys relative to the polarization of other actors involved in judicial selection. While they predict that polarization and politicization should go hand in hand at the federal level, that is not true in several states. As a result, US Circuit and District court judges are substantially more polarized than the population of attorneys. But state court judges are less polarized.

Polarization may strengthen the judiciary relative to Congress. There is good evidence that Congress overrides the Supreme Court less often as polarization has grown, as the SOP model described earlier would predict. In updating the data from William Eskridge, Richard Hasen finds that the rate at which Congress has overridden Supreme Court statutory decisions has fallen markedly.[33] From 1975 to 1990, Congress overrode an average of twelve Supreme Court decisions in every biennial term. But between 2001 and 2012, the rate was only 2.8 per term.[34]

But the effects of polarization within the judiciary may also undermine its effectiveness. Key values such as consistency, predictability, and restraint are undermined in a polarized judiciary. Appeals court decisions are increasingly related to the partisan composition of the circuit, which may make circuit splits more common. Small changes in the composition of the courts may lead to large shifts in the balance of political power and create demands for reversing precedents and doctrine. To the extent to which these changes reduce the perceived legitimacy of the courts, the legal system may suffer a loss in policy influence.

7.7 How has polarization affected the balance of power between the national and state governments?

A third set of actors who may derive some benefits from congressional dysfunction are the states. Federal gridlock may open spaces for states to adopt innovative policies without worries about federal preemption. Consider the liberalization of marijuana laws. Although Congress has not provided statutory authorization for states to legalize medical or recreational marijuana, President Obama's Department of Justice decided not to prosecute certain types of violations of federal marijuana law in those states that have a legal cannabis market.[35] States, through their ability to bring lawsuits, have also had a very important role in shaping policies related to the environment, tobacco, financial regulation, and immigration in the absence of congressional action.

Legislative gridlock has not only given states the space to pursue their own policy initiatives, but also the enhanced opportunity and incentive to actively resist federal policy. Legal scholars Jessica Bulman-Pozen and Heather Gerken have dubbed this new tendency "uncooperative federalism."[36] In their account, states are able to use their sovereign powers in a variety of ways that shape and constrain federal policy. They may shape national policy agendas through legislation or litigation or exploit their role as administrators of federal policies to force the federal government to heed state concerns. The power of the state's role in federal agenda setting is attested to by the increased activity of national interest groups such as the

American Legislative Exchange Council (ALEC) in promoting model legislation across states as a way of shaping the national policy agenda.

Polarization clearly enhances the incentives for state contestation of federal policy.[37] This is especially true in the case of unified party control at the federal level. In these situations, states controlled by the national out-party become the locus of opposition to federal policy. Just as Republican states resisted and challenged the Affordable Care Act, Democratic states are challenging Trump Administration policies on immigration and the environment. Consequently, states become the primary check on federal executive power when Congress has little incentive to play that role.

Of course, there are other political factors that shape the role of the states in national politics. An important one is the link between state and national election outcomes. Gubernatorial and state legislative elections are often determined by national-level economic and partisan factors.[38] On one hand, this may militate against state activity on national issues as the political payoffs from pursuing distinctive state-level political agendas may be minimal. But on the other hand, this nationalization of elections may leave state legislators less constrained by the wishes of their constituents.[39]

A second factor for state-level policymaking on national issues is that the exercise of the states' powers requires the complicity of the federal executive and judicial branches. As of this writing, it is expected that the Trump Administration will reverse the DOJ's memorandum on prosecution discretion for marijuana cases. Their ability to set policy as plaintiffs depends on a sympathetic judiciary. Moreover, congressional gridlock leaves the states in a vulnerable position. States can no longer depend on Congress to check executive encroachments or to override unfavorable statutory interpretations by the courts.

7.8 Has polarization affected policymaking in the states?

Given the importance of supermajoritarian institutions and the increasing frequency of divided government, gridlock has been the focus of studies of the effect of polarization on policymaking at the federal level. It is less clear, however, that the states face the same problems. First, it is less common for state legislatures to have supermajority voting or cloture requirements.[40] A few states have such requirements on specific legislation, such as budgets or tax increases,[41] but majority rule on other legislation is the norm.

Second, unified party government is far more frequent at the state level than at the national level. Jacob Grumbach reports that between 1970 and 2014, the federal government was unified 27% of the time, while the average state was unified 50% of the time.[42] Moreover, the fact that several states have veto-override requirements, less stringent than those at the federal level, suggests that divided government may be less of a problem in the states.

Despite the weaker expectations for polarization-induced gridlock in the states, a few recent studies have found evidence of such an effect. William Hicks finds that polarization reduces the number of statutory enactments in states where the parties are roughly balanced in the legislature.[43] To obviate concerns about comparing legislative productivity across states, Patricia Kirkland and Justin Phillips estimate the effects of divided government on whether or not a state passes its budget on time.[44] Using a variety of methods, they establish that a state is much more likely to miss the deadline when it switches from unified to divided government. The evidence that the effect of divided government has grown with polarization is not very strong, however.

Given the weak expectations and evidence about polarization and gridlock in the states, scholars have considered other effects that polarization might have on state-level policymaking. The most obvious is that polarization combined with unified government should produce wider variation in state policy outcomes and that policies in Republican-controlled states should increasingly diverge from the policies enacted in Democratic states. Devin Caughey, Yiqing Xu, and Christopher Warshaw use a measure of state policy liberalism to test whether partisan differences in policy outcomes have grown and whether that growth can be attributed to polarization in the states.[45] They find that before the 1990s, the policy change associated with shifting from a Republican-controlled government to a Democratical-controlled government was small and not statistically significant. But since that time, such a switch in party control has led to a statistically significant increase in the liberalism of a state's policies. In support of the idea that polarization can account for this increase, they find that switches in party control lead to bigger policy shifts when either the legislators or the electorate is more polarized. The authors find, however, that the effects of shifts in party control are still relatively small.

Jacob Grumbach undertakes a similar study.[46] But rather than focus on a summary measure of state party liberalism, he develops several scales associated with distinct policy domains. He also finds that there was little effect of party control on policy until the 1990s, but that partisan effects have become important over the past fifteen years—a process that he calls "policy polarization." He finds that the extent of policy polarization varies substantially across issues. For some issues, the policy changes associated with a change in party control have become substantial. These include taxes, labor policy, abortion, LGBT issues, the environment, and immigration. But other polices such as criminal justice and education are not correlated with partisan control of state government.[47] Importantly, Grumbach demonstrates that policy polarization has led to substantial partisan gaps in policy outcomes, such as revenue, spending, and health coverage.

It is worth noting that these studies have focused primarily on determining the "causal impact" of a switch in party control. This leads the authors to focus on states that are sufficiently competitive to have transitions in party control. This focus tends to understate the growing correlation between party control and policy choices in the states, as noncompetitive Republican states have adopted much more conservative polices, while noncompetitive Democratic states have moved in a liberal direction.[48] This increase in policy variation may well be one of the benefits of federalism, as states are better able to choose the policies preferred by their voters. But such variation may also lead the states into increased conflict with the federal government.

7.9 Has polarization increased the political power of the wealthy relative to others?

One of the most fertile research topics in recent years is the hyper-responsiveness to the interest and opinions of the wealthy in policymaking in the United States. Larry Bartels has shown that congressional roll-call voting behavior correlates very highly with the policy preferences of high-income voters but not with those of lower- and middle-income groups.[49] Moreover, scholars have found considerable evidence that wealthy individuals and economic interests have a large impact on determining those policies that get adopted and those that do not.[50]

Given the correlation of polarization with economic inequality, it is natural to ask whether these patterns of disproportionate influence by the wealthy are related to polarization. Several pieces of evidence point suggest no strong connection. First, much of the scholarship suggests that kowtowing to the wealthy is a bipartisan sin. In Bartel's study, Democrats and Republicans alike were highly responsive to high-income voters. Legislators of both parties voted in a more conservative direction when their high-income constituents had more conservative preferences. Democratic legislators, unlike Republican legislators, were responsive to the preferences of the middle-class, while neither party was responsive at all to the views of the bottom third of the income distribution.[51] An interpretation of this finding is that the polarization of preferences of wealthy citizens might play some role in legislative polarization.

A second piece of evidence complicating a direct relationship between polarization and the influence of the wealthy is that there is not strong evidence of any trend in our system's plutocratic tendencies. Consider the evidence provided by Martin Gilens.[52] Gilens collected information from more than 1,900 national polls from 1981 to 2002 that asked voters whether or not they support or oppose some policy change. For some analyses, he used additional data from the Johnson Administration and two years of the second George W. Bush Administration (2005–2006). In each of the polls used in his study, voters were also asked about their family income, allowing Gilens to calculate the likelihood that a policy changes (within a four-year window) as a function of the level of polling support for the change from different income groups.

Many of Gilens's findings are consistent with the conventional wisdom about political representation in the United States. New policies tend to move in directions favored by most voters. Yet the status quo bias of our system means that policy typically does not change unless there is a very high level of voter support. For example, when 80% of voters favor a policy change, there is only about a 40% chance that the change occurs within four years of the poll. When Gilens examines policy responsiveness to voters in different income groups, he finds only a modest difference between the effect of public opinions for low- and high-income voters. If 80% of the voters at the ninetieth percentile of incomes favor a change, it occurs within four years of the survey 45% of the time. If 80% of poorer voters (in the tenth percentile) favor it, it passes at an only slightly lower rate of 41%.

But Gilens argues that this triumph of democratic equality is illusory. The apparent finding of equality is due to the fact that rich and poor voters often have similar preferences on many policy questions. What is relevant, Gilens argues, is what happens when the rich and poor disagree. Here his findings are disquieting. When the rich and poor (ninetieth and tenth percentile incomes) disagree by more than 10 percentage points on a poll, the odds show a marked lack of responsiveness to the views of the poorer voters. Conversely, if 80% of high-income voters support a change, it has a 50% chance of passing, compared to only a 32% chance of passing with 80% support from the poor. Middle-income voters fare no better when pitted against high-income opposition: When the ninetieth percentile voters disagree with the fiftieth percentile voters, Gilens's findings are the same: policymaking is responsive to the higher-income group, but not the middle-income group.

When he considers trends in responsiveness to different income groups, his findings are surprising. He does not find that the political system was more responsive to middle- and low-income voices before the era of increasing inequality. Rather, his data show that Johnson's Great Society was not very responsive to voters anywhere in the income spectrum; much of the Great Society legislation passed despite its lack of public support. To the extent that one cares about democratic responsiveness, the early George W. Bush days were, to the surprise of some, quite good. Many pieces of legislation popular across income groups passed, while unpopular stuff was stymied by polarization and gridlock.

The lack of a trend in responsiveness is echoed in several other patterns of political inequality. Kay Schlozman and her coauthors find that social and economic gaps in most areas of political participation have not grown over the past thirty years.[53] In the 1960s, the gap between high Socio-Economic Status (SES) and low-SES groups for the percentage engaging in at least one political act other than voting was about thirty-five points. It rose to forty-five in 1990, but settled back to thirty-five by 2008. As a summary of inequality in political activities, the authors often use a ratio of participation rates of the top socialeconomic status (SES) group to the participation rates for the bottom SES group. Higher scores indicate more inequality. The specific trends are telling. For voting, the ratio declined from 1.84 in 1952 (high socioeconomic status citizens were 84% more likely to vote) to 1.36 in 1964, before climbing to over 2.0 in 1984.[54] But this measure has been declining ever since, and was at only 1.54 in 2008. Other trends are similar. The ratio for a broad composite measure of political activity has been generally declining since the early 1980s.

Of course, campaign finance is one important area where political inequality has grown in tandem with economic inequality. As illustrated in Figure 6.6, a growingly disproportionate share of political spending originates with wealthy donors. Adam Bonica and Howard Rosenthal argue that this concentration of campaign funding can largely be explained by increasing wealth inequality.[55] They find that wealthy citizens tend to spend approximately 1% more on campaign funding for every 1% increase in their wealth. Given that the bulk of the non-wealthy contribute little and in ways less directly related to their wealth, then wealth inequality automatically increases the skew in campaign finance.

There are other ways in which income and wealth inequality and polarization are related. One plausible channel is through the gridlock created by polarization. This gridlock may preclude redistributive policies that might mitigate or reduce income and wealth inequality. In this regard, it is worth noting that income inequality in the United States grew more rapidly than of any other wealthy democracy despite the fact that all such countries were hit by the economic and social transformations that are associated with increased inequality. Polarization-induced gridlock may well be responsible for the US failure to act as aggressively against these unleveling forces.

7.10 Does polarization have a conservative bias?

As I discussed earlier, the prevalent pattern for polarization over the past thirty years is that it reflects the movement of the Republican party to the right. This fact raises the question of the extent to which the Republican's behavioral shift is primarily ideological or whether it might have a tactical component such that the party's relatively extreme and uncompromising behavior directly produces better policy and electoral outcomes for the party.

One argument for a conservative advantage from polarization stems from the relationship between polarization and gridlock. There are a number of reasons why gridlock may serve conservative interests better than liberal interests. Generally speaking, liberals and progressives would like government to do more while conservatives and libertarians would like it to do less. So gridlock thwarts the aims of the left while benefiting the right. Gridlock may also allow policy outcomes to drift in ways that benefit conservatives. For example, many policies are denominated in nominal dollars and are not automatically adjusted for inflation. Thus, without new legislation, the real value of these policies may deteriorate. For example, the real value of the minimum wage fell from $11.63 in 1968 to $7.25 in 2018 (based on 2018 dollars). This conservative policy outcome was accomplished without a single decrease in the nominal value of the wage. Inflation and gridlock did all of the work.

But it is important to note that in principle gridlock can allow policy to drift in a liberal direction. This was true of federal income tax brackets until the 1980s. Until indexing was adopted in the Reagan tax bill, inflation could cause tax payers to move into a higher bracket even though their inflation-adjusted salary had not changed. This so-called bracket creep meant that real inflation-adjusted tax receipts would climb absent any change in the law. Clearly, the adoption of bracket indexing results in a substantial loss of liberal leverage in a polarized Congress. That Social Security benefits are indexed to wages rather than inflation is another example where gridlock may have a progressive effect. Gridlock may also work against Republicans and conservatives to the extent to which they would like to roll back or eliminate government programs.

A second argument for a conservative advantage from gridlock is that conservatives benefit less ideologically and electorally from government programs that are effective. An important tenet of conservative orthodoxy is that most government programs are inherently ineffective and inefficient. Thus, the impulse of a conservative who sees a struggling program is not to reform it, but to view the program's problems as confirmation of these basic beliefs. Moreover, conservative politicians might prefer to use examples of government ineffectiveness to persuade voters of the conservative viewpoint. An extreme form of this logic was on display during the early Trump Administration when the president mused aloud that it would be better to allow the Affordable Care Act (Obamacare) to implode rather than negotiate on reforms that minimize the loss of insurance coverage.

7.11 What have we learned?

Under many constitutional systems, party polarization might be largely beneficial. It would produce distinctive alternatives for the voters and facilitate their role in directing public policy and holding parties and elected officials accountable. Unfortunately, our Madisonian constitution of separation of powers, check and balances, and federalism is not one of those constitutions. By creating a supermajority system, these features tend to produce gridlock when the political parties are polarized and evenly balanced as they are today. This gridlock is far from neutral as it facilitates shifts in the balance of power between branches and levels of government, advantages the defenders of the status quo, and can lead to a deteriorating quality of governance. Poor governance may in turn undermine faith in our constitution, leading to even greater levels of polarization as politicians are incentivized to push the boundaries of the constitution—a concern I take up in the next chapter.

8

IS THE TRUMP PRESIDENCY
A NEW NORMAL OR MORE
OF THE SAME?

Perhaps the most important question in American politics in 2019 is what to make of Donald Trump's emergence as a presidential candidate and his subsequent electoral victory. Ever since he descended the golden escalators of Trump Tower to announce his seemingly quixotic presidential bid, pundits and analysts have battled over whether he and his movement represent an authentic re-emergence of popular control over moribund elite institutions, a dark new turn toward populism, nationalism, and authoritarianism, or simply a continuation of the long-term trends that I have outlined in this book.

There is much to be said in favor of the position of those observers that argue the Trump phenomenon represents something of a turn in American politics. The best evidence of such a turn is to recall how unseriously Trump's early electoral prospects were viewed by the elites of both parties. After all, his presidential resume was like no other. Not only had he not held elective office and had avoided military service, his record in business was spotty at best—heading a small privately held, family-run real estate firm that, following a string of bankruptcies, engaged in branding and licensing much more than it did in building. His only obvious electoral advantage was his popularity, born out of his success in reality television and conspiracy-mongering on social media.

A second unique factor in Trump's emergence was the extreme heterodoxy of his current and past political affiliations and policy positions. Consider his partisan trajectory. His first serious presidential flirtation was an effort in 2000 to obtain the nomination of the post–Ross Perot Reform party. At the time, Trump claimed to have left a Republican Party that had become "just too crazy right," and among his positions during that campaign were distinctly un-GOP proposals to tax the super-wealthy in order to retire the national debt and to create a single-payer health-care system.[1]

After dropping out of a collapsing Reform party, Trump was very slow to return to the GOP fold. According to voter registration records, Trump became a Democrat in 2001, switched back to the GOP in 2009, moved to a non-affiliated status in 2011, before moving back once again to the GOP in 2012.[2] He later justified his dalliance with the Democrats because

It just seems that the economy does better under the Democrats than the Republicans. Now, it shouldn't be that way. But if you go back, I mean it just seems that the economy does better under the Democrats . . . But certainly we had some very good economies under Democrats, as well as Republicans. But we've had some pretty bad disaster[s] under the Republicans.[3]

Moreover, before 2011, Trump often put his money where his mouth was in contributing hundreds of thousands of dollars to Democratic federal and state candidates.[4] Trump later defended these contributions as not reflecting his partisanship but his need as a real estate developer to "pay to play." In an era marked by tribal partisanship and affective polarization, one would generally think that such a promiscuous partisan history would be disqualifying in the minds of primary voters.

Many of Trump's policy views, both before and after he sought the GOP nomination, fell well outside the conservative mainstream. Most significantly, he was pro-choice and pro–gay rights in the 1990s and early 2000s. In 1999, Trump told Tim Russert of NBC News that he was "pro-choice in every respect" and that as president he would not seek to ban even late-term abortions.[5] In the same interview, he voiced an open mind on gay marriage at a time when even leading Democrats felt free to support civil unions in lieu of true marriage rights. By the time Trump began his 2016 campaign, he had repudiated his earlier support for abortion rights and mused that women who obtained abortions should be prosecuted.[6] His positions on marriage rights and legal protections for the LGBTQ community remained hedged during the campaign. Among these equivocations were that the issue of gay marriage had been settled by the Supreme Court and that he would defer to the "generals" on the issue of LGBTQ military service. The ambiguity was resolved only after the election when he appointed exclusively pro-life judges and moved to bar the military service of the transgender populations over the objections of the Pentagon.

His views in many other areas fell well outside those of the GOP establishment. In hindsight, it is hard to believe that Trump's proclamation that Mexico was sending us crime, drugs, and rapists was widely considered disqualifying. But, while anti-immigration sentiment had been brewing among the GOP base for sometime, GOP elites had determined that overt campaigning on the issue (especially in any way that could be deemed racially insensitive) had damaged the party in 2012, and they were determined not to repeat the mistake. Moreover, certain elements of the GOP coalition were supportive of high levels of immigration (especially high-skilled) and supported some proposals designed to provide legal status for undocumented immigrants. Trump's positioning on international trade also represented a conundrum for GOP elites. While hostility toward NAFTA and trade with China had been growing in some quarters of the GOP, the party's establishment comprised of corporate leaders and libertarian free-traders have long been cheerleaders for globalization. Trump also gored GOP sacred cows on issues ranging from entitlement reform to infrastructure spending to relations with Russia.

But despite these apparent discontinuities with the GOP's ideological trajectory, there were also important points of persistence. While Trump appeared more open to government spending on entitlements, he revealed no less enthusiasm when it came to reducing government revenues through tax cuts—especially those targeted to the wealthy. His views on economic and environmental regulation were also standard issue within a party where many cheered his claim that climate change was a hoax created by China. But almost all of the sixteen more qualified candidates also held these positions on taxes and regulation without Trump's baggage on the others.[7] So how did Trump get the nomination?

The answer might seem obvious. His celebrity status created a popularity and name-recognition among GOP primary voters that the better-qualified senators and governors could not match. Moreover, his hardline positions on immigration, trade, and political correctness sated an unmet demand among these voters. All of this is of course true. But the conventional wisdom among many political scientists was that what the voters want matters much less than what the party establishment wants—and the party establishment clearly did not want Trump.

The argument that party elites generally win out in presidential nomination contests was developed and popularized by a group of scholars associated with the University of California at Los Angeles. According to the "UCLA School," political parties are best thought of as a coalition of policy-demanding interest groups.[8] For example, we might think of the GOP as a coalition of corporate interests: the National Rifle Association, pro-life groups, and so on. These groups have very strong incentives for the party to nominate presidential candidates with policy positions that are broadly acceptable to all of the groups in the party. Thus, it is imperative for the groups to coalesce around such a candidate well before any voters have a chance to muck things up. So the UCLA scholars have argued that the key to obtaining a major party presidential nomination is to win the "invisible primary," where candidates compete for early group endorsements and campaign contributions. The authors provide evidence that pre–Iowa Caucus endorsements are an especially good predictor of major party nominees from 1980 to 2012, with the exception of Barack Obama in 2012.[9] But Donald Trump was the clear loser of the invisible primary, obtaining almost no high-profile endorsements before the Iowa Caucus. He did not do much better after Iowa. In fact, with the exceptions of Chris Christie and Ben Carson, none of the other sixteen Republican presidential candidates endorsed Trump until after his final rival, Ted Cruz, had dropped out.[10]

It is worth noting that the elites in the Democratic party fared only slightly better in controlling their nomination. There was a concerted effort among Democratic leaders to clear the field for Hillary Clinton as the heir apparent. However, despite crushing it during the "invisible primary," Clinton had to compete wire-to-wire against Bernie Sanders, who was not even a member of the party. The established party was dealt an even bigger blow later in 2018 when, under pressure from activists and Sanders supporters, the party dramatically reduced the role of the so-called super-delegates (convention delegates, usually office holders, who are free to support the candidate of their choice) in the presidential nomination contest.[11] While such a move may enhance intra-party "democracy," it certainly weakens the accountability of the party elite for its nominee and ultimately reduces the party's accountability to the voters.

In response to the failures of party elites to successfully coordinate in 2016, the UCLA school identifies three trends that may help explain why Trump was successful despite the strong elite opposition.[12] These include the emergence of new political media, a flood of early money, and enhanced conflict among party factions. While these are clearly important trends, it is not clear that they provide a causal explanation for the decline of elite control of nominations. It may well be that the declining influence of party elites caused these trends. Early fundraising may be a symptom of the decline of party control or a fracturing of the underlying network rather than a cause. Early news coverage of insurgent candidates may be a reflection of actual divisions within the party elite rather than the cause, as the press pays attention to conflicts evident on the ground. The proliferation of early debates may also be a symptom of party decline rather than a cause.[13]

In any case, the evidence seems clear that we are, in the words of Julia Azari, living in a world of "weak parties and strong partisanship."[14] Daniel Schlozman and Sam Rosenfeld argue that American parties are "hollow." While political parties command tremendous loyalties of the in-partisans and the enmity of the out-partisans, they are failing in their institutional role of "aggregating and integrating preferences and actors into ordered conflict, of mobilizing participation and linking the governed with the government."[15] That the beneficiaries of hollow parties are more extreme candidates like Donald Trump and Bernie Sanders seems to reinforce those arguments linking polarization to party weakness.[16]

So if Donald Trump's success should be chalked up to the voters wanting things that the establishment could not deliver, what exactly was it that the voters wanted? Much of the attention has focused on a horse race between the competing explanations of "economic anxieties," fostered by stagnating wages and living standards, and "racial anxieties," focused on the declining status of whites in American society.[17]

In the assessment of most scholars, the impact of economic anxiety was minimal. While it is true that Trump fared relatively well compared to previous Republican candidates in economically distressed regions of the country, such as the Rust Belt, the data do not show a large correlation between individual economic circumstances and voting for Trump.[18] However, decades of political science research show that voters "sociotropic" assessments of the broader economy generally play a much bigger role in voting than does individual economic factors. If sociotropic assessments were in play, voters who were not themselves unemployed or economically vulnerable may have nonetheless reacted to real or perceived economic decline in their extended families or local communities.[19] Thus, it seems premature to completely dismiss the role of economic stagnation, decline, and inequality.

Because of the stronger linkage between individual attitudes and vote choice, many scholars have focused much more on the role of racial attitudes in the 2016 election.[20] The basic thrust of these studies is that the correlation among white voters between racial attitudes and support for Trump is considerably higher than the correlation between those attitudes and support for previous Republican presidential candidates.[21] The implication of these findings is that Trump's base of core support overrepresents negative racial attitudes relative to the supporters of other candidates. Of course, this claim is substantially different than the common one that Trump owes his office to such voters.[22]

Such a claim is hard to prove. The high correlation between negative racial attitudes and Trump support has two sources. Clearly, some voters were drawn to Trump because of his ethnic-nationalist rhetoric. But some voters were turned off and defected to other candidates. It is notoriously difficult to do any analysis of the net flows, but it is worth remembering that Donald Trump lost the popular vote by almost 3 million in a year in which structural and economic factors might have advantaged a generic GOP candidate.[23] That Trump's victory was based on the Electoral College suggests that it was more important where the votes came from than from whom they came. Thus the geographical incidence of long-term economic decline may well have played a more significant role in determining the outcome than the individual-level analyses would suggest.

While the Republican party establishment could do little to derail Donald Trump during the primary, the party has alternated between constraining and enabling him in office. The constraints were largely an outgrowth of his ideological incompatibility with many of the party's elected officials and policy professionals. These tensions became very apparent during the transition when the president and his team worked to staff the new administration. Many top Republican officials and policy wonks were passed over due to disagreement with the president's policy priorities or because of previous criticisms of the president. As a result, the president had over 150 fewer confirmed appointees during his first year than either George W. Bush or Barack Obama.[24] And among those that were successfully confirmed and joined the administration, the turnover in key positions was unprecedented.[25]

The formation of Trump's foreign policy and national security teams typified his governing challenges. His anti-globalization, isolationist, "America First" approach meshed so poorly with the views of the Republican national security establishment that an open letter against Trump and his policy positions was signed by fifty high-ranking officials from previous GOP administrations.[26] The Trump Campaign was so frozen out by the GOP foreign policy establishment that his campaign's foreign policy advisory team took months to form and included as one of its members someone whose main credential was attending an international Model United Nations conference.[27] Things did not improve very much after Trump was elected. The signatories of the open letter were obviously out of the running, and many other top GOP policy hands declined to serve or were rejected due to previous criticism. The highest ranking appointment of a Republican regular was that of Nikki Haley, a governor with no foreign policy experience, to the ambassadorship of the United Nations.[28] The rest of the top jobs went to corporate executives or recently retired military leaders who had been minimally involved in Republican politics.

The slow, chaotic transition combined with policy differences with GOP leaders led to some notable policy failures during

Trump's first term. The drafting and roll out of his first executive order banning immigration from several majority Muslim countries is a case in point. The fear of opposition, not only from career bureaucrats but also from Trump appointees and congressional Republicans, resulted in the order being drafted secretly by a single hard-line adviser, Stephen Miller, and some of his former Hill colleagues. Because the standard interagency reviews were circumvented, the agencies who would have to implement the order were not given adequate notice to formulate protocols. The result was a chaotic implementation followed by the court striking down the order as unconstitutional.[29]

The failure of a unified Republican government to repeal the Affordable Care Act (ACA) represents another instance where Trump's ideological heterodoxy hindered his agenda. After the Republicans took over the House in 2010 and the Senate in 2014, they voted over three dozen times to repeal the ACA, secure in the knowledge that President Obama would veto it. Thus, the party never saw the need to reach any consensus about what sort of policy should replace it. When Trump was elected, however, the training wheels came off. The GOP would have to develop a clear alternative to the ACA. This problem was exacerbated by the fact that many of the act's provisions were quite popular, especially protections for those with preexisting conditions and the ability to keep children on parents' insurance through age twenty-six. Normally, a president would play a key role in either negotiating with the various factions or by imposing his own plan. But President Trump did not seem to have a clear idea of what kind of plan he wanted. His infidelity to ideological principles left him without the trust of any of the factions. Any such trust presumably evaporated when he called the leading House GOP proposal "mean." And negotiating with the Democrats was a bridge too far. Consequently repeal required pushing a complex and controversial plan through the eye of the procedural needle so that Senator John McCain's "thumb's down" was sufficient to kill the effort.

The administration has also repeatedly failed in areas where his ideological heterodoxy might have been a bipartisan asset. This is true of one of Trump's signature policies—huge increases in infrastructure spending. This was perhaps the only part of his agenda that intrinsically appealed more to Democrats than to Republicans. Yet the administration's repeated attempts to jumpstart the issue by declaring it "Infrastructure Week" became the fodder of numerous memes on social media. Trump's plans evolved over time into ones that were less attractive to Democrats. His proposals shied away from major government investments in favor of public-private partnerships focused on those that could be monetized, such as toll roads and airports. That more basic infrastructure such as water and sewage systems were deprioritized made the package less appealing to Democrats. Yet none of these changes elicited enough GOP support to mount a serious effort at legislating.[30]

Clearly, the Trump Administration has had some self-defined successes. The primary legislative achievement was the passage of the Tax Cut and Jobs Act that reduced corporate tax rates and provided personal income tax cuts heavily tilted to the well-off. But it is hard to imagine that a similar bill would not have passed (more easily) if the president had been any other generic Republican.

While Trump's unconventional policy positions may have mitigated his impact on ideological and policy polarization, the same cannot be said for his effect on affective polarization. It is often remarked how Donald Trump has energized his base with appeals to the identity of the white working class. The key to that strategy is, of course, delegitimizing the claims of other groups such as racial and ethnic minorities, immigrants, feminist women, and political and cultural elites. But in much of his rhetoric, the words Democrat or Liberal have become the catch-all descriptor for this collection of out-groups. But most importantly for the long run, Trump's actions serve to accelerate the trends of the partisan sorting of social identity groups identified by Lilianna Mason.[31]

The layering of high levels of affective polarization on top of ideological divides further shrink the window for the types of political compromises that are necessary to govern a democratic society. Even when ideological foes can find common ground, the partisan animosities of their constituents make deals hard to consummate. At a time when the United States faces daunting challenges related to economic inequality, climate change, and an uncertain world, the costs of the poor governance fostered by polarization will no doubt increase.

As these problems mount, citizens may well lose patience with the niceties of democratic governance and yearn for leaders willing to break norms to promote the interests of the "People." Indeed, the rise of Donald Trump coincides with the emergence of anti-liberal populist leaders across the globe including Hugo Chávez in Venezuela, Recep Tayyip Erdoğan in Turkey, and Viktor Orbán in Hungary. A common strategy of these leaders is to argue that the dysfunction of the political class justifies the weakening of civil liberties, the throttling of the free press, and the chipping away at the rule of law. Critics of the Trump Administration can certainly point to plenty of parallels, including his baseless allegations of voter fraud, demands that the Justice Department prosecute political opponents, the entanglements of his extensive financial interests, and his calling the news media the "enemy of the people."

Yet as of November 2018, our foundational institutions seem more tattered than torn. The press, the civil service, the states, and the judiciary continue to place formidable checks on the president's power. While the president's co-partisans in Congress should have challenged him more publicly and investigated his administration more thoroughly, they declined to move on some of his legislative priorities, opened independent investigations into his campaign, and refused to provide him cover should he have decided to fire Special Counsel Robert Mueller.[32]

Yet cloth can tatter only so long before it rips. The preservation of liberal democracy in the United States will eventually require overcoming our deep divisions in order to rekindle our faith in the virtues of compromise.

Appendix A

HOW ARE LEGISLATOR IDEAL POINTS ESTIMATED?

In interpreting the findings of Figure 3.2, it is useful to know something about the underlying mechanics of estimating ideal points. As described in chapter 3, the DW-NOMINATE model assumes that legislators vote according to the spatial theory of voting. This theory is based on three premises. First, it assumes that legislators have policy preferences that can be represented by a point on a line (e.g., an "unidimensional" model), or a point in a higher dimensional space (e.g., a "multidimensional" model).[1] The legislators' positions are known as ideal points. The second premise is that policy outcomes can also be represented by points on a line or higher dimensional space. In other words, a legislative alternative may be more liberal or conservative than some other alternative.

Given the locations of legislators and outcomes on the ideological map, the underlying assumption of the spatial model is that each legislator votes *yea* or *nay* depending on which outcome location is closer to his or her ideal point. As an example, consider voting on the minimum wage. Suppose the vote pits a fifteen-dollar wage against the status quo of seven dollars and twenty-five cents. All of those legislators whose ideal minimum wage is closer to fifteen dollars vote yea and all of those whose ideal point is closer to seven dollars and twenty-five cents vote nay. Typically, we assume that preferences are symmetric in that legislators value alternatives just above their ideal point equally to those the same distance below. In the minimum wage example, this implies that all of those legislators with ideal points $11.13 (= [$15 + $7.25]/2) and above prefer to vote for $15 while those with ideal points $11.12 and below vote against.[2] In the parlance of ideal point estimation, the point $11.125 is known as a cutpoint as it divides the supporters from the opponents of the yea outcome.

While we assume that legislators generally vote for the closest alternatives, they may, of course, make "mistakes" and depart from what would usually be expected. These deviations may be the result of pressures from campaign contributors, constituents, courage of conviction, or just plain randomness. But if we assume that legislators generally vote on the basis of the spatial map and that errors are infrequent, we can estimate the ideal points of the members of Congress directly from the hundreds or thousands of roll-call choices made by each legislator.

To understand better how ideal points are estimated, consider the three senator example in Table A.1. Suppose we observed only the following roll-call voting patterns from Senators Sanders, Feinstein, and Cruz.

Notice that all of these votes can be explained by a simple model where all senators are assigned an ideal point on a

Table A.1: Roll-Call Voting Example

Roll Call	Sanders	Feinstein	Cruz
1	YEA	NAY	NAY
2	YEA	YEA	NAY
3	NAY	YEA	YEA
4	NAY	NAY	YEA
5	YEA	YEA	YEA
6	NAY	NAY	NAY

left-right scale and every roll call is given a cutpoint that divides the senators who vote yea from those who vote nay. For example, if we assign ideal points ordered by Sanders to the left of Feinstein and Feinstein to the left of Cruz, the first vote can be perfectly explained by a cutpoint between Sanders and Feinstein, and the second vote can be explained by a cutpoint between Feinstein and Cruz. In fact, all six votes can be explained in this way. Note that a flipped scale with Cruz to the left of Feinstein to the left of Sanders works just as well. But a single cutpoint cannot explain votes 1–4 if the ideal points are ordered either Feinstein left of Sanders left of Cruz or Feinstein left of Cruz left of Sanders, Cruz left of Sanders left of Feinstein, or Sanders left of Cruz left of Feinstein. Therefore none of these orderings is consistent with a one-dimensional spatial model.

As two orderings of ideal points work equally well, which one should we choose? Given that Sanders espouses liberal (left-wing) views and Cruz is known for his conservative (right-wing) views, Sanders left of Feinstein left of Cruz seems like a logical choice.

The real world, however, is rarely so well behaved as to generate the nice patterns of the first 6 votes. What if we observed that Cruz and Sanders occasionally vote together against Feinstein, as in votes 7 and 8 shown in Table A.2? Such votes cannot be explained by the ordering Sanders left of Feinstein left of Cruz.

If there are only a few votes like 7 and 8 (relative to votes 1–6), it is reasonable to conclude that they may be generated by more or less random factors outside the model. If there are many more votes with patterns 1–6 than there are deviant

Table A.2: Unexplained Votes

Roll Call	Sanders	Feinstein	Cruz
7	YEA	NAY	YEA
8	NAY	YEA	NAY

votes, any of the common scaling procedures still generate the ordinal ranking Sanders left of Feinstein left of Cruz. As discussed, I focus on the DW-NOMINATE procedure for measuring ideology.[3] To match the common-language designation of liberals to the left and conservatives to the right, DW-NOMINATE scores are assigned so that each member's average score lies between −1 and +1, with −1 being the most liberal position and +1 the most conservative.

In the DW-NOMINATE model, the frequency of the deviant votes provides additional information about nominal values of the ideal points. For example, if there are few votes pitting Cruz and Sanders against Feinstein, DW-NOMINATE places Cruz and Sanders far apart, to mimic the improbability that random events lead them to vote together. Alternatively, if the Cruz-Sanders coalition were common, the model places them closer together, consistent with the idea that small random events can lead to such a pattern.

It is easy to measure the success of the one-dimensional spatial model. In the example, the "classification success" is simply the proportion of explained votes (i.e., types 1–6) of the total number of votes. Notice, however, that classification success will be inflated if there are lots of unanimous votes like 5 and 6, because any ranking of the senators can explain them. Thus, scholars typically measure classification success relative to what would be predicted if every member voted for the more popular position. This has the effect of netting out the contribution of the very lopsided votes.

A.1 What if the liberal-conservative dimension does not explain all voting?

Sometimes, however, there are so many votes like 7 and 8 that it becomes unreasonable to maintain that they are simply random. Perhaps there is some systematic reason why Cruz and Sanders often vote together against Feinstein. To capture this possibility, we might assume that a Cruz-Sanders coalition forms because there is some other policy dimension on which they are closer together than they are to Feinstein. DW-NOMINATE accommodates such behavior by estimating ideal points on a second dimension. In this example, a second dimension in which Cruz and Sanders share a position distinct from Feinstein's explains votes 7 and 8. Both dimensions combined explain all of the votes. Obviously, in a richer example with one hundred senators rather than three, two dimensions will not explain all the votes. Adding dimensions, however, generally adds explanatory power.

But the question is how much value higher dimensions add. Scholars tend to focus on one-dimensional models as they do a reasonably good job of explaining the bulk of congressional roll-call voting during the current era. But this does not mean that there are not higher dimensions to voting, just that they are not very informative. An analogy to maps is useful at this point. Consider Chile. Suppose instead of a full map, one were asked to predict only with latitude measures. Despite the fact that Chile has two dimensions, the North-South measure would do a very good job of prediction. Longitudes would help only marginally. Contrast that with the roughly rectangular United States. Latitude-only prediction would not be very good. One could hardly distinguish between Chicago and New Orleans. So when I describe American politics as one-dimensional, I mean that the ideological map looks more like the map of Chile than that of the United States.

A.2 Do members' ideal points move over time?

Ideological positions are quite stable for politicians throughout their career. Of course, there are a few prominent examples of politicians whose positions did change, such as the right to left movements of Wayne Morse, or the left to right movements of Richard Schweiker (R-PA), or the right to left to right movement of John McCain. A very small number of politicians have been nothing if not erratic, like William Proxmire (D-WI). But for the

most part, legislators' positions on our scale only move significantly if they switch parties (and, of course, party switching is
quite rare). Even a member whose constituency changes quite
dramatically either by elevation to the Senate or through major
redistricting rarely changes positions in a significant way. In a
very careful study, the assumption that legislators maintain the
same ideological position throughout their careers performs
just as well statistically as the assumption that legislators are
able to change positions in each biennial term.[4]

A.3 Can ideal points be compared over time?

An important feature of DW-NOMINATE is that we can use
overlapping cohorts of legislators to make inter-temporal
comparisons about the degree of polarization. For example, we
can establish that in relative terms Ted Cruz is more conservative than John Tower even though they never served in the
Senate together. We can do this by leveraging that John Tower
served with Phil Gramm, who served with Kay Hutchison,
who served with John Cornyn, who served with Ted Cruz.

It is important to recognize, however, that these comparisons
are only relative. For example, it is possible that the entire political spectrum may move to the right or the left over time.
Suppose that American politics moved uniformly leftward
from 1960 when Tower was elected. Then even though Ted
Cruz has a larger ideal point than John Tower, we would not
necessarily see that he was the more conservative. We could
say only that Cruz was relatively more conservative relative to
those he served with than was Tower. But when we measure
polarization, we are mostly interested in the relative position
of Republican and Democratic members so the practical importance of the issue is small.

It is also worth noting that changes in the level of polarization are driven in large part by cohort effects. This is especially true of the recent Republican party in which each new

class of first-term members has tended to be more conservative than the returning members. To the extent to which these comparisons hold, polarization measures are less dependent on the comparisons of individual ideal points over long periods of time.

A.4 Are there other methods for measuring ideal points and polarization from roll calls?

Over the past twenty years, scholars have developed a wide variety of alternative models for estimating ideal points from roll-call voting data.[5] But unlike DW-NOMINATE, these models are static in that they focus on estimating ideal points for a single or small number of legislative sessions. The contributions of these newer methods range from faster estimation, more transparent interpretation, the incorporation of information beyond roll calls, and alternative approaches to several technical issues. While there are subtle differences in the ideal points estimated by these different procedures, they all tend to correlate very highly with those from DW-NOMINATE. More importantly, all of the procedures produce estimates of ideal points consistent with the growing levels of partisan polarization.

All of the approaches just described are what statisticians call "parametric," because the random component is assumed to follow a specific random process. Poole (2000), however, develops a non-parametric algorithm that rank orders legislators in such a way as to minimize the number of classification errors. This procedure is dubbed OC for "optimal classification."

Other approaches have been developed to deal with dynamic ideal point estimation. Recall that DW-NOMINATE incorporates dynamics either by assuming that each individual member has a constant ideal point throughout her career or that each member moves according to a linear trend. The method developed by Groseclose, Levitt, and Snyder (1999) can be used to produce a dynamic model from static ideal points under the assumption that each member maintains a constant average ideal point but moves around this average from term to term. Martin and Quinn (2002) incorporates dynamics into an ideal point model by assuming that each member moves according to a "random walk."[6] Although these approaches produce different dynamic patterns for the ideal points of individual members, they don't produce substantially different patterns of partisan polarization. Nokken and Poole (2004) use a two-stage procedure in which the static DW-NOMINATE model is estimated in the first stage. In the second stage, the spatial positions of the yea and nay outcome from the first stage are held fixed, while estimating a unique ideal point for each legislator in each congressional term. Bonica (2014b) estimates senator ideal points based on a rolling average of the last fifty roll calls.[7]

Scholars have also used network analysis to measure the polarization of roll-call voting within Congress. The underlying idea is to treat two members who often vote together as connected nodes in a network. Intuitively, the separation of the Republican voting network from the Democratic one represents an analog to polarization. Waugh et al. (2009) applies a specific measure of network structure known as concept modularity. Modularity measures the division of the network into distinct groups or modules. An advantage of modularity measures are that they do not presume that the only network modules are those based on party. As applied to congressional voting, it measures the extent of the similarity of the voting records of legislators within a group and dissimilarity to legislators in other groups. Modularity measures in the Senate correlate well with DW-NOMINATE measures except during the middle of the twentieth century when the network measures show less polarization than DW-NOMINATE measures.[8]

A.5 What are the limitations of the roll-call–based measures of polarization?

While measures of polarization based on roll-call votes have proven very useful in studying polarization, and the findings on which they are based have been replicated on different data, there are a number of issues and limitations about their use. Several of these have already been addressed. The comparisons of ideal points over time requires strong assumptions about the stability of legislative preferences. While these assumptions and the cohort structure can make fairly accurate comparisons over short periods of time, comparisons of ideal points and polarization over longer periods of time is riskier. Also, uncertainties remain as to the extent to which ideal points reflect the true ideological positioning of legislators or are an amalgam of influences, such as constituency preferences, partisan pressures, and interest group influence.

A concern that I have not yet addressed is the extent to which polarization measures based on roll calls can be inflated (or deflated) by changes in the legislative agenda. One prominent argument in favor of this effect is based on the series of reforms undertaken in the House since the 1970s.[9] According to such accounts, power in Congress was decentralized among its committees until a series of post-Watergate reforms strengthened the majority party caucus at the expense of committees. Party power was further centralized in 1995 when Newt Gingrich and the Republican Conference exercised enormous discretion in the selection of committee chairs and imposed term limits on them.

This centralization of party power may affect polarization measured by NOMINATE scores in two ways. First, it may generate "artificial extremism" if party leaders use their agenda control to select issues on which to divide their partisans from the other side.[10] In the extreme, if every vote is on an issue that divides Democrats and Republicans, the voting patterns may look extremely polarized even if the parties are not very far apart. Polarization would be a statistical artifact. Second, increased party leadership might also exacerbate polarization if leaders were better able to force their moderate wings to vote with the party majority.

These claims, however, fail to explain some of the other patterns documented in this book. In particular, the explanations are very House-centered, so it is not clear that they are helpful in explaining the polarization of the Senate and various state legislatures. It is probably true that partisan leadership has become more prominent in the Senate but reform there has been less ambitious than in the House. The Senate's supermajority requirement embedded in its cloture rule also makes it extraordinarily difficult to pursue the partisan strategies that would create artificial extremism.

McCarty, Poole, and Rosenthal (2016) deal directly with these claims. First, they consider the effects of "artificial extremism." As I explain in chapter 3, this concept was first applied to the use of interest group ratings by Snyder (1992) who showed that if an interest group chooses votes to separate ideological friends from enemies, the distribution of ratings will be artificially bimodal. Similarly, if party leaders only allowed roll-call votes on issues that separate the parties, polarization would be inflated. Fortunately, we can be confident that this is not a large problem for NOMINATE. First, unlike interest group ratings, NOMINATE uses almost all the votes in a given term to estimate each ideal point. Interest groups can select only those votes that divide friend from foe, but any such selection bias is lessened when all votes are used. Thus, despite any increase in partisan control over the agenda, there are a wide variety of roll-call cutpoints each term. Second, there is a critical difference between interest group ratings and NOMINATE scalings. In an interest group rating, the distance between two legislators is directly proportional to the number of roll-call cutpoints that separate them. This is generally not the case for NOMINATE, because the "redundant" cutpoints do not change the estimates of the ideal points. So as long as the distribution of cutpoints is sufficiently wide, an increase in the number of cutting lines between the two parties will not automatically produce an increase in polarization.

To demonstrate how DW-NOMINATE polarization measures are robust to these concerns, Poole, Rosenthal, and I conducted an experiment. We reran NOMINATE for the 1st through the 113th Congresses constraining each House to have the same distribution of roll-call margins.[11] This experiment reflects the counterfactual of what would have happened if party leaders were not able to adjust the divisiveness of the bills on the roll-call agenda. We find that the pattern of polarization would be essentially the same even if the agenda were held constant. Of course, this experiment does not prove that the level of polarization is not inflated by artificial extremism, but it casts grave doubts on the role of artificial extremism in the increase of polarization.

I now turn to the concern that increased polarization is a reflection of the enhanced ability of party leaders to discipline backbenchers. This is a very challenging question methodologically because the observable manifestations of increased party pressure look a lot like ideological polarization. Both phenomena result in fewer observed bipartisan coalitions and thus less overlap in ideal point estimates. Moreover, it is hard to distinguish between pressures internal to the legislature, such as those from leaders and caucus majorities, and those that are external, emanating from primary electorates, partisan constituents, and contributors.

One approach to distinguishing between internal and external pressure is to look for "selective" party pressures on close or important votes. Essentially, this approach seeks to determine the extent to which certain roll calls are more partisan than others and postulates that the variation is due to the activity of party leaders and whips. A version of the approach was first developed by Snyder and Groseclose (2001). Because, as they argue, rational leaders would expend little effort whipping on lopsided votes, those votes can be used to estimate measures of preferences uncontaminated by party effects. Therefore, after estimating legislator preferences using sixty-five to thirty-five divisions or greater, they determine whether party continues to have predictive power on voting controlling for the "party-purged" ideal point estimates. They find that the party variable is statistically significant on a large percentage of the close roll calls, but, as expected, on few lopsided ones.

McCarty, Poole, and Rosenthal (2001) criticize this approach because of the possibility that the "party-purged" ideal points provide poor measures of moderates and that this measurement error is correlated with party. They provide an alternative methodology based on estimating distinct cutting lines for each party. If there is no party effect, the two cutting lines will be identical, just as in the standard model. If party discipline is applied, however, some Republicans to the left of the common cutpoint vote with their party and some Democrats to the right vote with theirs. The result is a separate cutpoint for each party. Because party discipline generally involves getting moderates to vote with extremists, the cutpoint for the Democrats should be to the right of the cutpoint for Republicans.

To assess the importance of selective party pressure, we simply compare the predictive success of the two-cutpoint model to that of a one-cutpoint model. When party pressure is important, the two-cutpoint model should perform much better. The upshot is that the correct classification gains of the two-cutpoint model are modest, and there is no evidence that selective party pressures have increased.

Of course, it is entirely possible that even if the ability to apply selective pressures has not increased, general party pressure (which would be reflected in each member's ideal point) has increased. But, as we have already noted, it is impossible at this point to distinguish between general party effects that are internal to the legislature and those that are external.

Appendix B

HOW DO WE MEASURE POLARIZATION IN THE PUBLIC?

With the exception of some of the studies described in chapter 3 that use text, campaign contributions, or social media data, the vast majority of our knowledge about polarization comes from public opinion surveys.[1] An evaluation of the strengths and weaknesses of these measures involves a little deeper dive into survey research.

B.1 What is a survey?

A survey is a tool that we can use to learn about aggregate features of social groups or collections of such groups. The basic mechanics of the survey are simple—we ask people questions. But as we will see, there is a great deal of subtlety involved in getting the sorts of answers that can be used in meaningful ways.

The uses of surveys are vast. One important set of uses involves inquiries about the beliefs, attitudes, and opinions of groups of individuals. Most people are surely aware of applications such as those measuring the public's preferences over various public policy issues or predicting turnout or vote choice in an election.

But surveys are also used to measure more objective features of groups, such as those related to their social, economic, and demographic profiles. Such surveys include the Census, the American Community Survey, and various other economic and social surveys.

B.2 What is a population and sample?

Clearly, with the possible exception of the Census, we are unable to ask questions of all members of the target groups. So we have to do what we can to estimate the features of a group based on the answers from a subset of that group. The key insight of survey research is that under certain conditions, we can make pretty reasonable inferences about the preferences, behavior, and demographic features of groups based on relatively small samples of responses.

So how do surveys accomplish this seemingly magical feat? To understand how surveys work, we need some definitions and terminology. The first thing a survey researcher must do is define a *population*. A population is simply the group about which the researcher wants to learn. The population might be all adults, all citizens, all likely voters, Princeton juniors, or African American voters in Wisconsin. Second, a researcher must identify a *sample*. The sample is the group of people who are actually interviewed or surveyed. Samples can be constructed in many different ways ranging from randomly selecting phone numbers or email addresses to grabbing people at the mall. As I will discuss, how a sample is constructed and contacted matters a great deal. Given a sample and a population, survey inference is the process of building bridges between what we learn about the sample and what we can say about the underlying population. These bridges are always probabilistic in that the features of the sample are likely to be true in the population, but not guaranteed to be so.

To make these ideas concrete, let's turn to an example of one of the most common uses of surveys in politics: the measurement of the president's approval rating. Since the 1950s, the Gallup Organization has been asking American adults "Do you approve or disapprove of the way President X is handling his job as president?" The respondents can answer "approve," "disapprove," or offer "no opinion." The approval rating is simply the percentage of those who say "approve." There is also a disapproval rating that is the percentage of disapprovers.

So the population for the Gallup survey is American adults. The weekly sample is 1500 adults, 40% of that are reached on landline phones and 60% through cell phones. So, like any survey, the goal of the presidential approval survey is to learn about the views of a population (all American adults) from a relatively small sample of interviews (1500). Gallup obtains an approval rating from the sample, but what does it imply about the approval rate of the population?

B.3 How do we draw inferences from surveys?

Inference is the bridge from the sample to the population. How do we build a bridge that is not going to collapse? The strongest bridges are built upon the foundation of random sampling. For our purposes, we say a sample is random if one of two conditions is met. The first is that all members of the population have an equal chance of being included in the survey and are equally likely to respond to the survey. Obviously, this condition is very hard to satisfy in practical terms. Some people are easier to reach than others. Some people have landline phones, some do not. Some people use the Internet, some do not. Some families are at home at six at night and some are not. Some people like to answer surveys, some do not.

Fortunately, there is a second condition that works almost as well. This condition requires that respondents and non-respondents be statistically identical. The respondents and non-respondents should, *on average*, have the same education, racial and ethnic composition, and should hypothetically answer the survey questions in the same way. Clearly, the demographic similarities can be checked against Census data, but the similarity of answers is obviously unverifiable. But we often base our inferences on the assumption that it is true.

It is important to note that condition one implies condition two. If the sample is a true random sample of the population, the respondents and non-respondents will be identical on average. But as we will see, there are ways to create a sample that is representative of the population without pure randomization.

B.4 Why is random sampling important?

Random sampling turns out to be the secret required for good inferences. If condition one or two holds, we can make strong statements about the population based on our survey samples. Consider the statements we can make about the population average or *mean*. First, if the conditions hold, then the sample mean matches the population mean on average. In technical language, this means that the sample mean is an unbiased estimate of the population mean. Importantly, it does not imply that the sample mean matches the true population mean exactly. Approximately half the time, the sample mean will be too low; approximately half the time it will be too high.

Let's go back to the example of presidential approval. On July 9, 2017, the Gallup Organization reported that President Trump's approval rating was 39%. Thus, the sample mean of the approval response was 0.39. Assuming that the samples were drawn randomly, we could say that 0.39 is an unbiased estimate of the proportion of US adults who supported the president. In reality, the proportion could be higher or lower, but 0.39 is the best prediction we can make based on the data.

I have stressed so far that the sample result gets things right on average. But the sample result generally deviates from the truth somewhat. What can we say about how much the sample result deviates from the population? In other words, what is the sampling error? Statistical theory, can tell us something about how far the sample result is from the true value. Many of you who have read about surveys are aware that they are often reported with a margin of error. For example, the Gallup approval rating has a margin of error of plus or minus three points. This means that if we took one hundred random samples, Trump's rating should lie between 36% and 42% in 95 of them.

In the case of random sampling, we can state very clearly how much variation in the outcomes of our sample we should expect. This sampling error has some very important properties. First, the error is decreasing in the size of the sample. Intuitively, if we have a larger sample, we have much more information on which to base our predictions about the population. But it turns out we do not need our samples to be too large. In fact, the sample error can get quite small based on as little as one thousand responses. Paradoxically, however, the sample error does not depend on the size of the population. One thousand respondents can approximate a population of a million just as well as it can a population of one hundred thousand.

Second, the sample error is maximized when the uncertainty about the population is highest. This occurs when the population is split fifty–fifty on some proposition (otherwise there is a clear majority position in the population and therefore less uncertainty).

These facts can be stated precisely in a formula for the *margin of error* of the poll. To state the formula let p be the proportion giving a particular survey response and n be the number of respondents. Then we can state the margin of error as approximately $1.96 \dfrac{\sqrt{p(1-p)}}{n}$. It is easy to see that the margin of error declines in n and is largest when $p = 0.5$.

Always remember the following caveat: the margin of error captures only that variability in the survey results associated with random sampling. As we will see, the survey results can deviate from the truth for many other reasons as well.

B.5 What happens when samples are not random?

As previously discussed, truly random samples are great. They give us an unbiased prediction of the attitudes, behavior, and other features of the population. Moreover, random samples reveal a very precise assessment of the variation of the sample results. But what if samples are not random? This is a clear concern because generating random samples is hard in practice. Clearly, the first condition where all members of the population are equally likely to be contacted and respond is nearly impossible. Moreover, there are some major impediments to generating a sample that satisfies the second weaker condition. For example, some groups are very difficult to contact because they do not have phones or Internet. If the hard-to-contact groups have different attitudes or behavior from the easy-to-contact groups, our survey results will be biased. Consider the 1936 Literary Digest poll that made the spectacularly bad prediction that Alf Landon would beat Franklin Roosevelt. It is widely believed that the erroneous prediction arose because FDR's supporters were less likely to be contacted by the pollsters.

It may also be the case that some groups are less likely to answer survey questions than others. For example, during the 2016 election, some people speculated that Trump supporters were less likely to answer survey questions about the election than were Clinton supporters. This would lead to survey responses that were biased in a pro-Clinton direction.

Of course it is possible that non-responders and responders are exactly alike on average, but that is a proposition that is very unlikely. Fortunately, there are some statistical corrections that can minimize (though not eliminate) the problems associated with nonrandom contact and response. The first and most common remedy is to *weight* the responses so that the weighted sample approximates a random sample as defined by condition two. A simple example will help explain this procedure. According to the Census, the US population is 12% black. But suppose for some reason, a sample comes back only 6% black. If this problem were ignored, the sample results would be biased against the views of black citizens. A solution is to make up for the low proportion of blacks by giving their responses more weight than those of non-blacks. The weights you would assign are two for blacks (12% divided by 6%) and 0.936 to non-blacks (88% divided by 94%). The weighted sample would therefore be 12% black and 88% non-black—the true proportions in the population.

Another problem with purely random samples is that the subsamples of particular groups might be quite small. Suppose we wanted to do a survey that would compare the political attitudes of Asian voters to those of non-Asian voters. A random sample might not obtain very many Asian respondents. Because Asians are 5.6% of the US population, a typical national sample would produce a dozen or so Asian voters. This is not really enough to learn much about Asians. The margins of error would be huge.

So a typical solution would be to stratify the sample. One could collect a large sample of Asians and a large sample of non-Asians. Or alternatively one could oversample Asians. These procedures can allow for precise predictions about both the Asian and non-Asian populations.

B.6 What are some of the problems associated with the design of surveys?

The cardinal rule of survey research is that the answers one gets depend on the questions asked. First, researchers should always avoid leading or loaded questions. Such questions tend to push respondents into certain answers even if those responses are not a true reflection of their views. Consider a question such as "do you support Republican efforts to reform health care by denying Medicaid coverage to millions of sick children?" Such phrasing certainly encourages the answer "no." Questions of this form are not only bad social science, but may blur the lines between research and advocacy.

Overly simple questions such as "do you want a tax cut?" or "do you want to reduce inequality?" are also not very informative. Many people like these things in the abstract, but in real life tax cuts and inequality reduction come with trade-offs. Lower taxes means less spending on something. Reducing inequality may mean higher taxes or policies that favor some groups over others. Respondents cannot clearly articulate how they view the trade-offs when the questions are so simple.

Survey responses may also be influenced by varying levels of numeracy in the population. People clearly vary in their abilities to understand and process quantitative information. So questions that present or elicit such information—such as questions about the ratio of CEO to worker pay—may be problematic for respondents who have difficulty thinking in ratio terms.

We also know from psychology that respondents may answer differently depending on whether a question is framed as a gain or a loss. Typically, people are adverse to losses and therefore respond more negatively to losses than they respond positively to gains. In a classic experiment, Amos Tversky and Daniel Kahneman ask people about a treatment for a disease affecting six hundred people. For some respondents, it is described as saving two hundred of the patients. For the other set of respondents, it is stated that four hundred will die. The drug is much more positively evaluated when it is described as saving two hundred than it is when four hundred die, even though the outcomes are logically the same.[2]

A second cardinal principle is that the answers one gets can depend on the order that questions are asked. A major concern in survey research is the effects of *priming*. Priming is where one stimulus influences the response to another stimulus. Priming has important implications for the study of voter polarization.

It is well known that survey respondents may answer public policy questions differently when they are perceived to relate to partisanship. Typically, they support the position advocated by their party. For this reason survey responses may differ to the extent to which partisanship is primed in the survey. If a policy question follows a series of questions about parties and their leaders, we might expect the respondents to answer in more partisan ways than they would if they had not been primed by partisanship. Clearly, other identities such as race, ethnicity, gender, and religion can be primed in ways that may influence answers. So researchers who would like to avoid priming effects should think carefully about the order of questions and ask those about partisanship, race, and ethnicity toward the end of the study. Of course, there are cases where the researcher wants to learn specifically about the effect of priming on identities. In this case, researchers often use survey experiments as discussed below.

Finally, it is possible that the answers to survey questions may not be meaningful. Clearly, there are a great many questions that citizens have not thought or care very much about. So unless there is a response option that allows them to express this uncertainty or ambivalence, the responses to the survey may reflect non-attitudes. Such responses could be random or driven by the answers that seem most socially desirable. But they would not reflect true opinion. Another concern is that it is not clear what incentives respondents have to answer truthfully. So there is always a cheap talk element to survey responses.

So many other motivations other than accuracy may come into play—we have already discussed one—social desirability. The respondent may give the answer she thinks looks good to the interviewer. Another concern is what one might call cheerleading—giving the answer designed to make one's preferred party or group look good. Consider an example: when voters are asked whether the economy is doing well, members of the president's party generally say yes, while members of the other party say no, independent of how well the economy is doing objectively. Of course, some of this could be the perceptual biases of partisans. But when researchers pay respondents for correctly predicting the unemployment or inflation rate, the magnitude of this partisan bias falls substantially. This suggests that cheerleading and cheap talk may influence survey responses.[3] Ultimately, however, we want survey responses to be predictive of actual behavior. So expressive behavior in surveys, such as cheerleading, might be quite informative in so far as that expressive behavior carries over to other forms of political action such as voting.

B.7 What are some limitations of using surveys to measure polarization?

Roughly speaking, there are two types of surveys. The first is the *cross-sectional* survey where a sample of voters is interviewed one time. The second is a *panel* survey where a sample of voters are interviewed on multiple occasions over time. Cross-sectional surveys are designed to capture a snapshot of the population at a given point in time. Panel studies allow researchers to understand how individuals within the population change over time.

Most surveys are designed as cross sections. Thus researchers who wish to understand how public opinion, partisanship, and polarization change over time must do so by comparing a series of these snapshots. An important limitation of this approach is that the actual voters sampled in each of the surveys will be different. So if we observe a difference in the polarization of two samples, it is difficult to infer whether those changes are due to changes in the population or changes in individual views.

A panel study avoids some of these problems. In such a study, the same set of voters are interviewed at different points in time. Thus, if we were to detect changes in the attitudes revealed, we would be able to attribute those to individual changes in attitudes. The ability to detect individual change is very important in the study of polarization. Recall the previous discussion about the difference between polarization and sorting in public opinion. Suppose the correlation between party identification and conservatism among voters was rising. This could occur for three distinct reasons. First, opinion might be polarizing such that Republicans were getting more conservative and Democrats were getting more liberal. Second, there could be ideology-driven sorting where conservative Democrats become Republicans and vice versa. Finally, the changes could be due to party-driven sorting where liberal Republicans become conservatives and conservative Democrats become liberals. Since all of these explanations depend on different types of individual behavioral changes, we cannot adjudicate based on looking at separate cross sections containing different sets of voters.[4] Panel data is crucial here. In comparing two points in time, we could assess how many voters switched their party but not their ideology; how many switched their ideology but not their party; how many switched both; and how many switched neither.[5] Unfortunately, unlike the fields of economics or sociology, there are very few political panel studies. The ones that exist tend to be short—either two or three election cycles or cover a single national campaign. Clearly, this lack of longitudinal data limits our knowledge about the long-term sources of voter polarization.

A second challenge to using surveys to measure polarization relates to the difficulty in securing sincere truthful responses from the voter. As I discussed earlier, there is the problem of cheerleading. When a voter is asked a survey question, there is always the possibility that she will offer the response that is more favorable to her party whether she believes it or not. For example, after the election of Donald Trump who campaigned on improving relations with Vladimir Putin's Russia, the approval of the Russian government by Republican voters surged. Clearly, there are (roughly) three possible explanations. The first is that support for improved Russian relations was seen by GOP voters as now central to their partisan identity. Second, GOP voters could have been persuaded by candidate Trump's arguments. Third, GOP voters might have understood the question about Russia to be a referendum on Donald Trump. These voters may have answered favorably about Russia to indicate support for the president even if their underlying views about the Russian government were unchanged. Clearly, each of these possibilities has different implications for the underlying social and psychological mechanisms underlying partisanship.

A related problem concerns *social desirability* bias. Many voters may be unwilling to share controversial or unpopular views with survey researchers. Thus, attitudes that might be deemed racist, sexist, or intolerant might well be underrepresented in conventional surveys. Consequently, polarization on a wide number of controversial issues related to race, gender, sexuality, or immigration may be underestimated.

To address these concerns and others, researchers have increasingly turned to survey experiments.

B.8 What is a survey experiment?

In a conventional survey, all respondents are asked the same set of questions. In a survey experiment, different respondents are asked different versions of a question to gauge the extent to which differences in the questions lead to a difference in response. In order to interpret any differences as caused by the difference in the survey question, the assignment of questions is usually done in a random fashion.

An example helps clarify. In policy debates over federal estate taxation, opponents of the tax took to calling it the "death tax." So scholars wanted to assess the extent to which framing the estate tax as a tax on dead people affected overall support and partisan differences. Obviously, one cannot just ask each respondent about both the estate tax and the death tax and then compare. Having answered a question about the death tax might influence her answer on the estate tax and vice versa. So a survey experiment would ask half the sample about the estate tax and the other half about the death tax. If the assignment of the questions is random, we can compare the average responses between the two groups to get the average effect of framing it as a death tax. The logic of randomly assigning the question is exactly the same as the argument for random sampling. Ideally we'd like the estate tax respondents to be similar to the death tax respondents so that the only thing that differs across the group is which question was asked.[6]

Survey experiments have come to play a prominent role in the study of polarization. As previously noted, the effects of priming and framing have the potential to complicate conventional surveys. But in the study of polarization, priming and framing are of central importance in understanding how voters of various stripes respond to cues and other information from candidates, the media, and other political elites. As I argued with the death tax example, survey experiments can help identify priming and framing effects and show how they may vary across partisans. Consider the earlier example of voter approval of the Russian government following the election of Donald Trump. A researcher interested in why GOP approval of the Russians grew might use a survey experiment that primes President Trump. In such an experiment, a *treatment* group receives a reminder of Trump's support for better relations with Russia, while a *control* group receives no such reminder. If respondents are randomly assigned to the two groups, any difference in approval for Russia would be attributable to the effect of the association with Donald Trump. For the purposes of studying polarization, researchers may primarily be interested as to whether this priming effect differs across members of the different parties (i.e., Republicans in the treatment group become more pro-Russian while Democrats in the treatment group become anti-Russian).[7]

Survey experiments can also be useful in eliciting responses to sensitive questions. A *list* experiment is one technique of doing so. For example, Redlawsk, Tolbert, and Franko (2010) were interested in determining the role of racial attitudes on support for the candidacy of Barack Obama in 2008. Of course, few Americans would readily admit to voting against him because he was black. So they conducted a list experiment by asking the following question to the treatment group:

Some people will vote for Barack Obama this fall and some people will not. Regardless of your overall feelings toward him, please indicate how many of the following five facts about Obama trouble you when you think about choosing the next president. We are not interested in WHICH ONES trouble you, only HOW MANY.

1. During the primary campaign, he described small-town Pennsylvanians as "bitter" and said that they "cling" to guns and religion.
2. He has served in the US Senate only since 2005.
3. He used to be a smoker.
4. He was a member of Jeremiah Wright's Trinity United Church of Christ for 20 years, before he resigned in May of 2008.
5. If elected, he will be the first black president.

The control group was only asked the first four questions, but not the one about Obama's race. Because respondents in the treatment group only reveal the number of concerns, they can answer truthfully because the surveyor will not know which of the reported number were actual concerns.[8]

Assuming that respondents in both the treatment and control groups answer truthfully, we can capture the share of the treatment group who were concerned about Obama's race by simply calculating the difference in the number of concerns in the treatment group with those from the control group. For example, among whites in the control group, the average number of concerns was 1.71 while the average number in the treatment group was 2.04. This difference of 0.33 implies that 33% of white respondents were troubled about the fact that Obama would be the first black president.[9] The researchers also find that a larger percentage of white Republicans and independents were concerned about race than of Democrats. They concede, however, that it is difficult to discern how much of that difference is associated with partisanship rather than racial attitudes.

B.9 What are survey scales?

While we could assess polarization among the general public one survey at a time, researchers generally combine responses to questions into *scales*. There are really two important uses of scales in the study of mass polarization. The first has to do with measurement error. A single survey question may not adequately capture the views of a voter for a variety of reasons. First, it is possible that the voter just answers erroneously. Perhaps she misunderstands the question or fails to see how it relates to her underlying views. For this reason, it may be useful to ask several questions about an issue or concept and combine the answers in some way. Because its less likely that a respondent gives mistaken answers to three questions about tax policy than one, the combined answer may contain less error.

A second rationale for creating scales from multiple questions is that the researcher may be interested in a broader ideological orientation than can be captured by a single question. He may, for example, want to know about the voters orientation toward government intervention into the economy. Therefore, he would want to ask about a number of interventions—taxes, regulations, public spending—and combine them in some way that can represent a summary of the voter's views.

The literature of the construction of survey scales is vast so I am not able to review it in any great detail. But intelligent consumption of the literature on mass polarization requires some exposure. The simplest way to construct a scale is to assign numerical values to specific responses and add these values together across multiple questions. One can either use the sum as the scale or divide by the number of items to take the average response. Such measures are known as *additive* scales. Either way we should expect there to be less measurement error and noise in the scales than in any of the individual survey items.

Of course, it is important that the individual survey questions be structured in similar ways so that the summation or average makes sense as a measure. First, the values assigned to responses should be structured so that high values have similar implications or meanings on each question. For example, if one were creating an additive scale to measure liberalism, the values should be assigned so that the liberal response on each question gets a high value and the conservative response gets a low value.

A standard structure for survey questions is designed specifically for the creation of additive scales. Many questions ask the respondent to evaluate some statement using the following responses:

1. Strongly disagree
2. Disagree
3. Neither agree nor disagree
4. Agree
5. Strongly agree

Such a question is known as a Likert item and the scale generated by the sum of the responses is known as a Likert scale. Of course, for the scale to make sense, all of the propositions should reflect a clear concept. In the example of a liberalism scale, all of the propositions should be ones in which liberals agree and conservatives disagree. The result would be nonsensical if some propositions were liberal and some were conservative. To avoid this problem, researchers reverse code the data so that "strongly disagree" with a liberal proposition is the same as "strongly agree" with a conservative one. A second concern with the Likert scale is that it assumes that each response is equally weighted. But some questions may be more informative about the respondent's overall orientation than others and should play a more prominent role in the summary measure.

A second type of additive scale is known as a Guttman scale. This scale is one constructed as the sum of binary (yes or no) responses to a series of questions that are ordered from one ideological extreme to another. For example, a Guttman scale for attitudes toward abortion might be based on the following questions from the General Social Survey:[10]

Please tell me whether or not you think it should be possible for a pregnant woman to obtain a legal abortion when . . .

1. The woman's own health is seriously endangered
2. She became pregnant as a result of rape
3. There is a strong chance of serious defect in the baby
4. The family has a very low income and cannot afford any more children
5. She is not married and does not want to marry the man
6. She is married and does not want any more children
7. The woman wants it for any reason

The underlying assumption is that these questions are ordered so that adherents of the most pro-life position would answer no to each (scoring a 0) and the most consistent adherents to the pro-choice position would answer yes to all seven (scoring a 7). Of course, it is possible that in the minds of some respondents the ordering is off. For example, some respondents might believe that a birth defect is a stronger rationale for abortion than rape. Such a concern should be examined before using the raw scale.

There are many cases however where researchers would like to construct scales using questions from a set of questions that mix the two formats or utilize an entirely different response format. Researchers may also worry that the Guttman questions are misordered or that different questions provide more information and should carry more weight. To deal with these issues and others, scholars have developed a large number of statistical models that can extract issue and ideological scales from such data. These come in a variety of flavors, ranging from plain-vanilla factor analysis to exotic ones like "Bayesian dynamic ordinal item response" models. Clearly, it is beyond the scope of this book to get into all of those approaches, but a rough understanding is useful for understanding arguments about polarization. First, many of these approaches are generally analogous to the estimation of ideal points discussed in chapter 3. Instead of legislators casting votes, we can think of voters as choosing between survey responses. These statistical techniques produce the equivalent of ideal points for the survey respondents. Moreover, these techniques can statistically handle questions that need to be reverse coded, or Guttman questions that are misordered, and can exploit the fact that some questions "discriminate" among voters better than others.

It is also worth noting an analogy of these statistical scales with a Guttman scale. Suppose the researcher had a set of binary questions but ones that were not obviously ordered like the abortion questions. A statistical procedure might start out by ordering them in an arbitrary way, computing the measure, and checking to see how well that measure predicts individual survey choices. If the fit is poor, the algorithm can reorder or reverse code some of the questions and check the quality of the new predictions. The procedure can continue with this process until it can no longer improve the fit by reordering or reverse coding. The result is a Guttman-like scale that can be interpreted somewhat analogously to an ideal point on one dimension.[11]

B.10 What is a thermometer rating?

A thermometer rating is a scale based on a question asking respondents to indicate the level of "warmth" they feel toward some person or institution. Typically, these scales range from 100 (very warm or favorable) to 0 (very cold or unfavorable). The midpoint 50 represents "no feeling at all." The American National Election Study (ANES) has asked thermometer scale questions about presidential candidates and political parties over many election cycles.[12]

B.11 What is party identification?

A standard question in political surveys asks respondents about their partisan loyalties. In light of scholarship showing that partisanship is a very stable marker of social identity,[13] the responses to these questions are generally referred to as reflecting partisan identification or party ID for short.

The canonical instrument for measuring party ID is that of the American National Election Study. The current version of their measure is based on the responses to a series of three questions. First, respondents are asked "Generally speaking, do you usually think of yourself as a Republican, a Democrat, an independent, or what?" If they respond that they are a Republican or Democrat, they are asked "Would you call yourself a strong (REPUBLICAN/DEMOCRAT) or a not very strong (REPUBLICAN/DEMOCRAT)." Finally, if the respondent said that she was an independent or declined to state a preference, she would be asked "Do you think of yourself as closer to the Republican or Democratic party?"

The responses to these questions can be used to generate a seven-point scale: strong Democrat, weak Democrat, Democratic-leaning independent, true independent, Republican-leaning independent, weak Republican, and strong Republican. Some care should be exercised, however, in assuming that the scale is strongly ordinal.[14] For example, in many cases, leaning independents behave almost identically to weak partisans, and "independent" may mean something different than "in-between the parties."[15] To elide these problems, analysts usually collapse the scale to Democrats, Republicans, and independents where each group's behavior is examined separately. Sometimes leaning independents are treated as partisans rather than independents.

Recently, some scholars have argued that the traditional scale is inadequate for the measurement of partisanship as a social identity. For example, Huddy, Mason, and Aarøe (2015) use a set of survey questions designed to tap the social identity aspects of partisanship. These questions include:

- How important is being a [Democrat/ Republican] to you?
- How well does the term [Democrat/ Republican] describe you?
- When talking about [Democrats/ Republicans], how often do you use "we" instead of "they"?
- To what extent do you think of yourself as being a [Democrat/ Republican]?

The authors show that an additive scale of these items outperforms the traditional measure of strong partisanship in predicting past electoral activity, current and future campaign activity, and anger and enthusiasm generated by an experimental measure provided to the respondents.[16]

B.12 What is an independent?

A central issue in understanding trends in voter polarization and partisanship is the question of how to interpret the responses of those voters who claim to be "independent" of any political party. In the popular image, an independent is a principled individual who sets aside partisan considerations to focus on the issues and candidates' performance in office. But others see independents as an alienated group increasingly disconnected from the political system. Obviously, these two views lead to very different conclusions about the desirability of the growing number of self-identified independents.

The truth about independents surely resides somewhere between these two poles. They are neither paragons of unbiasedness nor a set of disgruntleds waiting for a third-party savior. Most independents tend to lean to one party or another. And as mentioned earlier, such independents tend to behave very similarly to the partisans on their side.[17]

Only the so-called pure independent exhibits a distinctive behavioral profile. That profile falls much closer to the alienation image than the one of the engaged citizen shorn of partisan bias. Pure independents vote less often, are less attentive to politics, and more uninformed about public policy. But there seems to be no clear trend toward more pure independents—their numbers peaked in the 1970s and have declined gradually since.

Abrams and Fiorina (2011) argue, however, that the partisan behavior of leaning independents may be illusory. They suggest that partisan-leaning independents may be true independents who report leaning toward the party of their intended vote. Thus, for independents, the causality may run from vote choice to party ID rather than the other way around. Moreover, recent work by Klar and Krupnikov (2016) argues that independents exhibit certain anti-partisan preferences. In particular, independents associate partisanship with negative traits and perceive partisan associations to be socially damaging. These tendencies have been exacerbated by media coverage of politics that amplifies the extent of disagreement. This aversion to partisans and the resulting tendency to "go undercover" to hide their leanings may be an impediment to political participation and partisan mobilization.

B.13 What is ideological self-placement?

As with partisanship, surveys often ask respondents about their ideological commitments. For example, the ANES asks respondents: "Here is a 7-point scale on which the political views that people might hold are arranged from extremely liberal to extremely conservative." The response categories are extremely liberal, liberal, slightly liberal, moderate or middle of the road, slightly conservative, conservative, and extremely conservative.

The relationship between responses to this question and party ID are very important for debates about voter polarization and sorting. An important finding is that the statistical correlation between conservative ideological placement and Republican party ID (and liberal ideological placement and Democratic party ID) has risen substantially over the past three decades. According to the ANES, between 1972 and 2012, the percentage of Republican identifiers (including partisan leaners) who identified as conservative went from 42% to 70%. The similar change for Democrats identifying as liberal was from 26% to 45%.[18]

For reasons previously discussed, it is difficult to interpret these trends in isolation. In principle, they could arise from either polarization or sorting. Polarization is probably not a large part of the story given that the ideological groups that grew in size from the 1970s were the moderates (+5 points) and the conservatives (+8 points). The trends for the other groups are quite flat.[19] And of course, it is difficult to tell how much was ideology-driven sorting where conservatives became Republicans, or party-driven sorting where Republicans became conservatives.[20]

But there is a much bigger challenge to interpreting these results. The polarization and sorting interpretations require that voters have a decent understanding about what these ideological terms mean and how to apply them. There is considerable evidence that this is not the case. For example, many voters continue to rank Democratic presidential candidates as more conservative than Republican presidential candidates. Moreover, the correlation of ideological placement and preferences over specific public policies is not as high as one would expect. For example, many self-identified conservatives wish that taxes and the minimum wage were higher while liberals wish for lower taxes and regulation.[21]

B.14 Can we estimate ideal points of voters?

Scholars have approached the estimation of voter ideal points in two distinct ways. The first is to use responses to survey questions to estimate ideal points using methods similar to those used to estimate ideal points from roll-call votes. The main advantage of this approach is that in principle the data from any public opinion survey could be used to estimate ideal points for those taking the survey. The downside is that those ideal points cannot be compared to ideal points generated from other surveys and would therefore lead to relatively small samples. Such estimates may also not be useful in determining how polarized the respondents are relative to the parties and elected officials. Tausanovitch and Warshaw (2013) tackle the first problem by combining nine different surveys to obtain responses to policy questions by more than 275,000 respondents. Two of these surveys were Cooperative Congressional Election Survey (CCES) modules designed by the authors to include questions that had been asked in previous studies to facilitate comparisons across surveys. This allowed them to estimate the ideal points for all 275,000 respondents. With these estimates, they are able to use demographic and geographic data to generate accurate estimates of the aggregate public opinion for districts as small as those of state legislators.

To deal with the second problem, scholars have been designing surveys that ask respondents to vote on the same roll calls as members of Congress. For example, Bafumi and

Herron (2010) use the 33,000 respondents to the 2006 CCES to estimate voter ideal points. That survey asked respondents to take positions on a number of issues that were subject to roll-call votes in the 109th Congress (2005–2006), as well as a number of issues not directly related to votes. Therefore, using three sources of data, roll calls included on the CCES, roll calls not included on the CCES, and survey questions unrelated to roll calls, Bafumi and Herron are able to estimate ideal points for the voters and legislators on the same scale. The large number of voters per state allows them to compute overall median, median Democratic, and median Republican ideal points for each state. Their main substantive finding is that almost all House members and senators have ideal points considerably more extreme than the median of their partisan constituencies. They dub this finding "leapfrog representation" in that when voters replace a legislator of one party with another, the representatives ideal point "leaps" over almost all of the voters' ideal points.

There are several concerns about the estimation of voter ideal points that are worth noting. Palfrey and Poole (1987) were among the first to uncover a key problem with scaling voter ideal points. Those voters that are relatively uninformed or ambivalent about issues may choose either ideologically incoherent responses or a focal response such as the midpoint on survey questions. These voters would then appear as moderates when scaled alongside more informed voters. Once Palfrey and Poole filter out uninformed voters (those whose placement of candidates on a seven-point scale deviate the most from the average estimates across all voters), they recover a quite polarized distribution of voter ideal points.[22] These results are also consistent with those of Lauderdale (2013) who finds that providing more information experimentally leads the distribution of voter preferences on roll calls to polarize.

Broockman (2016) raises a second concern about voter ideal point estimates that also suggests an inflation of the number of moderate voters. He argues that voter preferences are far less ideologically constrained than is required by low-dimensional ideal point estimates. For example, he argues that many voters will have an extreme right-wing position on some issues and an extreme left-wing position on others. If one tried to estimate the ideal point of such a voter, they would appear as a moderate even though they did not hold a moderate view on any issues. Thus, Broockman argues against measuring voter polarization by the means of any summary ideological scale. His findings also question whether elected members of Congress are as out of step with their constituents as Bafumi and Herron's results imply.

Similarly, Jessee (2016) outlines another key problem associated with efforts to jointly estimate positions of legislators and voters: the assumption that preferences of the two groups of actors are representable by the same scale. He shows that ignoring this problem may have a large impact on the distribution of voter ideal points relative to legislator ideal points. Thus, assessments of whether the politicians are more polarized than the voters may be sensitive to the size of the voter survey. He proposes an alternative procedure where only the responses of one group (politicians or voters) are used to define the ideological scale, and the preferences of the other group are estimated taking that scale as fixed.

In summary, there remains an active debate about how best to measure ideal points and ideological polarization in the public.

NOTES

Acknowledgments
1. See Poole and Rosenthal (1997)
2. See McCarty, Poole, and Rosenthal (1997).
3. See McCarty, Poole, and Rosenthal (2006, 2016).
4. See McCarty, Poole, and Rosenthal (2001, 2009, 2013).

Chapter 1
1. See Fiorina (2005); and Mann and Ornstein (2016).
2. Because the debate about polarization and sorting hinges on some methodological nuances, I include an appendix that provides a primer on survey research.
3. Perhaps I should say almost nothing bipartisan happened. Both parties in Congress did overwhelmingly support a bill placing sanctions on Russia for its interference in the 2016 election *over the opposition of President Trump.*

Chapter 2
1. Oxford English Dictionary.
2. Some readers may object at this point that there are ideological orientations that do not fit neatly onto a left-right spectrum. For example, libertarianism represents a combination of socially liberal policy preferences with economic policy preferences associated with the right. This objection is considered extensively in chapter 3.
3. See Lee (2009, 2016a).
4. See Green, Palmquist, and Schickler (2002); and Achen and Bartels (2016).

5. See Lenz (2013).
6. With the retirements of Charlie Dent (PA) and Rodney Frelinghuysen (NJ) in 2018, there are no GOP members of the House of Representatives who support abortion rights. Two pro-choice Republicans remain in the Senate. See Kilgore (2018).
7. See Saad (2017); and General Social Survey (2012).
8. See Hartig (2018).
9. See Lunch and Sperlich (1979) for trends in public opinion on the Vietnam War; and McAdam and Su (2002) on the effects of protest and public opinion on congressional voting.
10. See Pew Research Center (2017).
11. See Green, Palmquist, and Schickler (2002).
12. See Rohde (1991); Sinclair (2006); Hacker and Pierson (2005); and Mann and Ornstein (2016).
13. See, for example, Kabaservice (2012); and Rosenfeld (2017).
14. See Rosenfeld (2017) for a history of these intra-party battles.
15. An exception to this pattern is the work of Caughey, Dunham, and Warshaw (2016). Those authors find that the public began sorting on economic issues in the 1970s, de-sorted in the 1980s, and began sorting again in the 1990s. This pattern is also quite different than what is observed among elites who continued to polarize through the 1980s.
16. The comparison does have its limitations in that Goldwater was more conservative than Reagan on race, social security, and the Cold War. But of course, Jimmy Carter took positions considerably more moderate than Johnson. So at least some of the differences in the elections must reflect some increased acceptance of conservative ideology.
17. See Fiorina (2005).
18. See also Ansolabehere, Rodden, and Snyder (2006); Fiorina and Abrams (2008); Levendusky, Pope, and Jackman (2008); and Bafumi and Herron (2010).
19. Clinton (2006); Bafumi and Herron (2010); but see Broockman (2016) for a methodological critique.
20. See Abramowitz (2010).
21. See American Political Science Association (1950), pp. 17–19. The report was not without its contemporary detractors (e.g., Ranney (1951)). Rosenfeld (2017) provides a detailed account of how Responsible Party Theory was invoked by officials and activists of both parties who wished to reorganize around ideological principles.

Chapter 3

1. See Scott and Kli (2017).
2. Not all Democratic proposals would call for the repeal of the ACA but many envision allowing individuals and groups to buy into Medicare. Waldman (2018).
3. Clearly, these measures only make sense when applied to a reasonably balanced two-party system. So 1877 is a reasonable starting point as the Democratic party returned to rough parity with the Republican party following the readmission of the southern states.
4. A small caveat is in order. This ability to discriminate between moderates and extremists requires that the interest group has an extreme preference on the issue that it is rating. In practice this condition is generally met.
5. As discussed later in this chapter, there are statistical procedures that can facilitate over-time comparisons of interest group ratings. See Groseclose, Levitt, and Snyder (1999).
6. See Fowler (1982); and Snyder (1992).
7. See Poole and Rosenthal (1984).
8. See McCarty, Poole, and Rosenthal (1997).
9. See Esteban and Ray (1994).
10. See Converse (1964).
11. See Poole and Rosenthal (2011).
12. See McCarty, Poole, and Rosenthal (2016).
13. See Gilens (2009).
14. See Ansolabehere, Snyder, and Stewart (2001)a; and Ansolabehere, Snyder, and Stewart III (2001b).
15. See Shor and McCarty (2011).
16. See McCarty and Poole (1998).
17. See Bonica (2014a).
18. See Harbridge (2015); and Canen, Jackson, and Trebbi (2017).
19. See Krehbiel (1998); and Brady and Volden (2005).
20. See Curry and Lee (2019).
21. See Gerrish and Blei (2011); and Kim, Londregan, and Ratkovic (2018).
22. See Gerrish and Blei (2012). Ben Lauderdale and Tom Clark apply a similar model to voting on the Supreme Court (Lauderdale and Clark 2014).
23. John Lapinski (2013) manually codes roll calls according to a predefined issue scheme. He also observes considerable variation in the history of partisan conflict across issues.

24. See Gentzkow and Shapiro (2010); Groseclose and Milyo (2005); Kim, Londregan, and Ratkovic (2018); and Noel (2014).
25. See Barberá (2014).
26. See McCarty, Poole, and Rosenthal (2001).
27. See Poole (2007).
28. The differences between Feinstein and Boxer are not an artifact of DW-NOMINATE. A similar gap exists in their CFscores. Feinstein has also generally been viewed by the media and the public as a relative moderate, see Wire (2018).
29. These are the same-party pairs from Kentucky, Massachusetts, Minnesota, South Carolina, Texas, Utah, and West Virginia. There would be eight if we included the difference between "Socialist" Bernie Sanders and Democrat Patrick Leahy in Vermont.
30. See Poole and Romer (1993).
31. See Lapinski (2013). Lapinski conducts a similar effort for the Senate, but he only codes Senate votes continuously through 1996. Given the large amount of polarization since 1996, I focus on the more complete House findings.
32. His method is to use the ideal point model of Clinton, Jackman, and Rivers (2004) for each issue in each House term. He then uses the procedure of Groseclose, Levitt, and Snyder (1999) to compare the issue ideal points over time. See the appendix for a discussion of these procedures. For some of the pitfalls of Lapinski's approach, see McCarty (2016).
33. At least in the case of the Senate, the Tea Party might have *decreased* polarization through its support of extreme candidates such as Christine O'Donnell, Richard Mourdock, and Todd Akin that ultimately cost the Republican party seats that were won by moderate Democrats.
34. See "Vital Statistics on Congress" (2018), Tables 1–16, 1–18, and 1–19.
35. See See McCarty, Poole, and Rosenthal (2016).
36. While there is more variation in the movements of the Democratic and Republican parties at the state level, Republicans have become more extreme on average in state legislatures. "Asymmetric Polarization in the State Legislatures? Yes and No" (2013).
37. For examples, see Aldrich and Battista (2002); Gerber and Lewis (2004); Kousser, Lewis, and Masket (2007); Wright and Schaffner (2002); and Jenkins (2006).

38. See also Appendix A.
39. See Shor and McCarty (2011).
40. See the earlier discussion of the NPAT.
41. See Clark (2008); and Esteban and Ray (1994). These scores are based on the Martin and Quinn (2002) dynamic ideal point estimates of judges. See Epstein et al. (2007) for details.
42. Clark also estimates polarization based on the scores of Segal and Cover (1989). These scores are based on news coverage of each justice at the time of their nomination and are fixed throughout a justice's term. Supreme Court polarization based on this measure shows a very different pattern. Polarization was low before the late 1960s and was high in the 1970s and 1980s before returning to the 1960s level in the 1990s.
43. I thank Tom Clark for providing me with updates to his polarization measure.
44. See Bartels (2015).
45. See Groseclose and Milyo (2005).
46. See Gentzkow and Shapiro (2010).
47. They do report similar conclusions when legislator ideology is measured by NOMINATE or interest group ratings.

Chapter 4
1. See DiMaggio, Evans, and Bryson (1996); Fiorina (2005); and Fiorina (2017).
2. See Abramowitz (2010).
3. Lelkes (2016) updates many of the measures used in the studies subsequently cited. The basic thrust of the earlier studies has not changed.
4. See DiMaggio, Evans, and Bryson (1996).
5. See Evans (2003) for an update. The most significant new finding was an increase in polarization of a broader set of issues related to sexuality.
6. See Fiorina (2005). Fiorina's arguments and data have been updated on a number of occasions, most recently in Fiorina (2017).
7. See Appendix B.9 for more information on this question. Fiorina (2017) updates this analysis.
8. See Hill and Tausanovitch (2015), especially Figure 4.
9. See Converse (1964).
10. See Baldassarri and Gelman (2008).

11. DiMaggio, Evans, and Bryson (1996) find little evidence for an increase in attitudinal constraint. Abramowitz and Saunders (2008) and Abramowitz (2010) use a somewhat different measure of ideological constraint and find that it grew between the 1980s and the 2000s. But the increase from 1984 to 2012 was very small—less than 10% of the total scale. See Boxell, Gentzkow, and Shapiro (2017), Figure 2.
12. See See Abramowitz (2010).
13. An increase in bimodality of engaged voters is hard to square with another of his claims—that levels of voter engagement are rising. Statistically, if the bimodality of engaged voters were increasing and engaged voters were an increasing share of the population, then overall bimodality should be increasing. There is little evidence that this is the case.
14. See Appendix B for a discussion of these measures.
15. See Kinder and Kalmoe (2017).
16. See Levendusky (2009).
17. See Appendix B.7 for a discussion of panel data.
18. See Carsey and Layman (2006).
19. See Baldassarri and Gelman (2008).
20. See Hill and Tausanovitch (2015).
21. See Mason (2016).
22. See Layman and Carsey (2002).
23. See Caughey, Dunham, and Warshaw (2016).
24. See Ansolabehere, Rodden, and Snyder (2006).
25. See Bartels (2006).
26. See Mason (2016).
27. See Hopkins (2017b).
28. See Tajfel (1970); and Tajfel and Turner (1979). An early application to partisanship is that of Greene (2004). Huddy and Bankert (2017) provide an extensive review of the application of SIT to partisan behavior.
29. See Tajfel and Turner (1979), p. 41.
30. Even among those who stress the sociological origins of partisanship, the SIT is far from universal. Green, Palmquist, and Schickler (2002) criticize the application of social identity theory.

> It seems to us unlikely that the pursuit of self-esteem drives the formation and adjustment of party attachment. One would think that self esteem-seeking voters would climb aboard the victorious party's bandwagon after a landslide

victory, yet we do not see citizens severing their party attachments in the wake of scandals or electoral defeats. Nor do we see adherents to the losing party resisting these bandwagon pressures by demonizing the victorious party and finding new virtues of their own.

31. See Iyengar, Sood, and Lelkes (2012).
32. These scores ask respondents to rate Republicans and Democrats. See Appendix 10 for a discussion of these measures.
33. See the ANES Guide to Public Opinion and Electoral Behavior. https://electionstudies.org/resources/anes-guide/top-tables/?id=21. Downloaded February 6, 2019.
34. See Layman and Carsey (2002); and Layman, Carsey, and Horowitz (2006) for the update through the 2004 election.
35. Of course, the causality is not clear—it is possible that Republicans with the most out-party hostility adopted economically conservative policy preferences.
36. See Iyengar and Westwood (2015).
37. Partisanship was cued based on extracurricular group memberships, race was cued by stereotypical names, and qualifications were manipulated using reported GPA.
38. The comparison of partisan and racial attitudes does come with an important caveat. Reported racial views on surveys are probably more prone to social desirability bias than are partisan views. Other experiments reported by Iyengar and Westwood, however, are less susceptible to this concern.
39. See Lelkes (n.d.).
40. See Webster and Abramowitz (2017).
41. See Rogowski and Sutherland (2016).
42. See Mason (2015).
43. See Mason and Wronski (2018).

Chapter 5

1. See Lee (2016a); and Fiorina (2017).
2. See Lee (2016b).
3. See McCarty (2016).
4. In the Senate, overall correlations are always above 0.9 while the within-party correlations vary between 0.4 and 0.8.
5. See Key (1949).
6. See Carmines and Stimson (1989).
7. See Schickler (2016).

8. See Shafer and Johnston (2009).
9. See McCarty, Poole, and Rosenthal (2016).
10. Gelman et al. (2005) find a general pattern of higher correlations between income and partisanship in low-income states.
11. See Valentino and Sears (2005).
12. Much of their analysis is based on a scale combining agreement with "it's really a matter of some people not trying hard enough; if blacks would only try harder they would be just as well off as whites" and disagreement with "generations of slavery and discrimination have created conditions that make it difficult for blacks to work their way out of the lower class."
13. See Kuziemko and Washington (2015).
14. See McCarty, Poole, and Rosenthal (2016), Figure 2.2.
15. See McCarty, Poole, and Rosenthal (2016).
16. See Piketty and Saez (2003).
17. See Voorheis, McCarty, and Shor (2015). Because this study can leverage variation across states and over time, it is less susceptible to biases caused by omitted variables. Moreover, we use a statistical procedure to minimize the effects of reverse causation.
18. See Rohde (1991); Sinclair (2006); and Theriault (2008, 2013).
19. See Aldrich and Rohde (2000).
20. See Heberlig, Hetherington, and Larson (2006).
21. See Jessee and Malhotra (2010).
22. See Snyder and Groseclose (2001).
23. See McCarty, Poole, and Rosenthal (2001). Party pressures on legislators suggest that a Democratic and Republican legislator with the same ideal point would be induced to vote against each other and with their party. This suggests that a model with two cutpoints—one for each party—might perform better than a model with only one (see Appendix A for a discussion of voting cutpoints). We test this prediction.
24. See Cox and Poole (2002). Their test shows that there is more variation in Rice party dissimilarity scores (the absolute difference in the proportion of Democrats and Republicans voting yea) than can be accounted for by the estimates of ideal points. This is equivalent to the observation that legislator voting errors are correlated within each party. Their approach treats both party-unifying forces and party-dividing forces as party effects.
25. See Lee (2016a).

26. This rule is named after Dennis Hastert who served as Speaker of the House from 1999–2007.
27. See Cox and McCubbins (2005).
28. In support of this hypothesis, Anzia and Jackman (2012) find that when a state legislature endows the majority party with substantive agenda setting powers, the majority party is rolled by the minority party less often. But Jackman (2014) concludes that these majority party advantages are offset in state legislatures where the floor votes on committee chairs; the floor can amend the legislative calendar; or where bills may be discharged from committee.
29. They argue that it originated under the speakership of Thomas Bracket Reed (1889–1891 and 1895–1899) who successfully stripped the minority party of many of its opportunities to obstruct the agenda of the majority party.
30. See McCarty, Poole, and Rosenthal (2016).
31. See Lee (2016a).
32. But as discussed in section 5.7 of this chapter, the impact on polarization as measured by DW-NOMINATE might be less substantial.
33. See Lee (2016b).
34. See Canes-Wrone, Brady, and Cogan (2002); Carson et al. (2010); and Hall (2015).
35. See Henderson (2016). Candidates do, however, stress partisan themes in their negative ads against opponents.
36. See chapter 6 of this book.
37. See Brady, Han, and Pope (2007).
38. See Thomsen (2017); and Hall (2018).
39. See Figure 1.3 and discussion on pp. 10–11 in Thomsen (2017). In these calculations, Thomsen defines a moderate as a Republican with a CFscore at least as liberal as Olympia Snow (R-ME) or a Democrat with a score at least as conservative as John Tanner (R-TN), the founder of the Blue Dog Coalition.
40. See Thomsen (2017), Figure 3.1.
41. Excluding elections following reapportionment where two incumbents are often pitted together by redistricting, less than 1% of House members running for re-election have been denied renomination. See Vital Statistics on Congress for the data.
42. See Stroud (2008).
43. See Iyengar and Hahn (2009).

44. See Gentzkow and Shapiro (2006).
45. See Gerber, Karlan, and Bergan (2009).
46. The news environment during the experimental period was very negative for the Republicans with significant Iraq War casualties; an investigation related to the leaking of the name of a covert CIA officer; and the failed Harriet Miers nomination to the Supreme Court.
47. See DellaVigna and Kaplan (2007).
48. By using a statistical model to adjust for the effects of various demographic, economic, and political differences between FNC and non-FNC towns, Hainmueller (2012) finds no effect of exposure to Fox News.
49. See Hopkins and Ladd (2014).
50. See Clinton and Enamorado (2014).
51. See Clinton and Enamorado (2012).
52. See Martin and Yurukoglu (2017).
53. The authors provide evidence that the positioning of the channel is unrelated to the partisanship of the subscribers and other demographics that are correlated with Fox viewership.
54. See Prior (2007).
55. See Snyder and Stromberg (2010).
56. They find that members from congruent districts from both parties are less likely to vote with party leadership. They also find that Democrats from congruent districts have more moderate voting records.
57. See Gentzkow (2006).
58. See George and Waldfogel (2006).
59. See Campante and Hojman (2013).
60. The other concern about cable TV—that it creates more diversions from engagement with politics—surprisingly plays less of a role in the commentary about social media.
61. See Sunstein (2018).
62. See, for example, Conover et al. (2012); and Colleoni, Rozza, and Arvidsson (2014).
63. See Gentzkow and Shapiro (2011).
64. See Guess (2018).
65. See Guess (2016).
66. See Barberá (2015).
67. Technically, his finding is that user ideal points of those in heterogeneous networks moderated. See chapter 3, for a discussion of Barberá's estimates of Twitter ideal points.

68. See Boxell, Gentzkow, and Shapiro (2017).
69. See Lelkes, Sood, and Iyengar (2017).
70. The authors address the obvious concern that the adoption of certain broadband regulations might be correlated with a state's partisanship. They find no evidence of such a pattern.
71. See Rehm and Reilly (2010).
72. The Organization for Economic Cooperation and Development represents the most economically advanced countries.
73. See Fiorina (2017).

Chapter 6

1. For a sampling, see any of the following: Toobin (2003); Eilperin (2006); Lessig (2011); Edwards (2012); Draper (2012); Nocera (2013); Nagourney (2013); Walter (2013); Schumer (2014); and *The Economist* (2014).
2. See McCarty, Poole, and Rosenthal (2009) for a more extensive discussion.
3. The term sorting in this context has a slightly different meaning than its usage to describe the sorting of voters into parties based on ideology.
4. See Bafumi and Herron (2010).
5. See McCarty et al. (2018).
6. See McCarty, Poole, and Rosenthal (2009).
7. See Shor and McCarty (2011).
8. See McCarty, Poole, and Rosenthal (2009).
9. Recall Figure 3.2.
10. I take up the possibility that polarization in the House caused polarization in the Senate in what follows.
11. See McCarty, Poole, and Rosenthal (2016), Figures 2.23a–e, pp. 65–67.
12. In rank terms, these post-redistricting elections represent the third, fifth, thirteenth, and fifteenth most polarizing of the twenty elections since 1976.
13. It is important to remember that reapportionment may affect polarization in ways unrelated to gerrymandering. For example, due to population shifts, the relatively unpolarized northeastern states have lost substantial congressional representation to the more polarized South and West. See McCarty, Poole, and Rosenthal (2016), p. 62.
14. See McCarty, Poole, and Rosenthal (2009). Shor and McCarty (2011) report similar findings for the states.

15. See Eilperin (2006); and Theriault (2013).
16. See McCarty, Poole, and Rosenthal (2016), p. 68.
17. While political scientists have used the presidential vote alongside a variety of other measures of competitiveness, the use of the presidential vote is very common in journalistic and activist circles. For example, see Monopoly Politics (n.d.).
18. Suppose one were to use legislative vote shares instead. Such a measure would conflate the underlying features of the district with decisions about candidate entry, quality, and spending.
19. The main purpose of the mean deviation is to eliminate election-specific effects unrelated to the underlying competitiveness of House districts.
20. See McCarty (2015b).
21. See McCarty (2015b).
22. See Brunell and Grofman (2008) for parallel evidence casting doubt on the idea that US House polarization is related to the degree of inter-party competition.
23. See Brunell (2010).
24. See Gerber and Lewis (2004).
25. See Levendusky and Pope (2010).
26. See McCarty et al. (2018).
27. See also Calvert (1985); and Wittman (1983).
28. See Tausanovitch and Warshaw (2013).
29. We replicate our analysis for the US House and for state lower chambers. The results for the US House are very similar. The results for state lower chambers are somewhat weaker because our measures of heterogeneity are far less precise at that level.
30. As an even stronger test for a causal relationship, we look at what happens when a district goes from Republican to Democratic hands or vice versa. The resulting difference in the ideal points of the new legislator and old legislator is considerably larger in the heterogeneous districts, as our argument would predict.
31. See Stephanopoulos (2011).
32. The main difference between the systems is that in Louisiana a candidate who obtains 50% of the primary vote is declared the winner without having to run in a general election.
33. See Hirano et al. (2010).
34. See McGhee et al. (2014).

35. It is possible in theory that open and semi-open primaries could produce more polarization if partisan voters strategically crossed over to the opposition party primary and cast votes for the extreme candidate in hopes of increasing their chance of winning in the general election; see Chen and Yang (2002). A second possibility is that moderate voters mistakenly cross over and tip the election to the more extreme candidate of their own party; see Oak (2006). There is little evidence that strategic cross-over behavior is significant enough to influence primary election outcomes. See Alvarez and Nagler (2002).

36. In an additional analysis, the authors considered whether the switch from nonpartisan primaries by California, Washington, and Alaska occasioned by the Supreme Court decision in *California Democratic Party v. Jones* (520 U.S. 567) increased polarization in those states. The evidence that it did so was quite weak.

37. See Sides et al. (2018).

38. These findings are consistent with earlier studies such as Geer (1988); and Norrander (1989).

39. See Bullock and Clinton (2011). A blanket primary differs from a top-two primary only in that a top-two primary may result in two general election candidates of the same party. In the California blanket primary, the highest Republican and Democratic vote-getters move to the general election.

40. See Ahler, Citrin, and Lenz (2016). They provide additional evidence that voters were unable to discern the more moderate candidate when presented the option to vote for her.

41. See Kousser, Phillips, and Shor (2018).

42. See Grose (2014).

43. See McCarty, Poole, and Rosenthal (2006).

44. See Barber (2016),Figure 1. The reliance of state candidates on individuals is 50%, also up from about 20% over the same period. See also Bonica (2013).

45. See Bonica (2014a).

46. See Table 3 in Barber (2016).

47. His research design does not utilize cross-state variation in the laws due to concerns about omitted variables that might be correlated with campaign finance laws and polarization.

48. Consistent with this finding, Barber also shows that tighter contribution limits lead to smaller contributions on average

and to more donors "maxing out" with a contribution at the legal limit.

49. Of course, there may be many reasons unrelated to polarization for tightening restrictions on corporate and labor union money.

50. See Hall (2014).

51. Masket and Miller (2015) use a slightly different methodology to compare the positions of members who accept public financing with those who opt out. They find no difference in the estimated ideal points of the two types. But it is possible that the existence of the laws has an effect even on those members who opt out.

52. See Bonica (2013) Figure 7, and the discussion on pp. 115–116.

53. See McCarty (2015a); Persily (2015); Pildes (2015); La Raja and Schaffner (2015); and Schlozman and Rosenfeld (2019).

54. See La Raja and Schaffner (2015).

55. See Krimmel (2013); McCarty (2015a); and Mayhew (1986).

56. See Cohen et al. (2009); and Bawn et al. (2012). See McCarty and Schickler (2018) for an assessment of the strengths and weaknesses of this approach.

57. McCutcheon v. Federal Election Commission, 572 U.S. (2014).

58. According to the Sunlight Foundation, the McCutcheon decision had a substantial impact on joint fundraising committees associated with 2016 presidential candidates. See Stewart (2016). Downloaded June 30, 2018.

59. See Drutman (2017); and Hopkins (2017b).

60. See Duverger (1954) for the classic work on this issue.

61. See Downs (1957).

62. Eggers and Lauderdale (2016) simulate what congressional polarization would be if the United States used proportional representation at the state level. They find that if seats were allocated proportionately to vote share within each state, polarization would be modestly lower because Congress would be composed of more southern Democrats and northeastern Republicans. But importantly, their analysis assumes that the behavior of voters and parties remains the same after a switch in systems. So the effects of the possible proliferation of parties under proportional representation are not accounted for.

63. Unlike the IRV, STV results may be sensitive to ties among parties for last place in a round. These are generally broken randomly, which produces some arbitrariness in the tabulation process.

64. Clearly, this example ignores a large number of incentives for voters to vote tactically.
65. See Donovan, Tolbert, and Gracey (2016).
66. See McDaniel (2015).
67. See Neely and McDaniel (2015). These disqualifications were associated with voters ranking too many candidates.
68. See Kimball and Anthony (2016).
69. Burnett and Kogan (2015) examine ballot image data from four elections and find that in all cases the election winner received less than a majority of the total votes cast. This ballot "exhaustion" effect would obviously be reduced if voters were allowed to rank all candidates. But, of course, such a change would dramatically increase the complexity of the ballot and the vote tabulation.
70. For this reason, RCV advocates would favor the elimination of primaries. But other forms of elite coordination would still be available. See Cohen et al. (2009).
71. In the other two cases, a Greens first-round winner lost to a Labor candidate and a Liberal candidate lost to the candidate of a minor centrist party. The data were obtained from "Federal Elections" (2016). http://www.abc.net.au/news/federal-election-2016/results/list/. The rate of first-round winners losing in later rounds is somewhat higher than the historical averages. See Bean (1997).
72. Instead it appears that Australian parties do a very good job of strategically coordinating the rank ordering of their loyal voters.
73. See Mainwaring (1993).

Chapter 7
1. See Krehbiel (1998); and Brady and Volden (2005).
2. See McCarty (2015a); and Pildes (2015).
3. For a general argument to this effect, see Levinson and Pildes (2006). In support of this claim, Kriner and Schickler (2016) find evidence that the effect of divided government on House investigatory activity of the executive branch has been magnified by polarization, but they find no similar effect for the Senate.
4. See Black (1948) on the median voter theorem. Technically, the median voter theorem requires that preferences be aligned on a single dimension. Unidimensionality is a reasonably good approximation of the contemporary Congress.

5. Westminster systems are those that are modeled on the UK parliament.
6. See Aldrich and Rohde (2000); and Cox and McCubbins (1993); Cox and McCubbins (2005).
7. See Cox and McCubbins (2005).
8. See Gilmour (1995); Groseclose and McCarty (2001); and Lee (2009).
9. See Lee (2016a).
10. For a detailed explication of the underlying theory, see Krehbiel (1998); and Brady and Volden (2005).
11. See McCarty (1997); Cameron (2000); and Cameron and McCarty (2004).
12. See McCarty, Poole, and Rosenthal (2016), Table 6.1.
13. See Mayhew (1991).
14. See also Binder (2003); and Binder (2015).
15. The gap would be even bigger except for the enormous legislative output following the September 11 terrorist attacks during the polarized 2000s.
16. It is an updated version of the analysis from McCarty (2007).
17. See, for example, Ferejohn and Shipan (1990); Moe and Howell (1999); Howell (2003); and Devins (2008).
18. See Krehbiel (1998).
19. See Cox and McCubbins (2005).
20. See Ferejohn and Shipan (1990); and Howell (2003).
21. Of course, whether the courts were overly restrictive in enjoining the immigration orders or whether President Obama overreached is a debatable question.
22. King v. Burwell 576 U.S. (2015). This case hinged on interpreting an ambiguous clause as to whether Congress intended citizens of states with state-run health-care exchanges to be eligible for subsidies.
23. See Joseph O'Connell (2009).
24. See Lewis (2010).
25. See Clinton et al. (2012).
26. See Devins and Lewis (2008).
27. See, for example, Segal and Spaeth (2002).
28. See Rosenberg (1991); and Clark (2009).
29. See Cameron, Kastellec, and Park (2013).
30. See Binder and Maltzman (2009).
31. See Bonica and Sen (2015).

32. There are a few states, however, where judges are more liberal than the underlying population of attorneys, possibly indicating some politicization by Democrats in those places.
33. See Eskridge (1991); and Hasen (2012).
34. Importantly, the decline in overrides cannot be explained by a decline in the number of statutory interpretation cases heard by the court. To the contrary, the number of such cases has been roughly constant since the early 1990s. See Hasen (2012), Figure 5.
35. See Cole (2013).
36. See Bulman-Pozen and Gerken (2009).
37. See Bulman-Pozen (2014).
38. See Rogers (2016); and Hopkins (2017a).
39. See Rogers (2017).
40. See Scobee (2016).
41. See http://www.ncsl.org/research/fiscal-policy/supermajority-vote-requirements-to-pass-the-budget635542510.aspx. Downloaded May 22, 2018.
42. See Grumbach (2018). Figure 8 of Grumbach's online appendix shows that the prevalence of unified government in the states has been growing in recent years.
43. See Hicks (2015).
44. See Kirkland and Phillips (2018).
45. See Caughey, Xu, and Warshaw (2017). See Caughey and Warshaw (2016) for the details of their measure.
46. See Grumbach (2018).
47. Thus, the small average effect found in Caughey, Xu, and Warshaw (2017) may be the result of their measure of policy liberalism—averaging issues that have some large partisan effects with those without such effects.
48. As demonstrated in Caughey, Xu, and Warshaw (2017), Figure 1, the total difference in policy liberalism between states with Democratic and Republican governors is much larger than their estimated effect of a party switch.
49. See Bartels (2016).
50. See Gilens (2012); Gilens and Page (2014); Hacker and Pierson (2010); and McCarty, Poole, and Rosenthal (2013).
51. Tausanovitch (2016), however, finds that low-income voters will be better represented by Democrats since the general liberal orientation of Democratic legislators better matches the preferences of low-income voters.

52. See Gilens (2012).
53. See Schlozman, Verba, and Brady (2012).
54. McCarty, Poole, and Rosenthal (2016) provide evidence that the increased disparity in voting rates between high-income and low-income residents is driven largely by the ineligible noncitizens that are clustered toward the bottom of the income scale.
55. See Bonica and Rosenthal (2015).

Chapter 8

1. Ironically, his opponent in the 2000 race was commentator Patrick Buchanan, who had long espoused the ethnic-nationalistic populism that became a central theme of Trump's 2016 campaign. But in 2000, Trump dismissed Buchanan as a "Hitler Lover." See Helmore (2017).
2. See "Donald Trump (NY-R-I-D-R-NP-R) Has Twice Dumped the GOP, But Remains a Republican at Press Time," 2015.
3. See Moody (2015).
4. See Eggen and Farnam (2011).
5. See "Trump in 1999: I Am Very Pro-Choice" (2015).
6. His campaign later walked this statement back, suggesting he intended the punishment to apply only to practitioners who performed abortions. See Flegenheimer and Haberman (2016).
7. Fifteen of the other candidates were current or former senators and governors. Carly Fiorina was the executive of a Fortune 500 company and a former Senate candidate. Only Ben Carson, a neurosurgeon with a compelling life story, could be classified as having less experience in public affairs.
8. See Cohen et al. (2009); and Bawn et al. (2012).
9. But see McCarty and Schickler (2018) for some concerns about this analysis.
10. Three candidates never endorsed Trump (Jeb Bush, John Kasich, and George Pataki) while Carly Fiorina rescinded her endorsement after a tape of Trump boasting of sexual assault became public.
11. Super-delegates will only be allowed to vote on nominations if the delegates elected through primaries and caucuses are deadlocked at the convention. See Herndon (2018).
12. See Cohen et al. (2016).
13. See McCarty and Schickler (2018) for an extended discussion.

14. See Azari (2016).
15. See Schlozman and Rosenfeld (2019).
16. See section 6.9.
17. A related third might be called "gender-role anxiety" created by the declining status of men.
18. Kramer (1983), however, suggests the pitfalls of favoring the individual over aggregate-level predictions.
19. Early work on sociotropic voting focused on voters' assessments of the national economy (e.g., Kinder and Kiewiet (1981)). But recently, scholars have found that these perceptions are driven in large part by local economic conditions. See Ansolabehere, Meredith, and Snowberg (2014).
20. See Schaner, MacWilliams, and Nteta (2018).
21. Matt Grossmann (2018) makes a somewhat distinctive argument that Trump voters were motivated by his opposition to political correctness.
22. Ironically in a period of polarization, this interpretation seems to have been accepted by the left (explicitly) and the right (implicitly). The left argues it to de-legitimize the president, and the president's supporters often resort to racialized appeals in the belief that they will continue to mobilize Trump's base.
23. Many pre-election forecasts that did not use polling data predicted a GOP popular vote victory. See, for example, "Post-Mortem" (n.d.); and see Dickinson (2016).
24. The differences can mainly be accounted for by the slow pace at which nominations were made. See Diehm et al. (2017).
25. See Lu and Yourish (2019).
26. See "Statement by Former National Security Officials" (n.d.).
27. The campaign presumably now regrets that appointment, given George Papadopoulous's later role in the investigation of Russian election interference. See Ryan and Mufson (2016).
28. Two Republican legislators, Dan Coats and Mike Pompeo, were appointed director of National Intelligence and director of the CIA, respectively.
29. See Shear and Nixon (2017). The administration later issued a ban that included the citizens of non-Muslim countries, which was upheld by the courts.
30. See Berman (2018).
31. See Mason (2016).
32. See Lee and McCarty (2019).

Appendix A

1. For example, a two-dimensional model assumes that these are points on a plane.
2. This example reveals another possible limitation of ideal point estimates. The model assumes that legislators vote *sincerely* for the most preferred outcome of a pair of alternatives. This rules out *strategic* voting -where legislators cast votes with expectations about how the current outcome might affect the future agenda. In the minimum wage example, one might imagine a legislator with an ideal point of $20 voting against $15 in the hopes of securing an even higher wage in the future.
3. See McCarty (2011) for a discussion of other alternatives.
4. See Poole (2007).
5. For examples, see Heckman and Snyder (1997); Clinton, Jackman, and Rivers (2004); and Fowler and Hall (2013).
6. A random walk assumes that, on average, a member's position in time t is the same as that in time $t-1$, but that she might randomly move left or right.
7. See McCarty (2016) for a discussion of the pros and cons of these approaches.
8. During this period, polarization is low in part because southern Democrats often voted with Republicans. But the modularity measures identify three distinct factions: northern Democrats, southern Democrats, and Republicans.
9. See Rohde (1991).
10. See Snyder (1992).
11. The average distribution of margins for all 113 Houses was used as the common margin.

Appendix B

1. Obviously, data on political text, campaign contributions, and media usage exist only for a very highly active segment of the electorate.
2. See Tversky and Kahneman (1981).
3. See Prior, Sood, and Khanna (2015); and Bullock et al. (2015) for evidence of partisan cheerleading. But see Berinsky (2018).
4. Any assessment based on cross sections would need to be done at the group level by examining changes related to females, blacks, Hispanics, college grads, and so on.

5. It is important to point out, however, that panel data is not magic, as we must still worry that some of the switches in party or ideology were driven by measurement error rather than true changes.

6. Such an experiment was conducted for the 2002 American National Election survey. Based on the analysis of Bartels (2016), the death tax framing had no overall impact on support for repeal of the estate tax that was part of President George W. Bush's first tax bill (Table 7.2). But he finds that Republican respondents favored repealing the death tax more than they did the estate tax (Table 7.3).

7. It has become conventional to interpret such a priming effect as a reflection of how partisanship drives the stated preferences of voters. But other interpretations are also possible. The association with Trump might remind voters about specific pieces of information on Russia that they had forgotten. Or the Trump prime might be seen as an invitation to cheerlead.

8. There is a slight concern in that a respondent who had all five concerns might not be willing to answer truthfully and reveal that race was a concern. Thus, the relatively trivial smoking item was included to make it unlikely that many voters had all five concerns.

9. If we assume that due to random assignment the control and treatment groups were troubled in equal measure by the first four facts, then the difference of 0.33 arises because one-third of the treatment sample was concerned about race.

10. See "General Social Survey 2012" (2013).

11. This example does not address how the procedures take advantage of more informative questions. The intuition is that the procedure can assign more or fewer points to certain responses.

12. An example of ANES Thermometer questions:

> I'd like to get your feelings toward some of our political leaders and other people who are in the news these days. I'll read the name of a person and I'd like you to rate that person using something we call the feeling thermometer. Ratings between 50 degrees and 100 degrees mean that you feel favorable and warm toward the person. Ratings between 0 degrees and 50 degrees mean that you don't feel favorable

toward the person and that you don't care too much for that person. You would rate the person at the 50 degree mark if you don't feel particularly warm or cold toward the person. If we come to a person whose name you don't recognize, you don't need to rate that person. Just tell me and we'll move on to the next one.

13. See especially Campbell et al. (1960).
14. See Weisberg (1980).
15. See Magleby, Nelson, and Westlye (2011).
16. Caution is in order for interpreting these results. Additive scales are generally less prone to measurement error than single items. Greater measurement error in the traditional measure may also account for its relatively worse performance.
17. See Magleby, Nelson, and Westlye (2011).
18. See https://electionstudies.org/resources/anes-guide/second-tables/?id=123 and https://electionstudies.org/resources/anes-guide/second-tables/?id=127.
19. Kinder and Kalmoe (2017) report some modest polarization reflected in a high proportional increase in the numbers choosing one of the extreme options.
20. Given that party ID is more persistent than ideological identification, it stands to reason that the majority of these shifts are party-driven. See Kinder and Kalmoe (2017).
21. See Converse (1964); and Kinder and Kalmoe (2017). Kinder and Kalmoe find that the average correlation between policy issue questions and ideological position is 0.23 and has not grown since the 1970s.
22. See Hare et al. (2015) for an update based on a similar model. They also show considerable polarization among the informed electorate.

BIBLIOGRAPHY

Abramowitz, Alan. 2010. *The Disappearing Center: Engaged Citizens, Polarization, and American Democracy.* New Haven, CT: Yale University Press.

Abramowitz, Alan I., and Kyle L. Saunders. 2008. "Is Polarization a Myth?" *Journal of Politics* 70(2): 542–555.

Abrams, Samuel J., and Morris P. Fiorina. 2011. "Are Leaning Independents Deluded or Dishonest Weak Partisans?" CISE-ITANES Conference, "Revisiting Party Identification," Luiss School of Government, Roma, Italy. https://cise.luiss.it/cise/wp-content/uploads/2011/10/Are-Leaners-Partisans.pdf.

Achen, Christopher H., and Larry M. Bartels. 2016. *Democracy for Realists: Why Elections Do Not Produce Responsive Government.* Princeton, NJ: Princeton University Press.

Ahler, Douglas J., Jack Citrin, and Gabriel S. Lenz. 2016. "Do Open Primaries Improve Representation? An Experimental Test of California's 2012 Top-Two Primary." *Legislative Studies Quarterly* 41(2): 237–268.

Aldrich, John H., and David W. Rohde. 2000. "The Logic of Conditional Party Government: Revisiting the Electoral Connection." In *Congress Reconsidered, 7th Edition*, edited by Lawrence Dodd and Bruce Oppenheimer, 269–292. Washington DC: CQ Press.

Aldrich, John H., and James S. Coleman Battista. 2002. "Conditional Party Government in the States." *American Journal of Political Science* 46(January): 164–172.

Alvarez, R. Michael, and Jonathan Nagler. 2002. "Should I Stay or Should I Go?" In *Voting at the Political Fault Line: California's*

Experiment with the Blanket Primary, 107. Berkeley: University of California Press.

American Political Science Association. 1950. "Toward a More Responsible Two-Party System: A Report of the Committee on Political Parties." 44(3): part 2, Supplement.

Ansolabehere, Stephen, James M. Snyder, and Charles Stewart, III. 2001a. "Candidate Positioning in U.S. House Elections." *American Journal of Political Science* 45(1): 136–159.

Ansolabehere, Stephen, James M. Snyder, and Charles Stewart, III. 2001b. "The Effects of Party and Preferences on Congressional Roll-Call Voting." *Legislative Studies Quarterly* 26(4): 533–572.

Ansolabehere, Stephen, Jonathan Rodden, and James M. Snyder. 2006. "Purple America." *Journal of Economic Perspectives* 20(2): 97–118.

Ansolabehere, Stephen, Marc Meredith, and Erik Snowberg. 2014. "Mecro-economic Voting: Local Information and Micro-Perceptions of the Macro-Economy." *Economics & Politics* 26(3): 380–410.

Anzia, Sarah F., and Molly C. Jackman. 2012. "Legislative Organization and the Second Face of Power: Evidence from US State Legislatures." *Journal of Politics* 75(1): 210–224.

"Asymmetric Polarization in the State Legislatures? Yes and No." 2013. American Legislatures.com, July 19, https://americanlegislatures. com/2013/07/29/partisan-polarization-in-state-legislatures/.

Azari, Julia. 2016. "Weak Parties and Strong Partisanship Are a Bad Combination." Vox, November 3, https://www. vox.com/mischiefs-of-faction/2016/11/3/13512362/ weak-parties-strong-partisanship-bad-combination.

Bafumi, Joseph, and Michael C. Herron. 2010. "Leapfrog Representation and Extremism: A Study of American Voters and Their Members in Congress." *American Political Science Review* 104(3): 519–542.

Baldassarri, Delia, and Andrew Gelman. 2008. "Partisans without Constraint: Political Polarization and Trends in American Public Opinion." *American Journal of Sociology* 114(2): 408–446.

Barber, Michael J. 2016. "Ideological Donors, Contribution Limits, and the Polarization of American Legislatures." *Journal of Politics* 78(1): 296–310.

Barberá, Pablo. 2014. "Birds of the Same Feather Tweet Together: Bayesian Ideal Point Estimation using Twitter Data." *Political Analysis* 23(1): 76–91.

Barberá, Pablo. 2015. "How Social Media Reduces Mass Political Polarization. Evidence from Germany, Spain, and the US." Paper Prepared for 2015 APSA Conference.

Bartels, Brandon. 2015. "Sources and Consequences of Polarization on the US Supreme Court." In *American Gridlock: The Sources, Character, and Impact of Political Polarization*, edited by James Thurber and Antoine Yoshinaka, 171–200. Cambridge, UK: Cambridge University Press.

Bartels, Larry M. 2006. "What's the Matter with *What's the Matter with Kansas?" Quarterly Journal of Political Science* 1(2): 201–226.

Bartels, Larry M. 2016. *Unequal Democracy: The Political Economy of the New Gilded Age*. Princeton, NJ: Princeton University Press.

Bawn, Kathleen, Martin Cohen, David Karol, Seth Masket, Hans Noel, and John Zaller. 2012. "A Theory of Political Parties: Groups, Policy Demands and Nominations in American Politics." *Perspectives on Politics* 10(03): 571–597.

Bean, Clive. 1997. "Australia's Experience with the Alternative Vote." *Representation* 34(2): 103–110.

Berinsky, Adam J. 2018. "Telling the Truth about Believing the Lies? Evidence for the Limited Prevalence of Expressive Survey Responding." *Journal of Politics* 80(1): 211–224.

Berman, Russell. 2018. "Infrastructure Week Is Always Next Week." *Atlantic*, February 1, https://www.theatlantic.com/politics/archive/2018/02/infrastructure-week-is-always-next-week/552047/.

Binder, Sarah. 2015. "The Dysfunctional Congress." *Annual Review of Political Science* 18: 85–101.

Binder, Sarah A. 2003. *Stalemate: Causes and Consequences of Legislative Gridlock*. Washington, DC: Brookings Institution Press.

Binder, Sarah A. 2008. "Consequences for the Courts: Polarized Politics and the Judicial Branch." In *Red and Blue Nation: Consequences and Correction of America's Polarized Politics*, edited by Pietro S. Nivola and David W. Brady, 107–133. Washington, DC: Brookings Institution Press.

Binder, Sarah A., and Forrest Maltzman. 2009. *Advice and Dissent: The Struggle to Shape the Federal Judiciary*. Washington, DC: Brookings Institution Press.

Black, Duncan. 1948. "The Decisions of a Committee Using a Special Majority." *Econometrica* 16(3): 245–261.

Bonica, Adam. 2013. "Ideology and Interests in the Political Marketplace." *American Journal of Political Science* 57(2): 294–311.

Bonica, Adam. 2014a. "Mapping the Ideological Marketplace." *American Journal of Political Science* 58(2): 367–386.

Bonica, Adam. 2014b. "The Punctuated Origins of Senate Polarization." *Legislative Studies Quarterly* 39(1): 5–26.

Bonica, Adam, and Howard Rosenthal. 2015. "The Wealth Elasticity of Political Contributions by the Forbes 400."Social Science Research Network.

Bonica, Adam, and Maya Sen. 2015. "The Politics of Selecting the Bench from the Bar: The Legal Profession and Partisan Incentives to Politicize the Judiciary." *Journal of Law and Economics* 60: 559–595.

Bonica, Adam, Nolan McCarty, Keith T. Poole, and Howard Rosenthal. 2013. "Why Hasn't Democracy Slowed Rising Inequality?" *Journal of Economic Perspectives* 27(3): 103–123.

Boxell, Levi, Matthew Gentzkow, and Jesse M Shapiro. 2017. "Is the Internet Causing Political Polarization? Evidence from Demographics." NBER Working Papers 23258. National Bureau of Economic Research.

Brady, David W., and Craig Volden. 2005. *Revolving Gridlock: Politics and Policy from Jimmy Carter to George W. Bush.* Boulder, CO: Westview Press.

Brady, David W., Hahrie Han, and Jeremy C. Pope. 2007. "Primary Elections and Candidate Ideology: Out of Step with the Primary Electorate?" *Legislative Studies Quarterly* 32(1): 79–105.

Broockman, David E. 2016. "Approaches to Studying Policy Representation." *Legislative Studies Quarterly* 41(1): 181–215.

Brunell, Thomas. 2010. *Redistricting and Representation: Why Competitive Elections Are Bad for America.* New York: Routledge.

Brunell, Thomas L., and Bernie Grofman. 2008. "Evaluating the Impact of Redistricting on District Homogeneity, Political Competition, and Political Extremism in the US House of Representatives, 1962–2000." In *Designing Democratic Government: Making Institutions Work*, edited by Margaret Levi, James Johnson, Jack Knight, and Susan Stokes, 117–140. New York: Russell Sage Foundation.

Bullock, John G., Alan S. Gerber, Seth J. Hill, and Gregory A. Huber. 2015. "Partisan Bias in Factual Beliefs about Politics." *Quarterly Journal of Political Science* 10(4): 519–578.

Bullock, Will, and Joshua D. Clinton. 2011. "More a Molehill Than a Mountain: The Effects of the Blanket Primary on Elected Officials' Behavior from California." *Journal of Politics* 73(3): 915–930.

Bulman-Pozen, Jessica. 2014. "Partisan Federalism." *Harvard Law Review* 127(4): 1077–1146.

Bulman-Pozen, Jessica, and Heather K. Gerken. 2009. "Uncooperative Federalism." *Yale Law Journal* 118: 1256–1310.

Burnett, Craig M., and Vladimir Kogan. 2015. "Ballot (and Voter) "Exhaustion" under Instant Runoff Voting: An Examination of Four Ranked-Choice Elections." *Electoral Studies* 37: 41–49.

Calvert, Randall L. 1985. "Robustness of the Multidimensional Voting Model: Candidate Motivations, Uncertainty, and Convergence." *American Journal of Political Science* 29(1): 69–95.

Cameron, Charles M. 2000. *Veto Bargaining: Presidents and the Politics of Negative Power.* Cambridge, UK: Cambridge University Press.

Cameron, Charles M., and Nolan McCarty. 2004. "Models of Vetoes and Veto Bargaining." *Annual Review Political Science* 7: 409–435.

Cameron, Charles M., Jonathan P. Kastellec, and Jee-Kwang Park. 2013. "Voting for Justices: Change and Continuity in Confirmation Voting, 1937–2010." *Journal of Politics* 75(2): 283–299.

Campante, Filipe R., and Daniel A. Hojman. 2013. "Media and Polarization: Evidence from the Introduction of Broadcast TV in the United States." *Journal of Public Economics* 100: 79–92.

Campbell, Angus, Philip E. Converse, Warren E. Miller, and Donald E. Stokes. 1960. *American Voter.* New York: Wiley.

Canen, Nathan, Matthew O. Jackson, and Francesco Trebbi. 2017. "Endogenous Networks and Legislative Activity." Social Science Research Network.

Canes-Wrone, Brandice, David W. Brady, and John F. Cogan. 2002. "Out of Step, Out of Office: Electoral Accountability and House Members' Voting." *American Political Science Review* 96(1): 127–140.

Carmines, Edward G., and James A. Stimson. 1989. *Issue Evolution: Race and the Transformation of American Politics.* Princeton, NJ: Princeton University Press.

Carsey, Thomas M., and Geoffrey C. Layman. 2006. "Changing Sides or Changing Minds? Party Identification and Policy Preferences in the American Electorate." *American Journal of Political Science* 50(2): 464–477.

Carson, Jamie L., Gregory Koger, Matthew J. Lebo, and Everett Young. 2010. "The Electoral Costs of Party Loyalty in Congress." *American Journal of Political Science* 54(3): 598–616.

Caughey, Devin, and Christopher Warshaw. 2016. "The Dynamics of State Policy Liberalism, 1936–2014." *American Journal of Political Science* 60(4): 899–913.

Caughey, Devin, James Dunham, and Christopher Warshaw. 2016. "Polarization and Partisan Divergence in the American Public, 1946–2012." Midwest Political Science Association Conference, 2016; MIT Political Science Department Research Paper No. 2016-13.

Caughey, Devin, Yiqing Xu, and Christopher Warshaw. 2017. "Incremental Democracy: The Policy Effects of Partisan Control of State Government." *Journal of Politics* 79(4): 1342–1358.

Chen, Kong-Pin, and Sheng-Zhang Yang. 2002. "Strategic Voting in Open Primaries." *Public Choice* 112(1): 1–30.

Clark, Tom S. 2008. "Measuring Ideological Polarization on the United States Supreme Court." *Political Research Quarterly* 62(1): 146–157.

Clark, Tom S. 2009. "The Separation of Powers, Court Curbing, and Judicial Legitimacy." *American Journal of Political Science* 53(4): 971–989.

Clinton, Joshua D. 2006. "Representation in Congress: Constituents and Roll Calls in the 106th House." *Journal of Politics* 68(2): 397–409.

Clinton, Joshua D., and Ted Enamorado. 2012. "The Fox News Factor: How the Spread of Fox News Affects Position Taking in Congress." Social Science Research Network, May 3, https://papers.ssrn.com/sol3/papers.cfm?abstract_id=2050570.

Clinton, Joshua D., and Ted Enamorado. 2014. "The National News Media's Effect on Congress: How Fox News Affected Elites in Congress." *Journal of Politics* 76(4): 928–943.

Clinton, Joshua D., Anthony Bertelli, Christian R. Grose, David E. Lewis, and David C. Nixon. 2012. "Separated Powers in the United States: The Ideology of Agencies, Presidents, and Congress." *American Journal of Political Science* 56(2): 341–354.

Clinton, Joshua, Simon Jackman, and Douglas Rivers. 2004. "The Statistical Analysis of Roll Call Data." *American Political Science Review* 98(02): 355–370.

Cohen, Marty, David Karol, Hans Noel, and John Zaller. 2009. *The Party Decides: Presidential Nominations Before and After Reform.* Chicago: University of Chicago Press.

Cohen, Marty, David Karol, Hans Noel, and John Zaller. 2016. "Party Versus Faction in the Reformed Presidential Nominating System." *PS: Political Science & Politics* 49(4): 701–708.

Cole, James. 2013. "Guidance Regarding Marijuana Enforcement." US Department of Justice, August 29, https://www.justice.gov/iso/opa/resources/3052013829132756857467.pdf.

Colleoni, Elanor, Alessandro Rozza, and Adam Arvidsson. 2014. "Echo Chamber or Public Sphere? Predicting Political Orientation and Measuring Political Homophily in Twitter Using Big Bata." *Journal of Communication* 64(2): 317–332.

Conover, Michael D., Bruno Gonçalves, Alessandro Flammini, and Filippo Menczer. 2012. "Partisan Asymmetries in Online Political Activity." *EPJ Data Science* 1(June): 6.

Converse, Philip E. 1964. "The Nature of Belief Systems in Mass Publics." In *Ideology and Discontent,* edited by David Apter, 206–261. New York: Free Press.

Cox, Gary W., and Keith T. Poole. 2002. "On Measuring Partisanship in Roll-Call Voting: The US House of Representatives, 1877–1999." *American Journal of Political Science* 46(3): 477–489.

Cox, Gary W., and Mathew D. McCubbins. 1993. *Legislative Leviathan: Party Government in the House.* Berkeley: University of California Press.

Cox, Gary W., and Mathew D. McCubbins. 2005. *Setting the Agenda: Responsible Party Government in the US House of Representatives.* Cambridge, UK: Cambridge University Press.

Curry, James, and Frances Lee. 2019. "Congress at Work: Legislative Capacity and Entrepreneurship in the Contemporary Congress." In *Can America Govern Itself?,* edited by Frances Lee and Nolan McCarty, 181–219. Cambridge, UK: Cambridge University Press.

DellaVigna, Stefano, and Ethan Kaplan. 2007. "The Fox News Effect: Media Bias and Voting." *Quarterly Journal of Economics* 122(3): 1187–1234.

Devins, Neal. 2008. "Presidential Unilateralism and Political Polarization: Why Today's Congress Lacks the Will and the Way to Stop Presidential Initiatives." *Willamette Law Review* 45: 395.

Devins, Neal, and David E. Lewis. 2008. "Not-So Independent Agencies: Party Polarization and the Limits of Institutional Design." *Boston University Law Review* 88: 459.

Dickinson, Matthew. 2016. "Who Do You Trust: The Polls or the Forecast Models?" Middlebury College College, Presidential Power [blog], August 31, https://sites.middlebury.edu/presidentialpower/2016/08/31/who-do-you-trust-the-polls-or-the-forecast-models/.

Diehm, Jan, Sergio Hernandez, Aaron Kessler, Tal Kopan, Curt Merrill, and Sean O'Key. 2017. "Tracking Trump's Nominations." CNN,

December 31, http://www.cnn.com/interactive/2017/politics/
trump-nominations/.

DiMaggio, Paul, John Evans, and Bethany Bryson. 1996. "Have
American's Social Attitudes Become More Polarized?" *American
Journal of Sociology* 102(3): 690–755.

"Donald Trump Has Twice Dumped the GOP, But Remains a
Republican at Press Time." 2015. Smoking Gun, June 16,
https://www.thesmokinggun.com/buster/donald-trump/
donald-trump-voter-history-567920.

Donovan, Todd, Caroline Tolbert, and Kellen Gracey. 2016. "Campaign
Civility under Preferential and Plurality Voting." *Electoral Studies*
42(06): 157–163.

Downs, Anthony. 1957. *An Economic Theory of Democracy.*
New York: Columbia University Press.

Draper, Robert. 2012. "The League of Dangerous Mapmakers." *Atlantic*,
October.

Drutman, Lee. 2017. "The Case for Proportional Voting." *National Affairs*
34(Winter): 50–63.

Duverger, Maurice. 1954. *Political Parties.* Translated by B. North and
R. North. London: Methuen.

Edwards, Mickey. 2012. *The Parties Versus the People: How to Turn
Republicans and Democrats into Americans.* New Haven, CT: Yale
University Press.

Eggen, Dan, and T. W. Farnam. 2011. "Trump's Donation History Shows
Democratic Favoritism." *Washington Post*, April 26, https://www.
washingtonpost.com/politics/trumps-donation-history-shows-
democratic-favoritism/2011/04/25/AFDUddtE_story.html?utm_
term=.f0bc07c524ec.

Eggers, Andrew C., and Benjamin E. Lauderdale. 2016. "Simulating
Counterfactual Representation." *Political Analysis* 24(2): 281–290.

Eilperin, Juliet. 2006. *Fight Club Politics: How Partisanship Is Poisoning the
U.S. House of Representatives.* Lanham, MD: Rowman & Littlefield.

Epstein, Lee, Andrew D. Martin, Jeffrey A. Segal, and Chad Westerland.
2007. "The Judicial Common Space." *Journal of Law, Economics, and
Organization* 23(2): 303–325.

Eskridge, William N. 1991. "Overriding Supreme Court Statutory
Interpretation Decisions." *Yale Law Journal* 101(2): 331–455.

Esteban, Joan-Maria, and Debraj Ray. 1994. "On the Measurement of
Polarization." *Econometrica* 62(4): 819–851.

Evans, John H. 2003. "Have Americans' Attitudes Become More Polarized?—An Update." *Social Science Quarterly* 84(1): 71–90.

"Federal Elections 2016." 2016. ABC.net, https://www.abc.net.au/news/federal-election-2016/results/list/.

Ferejohn, John, and Charles Shipan. 1990. "Congressional Influence on Bureaucracy." *Journal of Law, Economics, & Organization* 6: 1–20.

Fiorina, Morris. 2017. *Unstable Majorities: Polarization, Party Sorting, and Political Stalemate.* Stanford, CA: Hoover Press.

Fiorina, Morris P., and Samuel J. Abrams. 2008. "Political Polarization in the American Public." *Annual Review of Political Science* 11: 563–588.

Fiorina, Morris P., with Samuel J. Abrams and Jeremy C. Pope. 2005. *Culture War? The Myth of a Polarized America.* New York: Pearson Longman.

Flegenheimer, Matt, and Maggie Haberman. 2016. "Donald Trump, Abortion Foe, Eyes 'Punishment' for Women, Then Recants." *New York Times,* March 30, https://www.nytimes.com/2016/03/31/us/politics/donald-trump-abortion.html.

Fowler, Anthony, and Andrew Hall. 2013. "Conservative Vote Probabilities: An Easier Method for Summarizing Roll-Call Data." Working Paper. Chicago: University of Chicago.

Fowler, Linda L. 1982. "How Interest Groups Select Issues for Rating Voting Records of Members of the US Congress." *Legislative Studies Quarterly* 7(3): 401–413.

Geer, John G. 1988. "Assessing the Representativeness of Electorates in Presidential Primaries." *American Journal of Political Science* 32(4): 929–945.

Gelman, Andrew, Boris Shor, Joseph Bafumi, and David Park. 2005. *Rich State, Poor State, Red State, Blue State: What's the Matter with Connecticut?* Princeton, NJ: Princeton University Press.

"General Social Survey 2012." 2013. NORC, http://www.norc.org/PDFs/GSS%20Reports/Trends%20in%20Attitudes%20About%20Abortion_Final.pdf.

Gentzkow, Matthew. 2006. "Television and Voter Turnout." *Quarterly Journal of Economics* 121(3): 931–972.

Gentzkow, Matthew, and Jesse M. Shapiro. 2006. "Media Bias and Reputation." *Journal of Political Economy* 114(2): 280–316.

Gentzkow, Matthew, and Jesse M. Shapiro. 2010. "What Drives Media Slant? Evidence from US Daily Newspapers." *Econometrica* 78(1): 35–71.

Gentzkow, Matthew, and Jesse M. Shapiro. 2011. "Ideological Segregation Online and Offline." *Quarterly Journal of Economics* 126(4): 1799–1839.

George, Lisa M., and Joel Waldfogel. 2006. "The New York Times and the Market for Local Newspapers." *American Economic Review* 96(March): 435–447.

Gerber, Alan S., Dean Karlan, and Daniel Bergan. 2009. "Does the Media Matter? A Field Experiment Measuring the Effect of Newspapers on Voting Behavior and Political Opinions." *American Economic Journal: Applied Economics* 1(2): 35–52.

Gerber, Elisabeth R., and Jeffrey B. Lewis. 2004. "Beyond the Median: Voter Preferences, District Heterogeneity, and Political Representation." *Journal of Political Economy* 112(December): 1364–1383.

Gerrish, Sean, and David M. Blei. 2011. Predicting Legislative Roll Calls from Text. In *Proceedings of the 28th International Conference on Machine Learning (icml-11)*, 489–496. Bellevue, WA: Omnipress.

Gerrish, Sean, and David M. Blei. 2012. How They Vote: Issue-Adjusted Models of Legislative Behavior. In *Advances in Neural Information Processing Systems* 4: 2753–2761.

Gilens, Martin. 2009. *Why Americans Hate Welfare: Race, Media, and the Politics of Antipoverty Policy.* Chicago: University of Chicago Press.

Gilens, Martin. 2012. *Affluence and Influence: Economic Inequality and Political Power in America.* Princeton, NJ: Princeton University Press.

Gilens, Martin, and Benjamin I. Page. 2014. "Testing Theories of American Politics: Elites, Interest Groups, and Average Citizens." *Perspectives on Politics* 12(3): 564–581.

Gilmour, John B. 1995. *Strategic Disagreement: Stalemate in American Politics.* Pittsburgh, PA: University of Pittsburgh Press.

Green, Donald, Bradley Palmquist, and Eric Schickler. 2002. *Partisan Hearts and Minds.* New Haven, CT: Yale University Press.

Greene, Steven. 2004. "Social Identity Theory and Party Identification." *Social Science Quarterly* 85(1): 136–153.

Grose, Christian. 2014. "The Adoption of Electoral Reforms and Ideological Change in the California State Legislature." Report. Swartzenegger Institute, University of Southern California.

Groseclose, Tim, and Jeffrey Milyo. 2005. "A Measure of Media Bias." *Quarterly Journal of Economics* 120(4): 1191–1237.

Groseclose, Tim, and Nolan McCarty. 2001. "The Politics of Blame: Bargaining Before an Audience." *American Journal of Political Science* 45(1): 100–119.

Groseclose, Tim, Steven D. Levitt, and James M. Snyder. 1999. "Comparing Interest Group Scores across Time and Chambers: Adjusted ADA Scores for the US Congress." *American Political Science Review* 93(1): 33–50.

Grossman, Matt. 2018. "Racial Attitudes and Political Correctness in the 2016 Presidential Election." Niskanen Center, May 10, https://niskanencenter.org/blog/racial-attitudes-and-political-correctness-in-the-2016-presidential-election/.

Grumbach, Jacob M. 2018. "From Backwaters to Major Policymakers: Policy Polarization in the States, 1970–2014." *Perspectives on Politics* 16(2): 416–435.

Guess, Andrew M. 2016. "Media Choice and Moderation: Evidence from Online Tracking Data." Unpublished manuscript, New York University, October 7.

Guess, Andrew M. 2018. "(Almost) Everything in Moderation: New Evidence on Americans' Online Media Diets." Unpublished manuscript, New York University, July 2.

Hacker, Jacob, and Paul Pierson. 2005. *Off Center: The Republican Revolution and the Erosion of American Democracy.* New Haven, CT: Yale University Press.

Hacker, Jacob S., and Paul Pierson. 2010. *Winner-Take-All Politics: How Washington Made the Rich Richer—and Turned Its Back on the Middle Class.* New York: Simon and Schuster.

Hainmueller, Jens. 2012. "Entropy Balancing for Causal Effects: A Multivariate Reweighting Method to Produce Balanced Samples in Observational Studies." *Political Analysis* 20(1): 25–46.

Hall, Andrew B. 2014. "How the Public Funding of Elections Increases Candidate Polarization." Unpublished manuscript, Harvard University, August 13.

Hall, Andrew B. 2015. "What Happens When Extremists Win Primaries?" *American Political Science Review* 109(1): 18–42.

Hall, Andrew B. 2018. *Who Wants to Run? How the Devaluing of Political Office Drives Polarization.* Chicago: University of Chicago Press.

Harbridge, Laurel. 2015. *Is Bipartisanship Dead?: Policy Agreement and Agenda-Setting in the House of Representatives.* Cambridge, UK: Cambridge University Press.

Hare, Christopher, David A. Armstrong, Ryan Bakker, Royce Carroll, and Keith T. Poole. 2015. "Using Bayesian Aldrich-McKelvey Scaling to Study Citizens' Ideological Preferences and Perceptions." *American Journal of Political Science* 59(3): 759–774.

Hartig, Hannah. 2018. "Nearly Six in Ten Americans Say Abortion Should Be Legal in All or Most Cases." Pew Research Center, http://www.pewresearch.org/fact-tank/2018/10/17/nearly-six-in-ten-americans-say-abortion-should-be-legal/.

Hasen, Richard L. 2012. "End of the Dialogue: Political Polarization, the Supreme Court, and Congress." *Southern California Law Review* 86: 205.

Heberlig, Eric, Marc Hetherington, and Bruce Larson. 2006. "The Price of Leadership: Campaign Money and the Polarization of Congressional Parties." *Journal of Politics* 68(4): 992–1005.

Heckman, James, and James Snyder. 1997. "Linear Probability Models of the Demand for Attributes with an Empirical Application to Estimating the Preferences of Legislators." *Rand Journal of Economics* 28: s142–189.

Helmore, Edward. 2017. "How Trump's Political Playbook Evolved since He First Ran for President in 2000." *Guardian*, February 5, https://www.theguardian.com/us-news/2017/feb/05/donald-trump-reform-party-2000-president.

Henderson, John A. 2016. "Issue Distancing in Congressional Elections." Working Paper, Yale University.

Herndon, Astead W. 2018. "Democrats Overhaul Controversial Superdelegate System." *New York Times*, April 25, https://www.nytimes.com/2018/08/25/us/politics/superdelegates-democrats-dnc.html.

Hicks, William D. 2015. "Partisan Competition and the Efficiency of Lawmaking in American State Legislatures, 1991–2009." *American Politics Research* 43(5): 743–770.

Hill, Seth J., and Chris Tausanovitch. 2015. "A Disconnect in Representation? Comparison of Trends in Congressional and Public Polarization." *Journal of Politics* 77(4): 1058–1075.

Hirano, Shigeo, James M. Snyder, Stephen Ansolabehere, and John Mark Hanson. 2010. "Primary Elections and Partisan Polarization in U.S. Congressional Elections." *Quarterly Journal of Political Science* 5(2): 169–191.

Hopkins, Daniel J., and Jonathan M. Ladd. 2014. "The Consequences of Broader Media Choice: Evidence from the Expansion of Fox News." *Quarterly Journal of Political Science* 9(1): 115–135.

Hopkins, Daniel J. 2017a. *The Increasingly United States: How and Why American Political Behavior Nationalized*. Chicago: University of Chicago Press.

Hopkins, David A. 2017b. *Red Fighting Blue: How Geography and Electoral Rules Polarize American Politics*. New York: Cambridge University Press.

Howell, William G. 2003. *Power without Persuasion: The Politics of Direct Presidential Action*. Princeton, NJ: Princeton University Press.

Huddy, Leonie, and Alexa Bankert. 2017. "Political Partisanship as a Social Identity." *Oxford Research Encyclopedia of Politics*. May 24.

Huddy, Leonie, Lilliana Mason, and Lene Aarøe. 2015. "Expressive Partisanship: Campaign Involvement, Political Emotion, and Partisan Identity." *American Political Science Review* 109(1): 1–17.

Iyengar, Shanto, and Kyu S. Hahn. 2009. "Red Media, Blue Media: Evidence of Ideological Selectivity in Media Use." *Journal of Communication* 59(1): 19–39.

Iyengar, Shanto, and Sean J. Westwood. 2015. "Fear and Loathing across Party Lines: New Evidence on Group Polarization." *American Journal of Political Science* 59(3): 690–707.

Iyengar, Shanto, Gaurav Sood, and Yphtach Lelkes. 2012. "Affect, Not Ideology: A Social Identity Perspective on Polarization." *Public Opinion Quarterly* 76(3): 405–431.

Jackman, Molly C. 2014. "Parties, Median Legislators, and Agenda Setting: How Legislative Institutions Matter." *Journal of Politics* 76(1): 259–272.

Jenkins, Shannon. 2006. "The Impact of Party and Ideology on Roll-Call Voting in State Legislatures." *Legislative Studies Quarterly* 31: 235–257.

Jessee, Stephen. 2016. "(How) Can We Estimate the Ideology of Citizens and Political Elites on the Same Scale?" *American Journal of Political Science* 60(4): 1108–1124.

Jessee, Stephen, and Neil Malhotra. 2010. "Are Congressional Leaders Middlepersons or Extremists? Yes." *Legislative Studies Quarterly* 35(3): 361–392.

Joseph O'Connell, Anne. 2009. "Vacant Offices: Delays in Staffing Top Agency Positions." *Southern California Law Review* 82: 913.

Kabaservice, Geoffrey. 2012. *Rule and Ruin: The Downfall of Moderation and the Destruction of the Republican Party, from Eisenhower to the Tea Party*. Oxford, UK: Oxford University Press.

Key, V. O. 1949. *Southern Politics in State and Nation*. New York: Knopf.

Kilgore, Ed. 2018 "The Near Extinction of Pro-Choice Republicans in Congress." *New York*, June 28, http://nymag.com/intelligencer/2018/06/pro-choice-republicans-in-congress-are-nearly-extinct.html?gtm=bottom&gtm=top/.

Kim, In Song, John Londregan, and Marc Ratkovic. 2018. "Estimating Spatial Preferences from Votes and Text." *Political Analysis* 26(2): 210–229.

Kimball, David C., and Joseph Anthony. 2016. Voter Participation with Ranked Choice Voting in the United States. Paper presented at annual meeting of the American Political Science Association, Philadelphia.

Kinder, Donald R., and D. Roderick Kiewiet. 1981. "Sociotropic Politics: The American Case." *British Journal of Political Science* 11(2): 129–161.

Kinder, Donald R., and Nathan P. Kalmoe. 2017. *Neither Liberal nor Conservative: Ideological Innocence in the American Public.* Chicago: University of Chicago Press.

Kirkland, Patricia A., and Justin H. Phillips. 2018. "Is Divided Government a Cause of Legislative Delay?" *Quarterly Journal of Political Science* 13(2): 173–206.

Klar, Samara, and Yanna Krupnikov. 2016. *Independent Politics.* Cambridge, UK: Cambridge University Press.

Kousser, Thad, Jeffrey B. Lewis, and Seth E. Masket. 2007. "Ideological Adaptation? The Survival Instinct of Threatened Legislators." *Journal of Politics* 69(3): 828–843.

Kousser, Thad, Justin Phillips, and Boris Shor. 2018. "Reform and Representation: A New Method Applied to Recent Electoral Changes." *Political Science Research and Methods* 6(4): 809–827.

Kramer, Gerald H. 1983. "The Ecological Fallacy Revisited: Aggregate Versus Individual-Level Findings on Economics and Elections, and Sociotropic Voting." *American Political Science Review* 77(1): 92–111.

Krehbiel, Keith. 1998. *Pivotal Politics: A Theory of U.S. Lawmaking.* Chicago: University of Chicago Press.

Krimmel, Katherine. 2013. "Special Interest Partisanship: The Transformation of American Political Parties in Government." PhD thesis, Columbia University.

Kriner, Douglas L., and Eric Schickler. 2016. *Investigating the President: Congressional Checks on Presidential Power.* Princeton, NJ: Princeton University Press.

Kuziemko, Ilyana, and Ebonya Washington. 2015. "Why did the Democrats Lose the South? Bringing New Data to an Old Debate." NBER Working Paper 21703, November.

La Raja, Raymond J., and Brian F. Schaffner. 2015. *Campaign Finance and Political Polarization: When Purists Prevail.* Ann Arbor, MI: University of Michigan Press.

Lapinski, John S. 2013. *The Substance of Representation: Congress, American Political Development, and Lawmaking.* Princeton, NJ: Princeton University Press.

Lauderdale, Benjamin E. 2013. "Does Inattention to Political Debate Explain the Polarization Gap between the US Congress and Public?" *Public Opinion Quarterly* 77(S1): 2–23.

Lauderdale, Benjamin E., and Tom S. Clark. 2014. "Scaling Politically Meaningful Dimensions Using Texts and Votes." *American Journal of Political Science* 58(3): 754–771.

Layman, Geoffrey C., and Thomas M. Carsey. 2002. "Party Polarization and 'Conflict Extension' in the American Electorate." *American Journal of Political Science* 46(4): 786–802.

Layman, Geoffrey C., Thomas M. Carsey, and Juliana Menasce Horowitz. 2006. "Party Polarization in American Politics: Characteristics, Causes, and Consequences." *Annual Review Political Science* 9: 83–110.

Lee, Frances, and Nolan McCarty. 2019. "Democratic Anxieties: Present and Emergent." In *Can America Govern Itself?*, edited by Frances Lee, and Nolan McCarty, 329–344. Cambridge, UK: Cambridge University Press.

Lee, Frances E. 2009. *Beyond Ideology: Politics, Principles, and Partisanship in the US Senate.* Chicago: University of Chicago Press.

Lee, Frances E. 2016a. *Insecure Majorities: Congress and the Perpetual Campaign.* Chicago: University of Chicago Press.

Lee, Frances E. 2016b. "Patronage, Logrolls, and "Polarization": Congressional Parties of the Gilded Age, 1876–1896." *Studies in American Political Development* 30(2): 116–127.

Lelkes, Yphtach. 2016. "Mass Polarization: Manifestations and Measurements." *Public Opinion Quarterly* 80(S1): 392–410.

Lelkes, Yphtach. n.d. "Policy over Party: The Relative Effects of Candidate Ideology and Party on Affective Polarization." *Political Science Research Methods.*

Lelkes, Yphtach, Gaurav Sood, and Shanto Iyengar. 2017. "The Hostile Audience: The Effect of Access to Broadband Internet on Partisan Affect." *American Journal of Political Science* 61(1): 5–20.

Lenz, Gabriel S. 2013. *Follow the Leader?: How Voters Respond to Politicians' Policies and Performance*. Chicago: University of Chicago Press.

Lessig, Lawrence. 2011. *Republic, Lost: How Money Corrupts Congress—and a Plan to Stop It*. New York: Hachette.

Levendusky, Matthew S. 2009. *The Partisan Sort: How Liberals Became Democrats and Conservatives Became Republican*. Chicago: University of Chicago Press.

Levendusky, Matthew S., and Jeremy C. Pope. 2010. "Measuring Aggregate-Level Ideological Heterogeneity." *Legislative Studies Quarterly* 35(2): 259–282.

Levendusky, Matthew S., Jeremy C. Pope, and Simon D. Jackman. 2008. "Measuring District-Level Partisanship with Implications for the Analysis of U.S. Elections." *Journal of Politics* 70(03): 736–753.

Levinson, Daryl J., and Richard H. Pildes. 2006. "Separation of Parties, Not Powers." *Harvard Law Review* 119: 2311–2386.

Lewis, David E. 2010. *The Politics of Presidential Appointments: Political Control and Bureaucratic Performance*. Princeton, NJ: Princeton University Press.

Lu, Denise, and Karen Yourish. 2019. "The Turnover at the Top of the Trump Administration Is Unprecedented." *New York Times*, January 14, https://www.nytimes.com/interactive/2018/03/16/us/politics/all-the-major-firings-and-resignations-in-trump-administration.html.

Lunch, William L., and Peter W. Sperlich. 1979. "American Public Opinion and the War in Vietnam." *Western Political Quarterly* 32(1): 21–44.

Magleby, David B., Candice J. Nelson, and Mark C. Westlye. 2011. "The Myth of the Independent Voter Revisited." In *Facing the Challenge of Democracy: Explorations in the Analysis of Public Opinion and Political Participation*, 238–266. Princeton, NJ: Princeton University Press.

Mainwaring, Scott. 1993. "Presidentialism, Multipartism, and Democracy: The Difficult Combination." *Comparative Political Studies* 26(2): 198–228.

Mann, Thomas E., and Norman J. Ornstein. 2016. *It's Even Worse Than It Looks: How the American Constitutional System Collided with the New Politics of Extremism*. New York: Basic Books.

Martin, Andrew D., and Kevin M. Quinn. 2002. "Dynamic Ideal Point Estimation via Markov Chain Monte Carlo for the US Supreme Court, 1953–1999." *Political Analysis* 10(2): 134–153.

Martin, Gregory J., and Ali Yurukoglu. 2017. "Bias in Cable News: Persuasion and Polarization." *American Economic Review* 107(9): 2565–2599.

Masket, Seth E., and Michael G. Miller. 2015. "Does Public Election Funding Create More Extreme Legislators? Evidence from Arizona and Maine." *State Politics & Policy Quarterly* 15(1): 24–40.

Mason, Lilliana. 2015. "'I Disrespectfully Agree': The Differential Effects of Partisan Sorting on Social and Issue Polarization." *American Journal of Political Science* 59(1): 128–145.

Mason, Lilliana. 2016. "A Cross-Cutting Calm: How Social Sorting Drives Affective Polarization." *Public Opinion Quarterly* 80(S1): 351–377.

Mason, Lilliana, and Julie Wronski. 2018. "One Tribe to Bind Them All: How Our Social Group Attachments Strengthen Partisanship." *Political Psychology* 39(S1): 257–277.

Mayhew, David. 1986. *Placing Parties in American Politics.* Princeton, NJ: Princeton University Press.

Mayhew, David R. 1991. *Divided We Govern.* New Haven, CT: Yale University.

McAdam, Doug, and Yang Su. 2002. "The War at Home: Antiwar Protests and Congressional Voting, 1965 to 1973." *American Sociological Review* 67(5): 696–721.

McCarty, Nolan. 1997. "Presidential Reputation and the Veto." *Economics & Politics* 9(1): 1–26.

McCarty, Nolan. 2007. "The Policy Effects of Political Polarization." In *Transformation of American Politics*, edited by Paul Pierson and Theda Skocpol, 211–255. Princeton, NJ: Princeton University Press.

McCarty, Nolan. 2011. "Measuring Legislative Preferences." In *Oxford Handbook of the American Congress*, edited by Frances Lee and Eric Schickler, 66–94. New York: Oxford University Press.

McCarty, Nolan. 2015a. "Reducing Polarization by Making Parties Stronger." In *Solutions to Political Polarization in America*, edited by Nathaniel Persily, 136–145. New York: Cambridge University Press.

McCarty, Nolan. 2015b. "Reducing Polarization: Some Facts for Reformers." *University of Chicago Legal Forum* 2015: 243–278.

McCarty, Nolan. 2016. "In Defense of DW-NOMINATE." *Studies in American Political Development* 30(2): 172–184.

McCarty, Nolan, and Eric Schickler. 2018. "On the Theory of Parties." *Annual Review of Political Science* 21: 175–193.

McCarty, Nolan, and Keith T. Poole. 1998. "An Empirical Spatial Model of Congressional Campaigns." *Political Analysis* 7: 1–30.

McCarty, Nolan, Jonathan Rodden, Boris Shor, Chris Tausanovitch, and Christopher Warshaw. 2018. "Geography, Uncertainty, and Polarization." *Political Science Research and Methods*: 1–20.

McCarty, Nolan, Keith T. Poole, and Howard Rosenthal. 1997. *Income Redistribution and the Realignment of American Politics*. Washington, DC: AEI Press.

McCarty, Nolan, Keith T. Poole, and Howard Rosenthal. 2001. "The Hunt for Party Discipline in Congress." *American Political Science Review* 95: 673–687.

McCarty, Nolan, Keith T. Poole, and Howard Rosenthal. 2006. *Polarized America: The Dance of Ideology and Unequal Riches*. Cambridge, MA: MIT Press.

McCarty, Nolan, Keith T. Poole, and Howard Rosenthal. 2009. "Does Gerrymandering Cause Polarization?" *American Journal of Political Science* 53(3): 666–680.

McCarty, Nolan, Keith T. Poole, and Howard Rosenthal. 2013. *Political Bubbles: Financial Crises and the Failure of American Democracy*. Princeton, NJ: Princeton University Press.

McCarty, Nolan, Keith T. Poole, and Howard Rosenthal. 2016. *Polarized America: The Dance of Ideology and Unequal Riches*. Cambridge, MA: MIT Press.

McDaniel, Jason A. 2015. "Writing the Rules to Rank the Candidates: Examining the Impact of Instant Runoff Voting on Racial Group Turnout in San Francisco Mayoral Elections." *Journal of Urban Affairs* 38(3): 387–408.

McGhee, Eric, Seth Masket, Steven Rogers, Boris Shor, and Nolan McCarty. 2014. "A Primary Cause of Partisanship? Nomination Systems and Legislator Ideology." *American Journal of Political Science* 58(2): 337–351.

Moe, Terry M., and William G. Howell. 1999. "The Presidential Power of Unilateral Action." *Journal of Law, Economics, and Organization* 15(1): 132–179.

Monopoly Politics (n.d.). FairVote, https://www.fairvote.org/ monopoly_politics_2018former#overview-2018.

Moody, Chris. 2015. "Trump in '04: 'I Probably Identify More as a Democrat.'" CNN, July 22, https://www.cnn.com/2015/07/21/ politics/donald-trump-election-democrat/index.html.

Nagourney, Adam. 2013. "California Sees Gridlock Ease in Governing."
    New York Times, October 18.
Neely, Francis, and Jason McDaniel. 2015. "Overvoting and the Equality
    of Voice under Instant-Runoff Voting in San Francisco." *California
    Journal of Politics and Policy* 7(4), http://dx.doi.org/10.5070/
    P2cjpp7428929.
Nocera, Joe. 2013. "Fixing the System." *New York Times*, November 4.
Noel, Hans. 2014. *Political Ideologies and Political Parties in America*.
    Cambridge, UK: Cambridge University Press.
Nokken, Timothy P., and Keith T. Poole. 2004. "Congressional Party
    Defection in American History." *Legislative Studies Quarterly*
    29(4): 545–568.
Norrander, Barbara. 1989. "Ideological Representativeness of
    Presidential Primary Voters." *American Journal of Political Science*
    33(3): 570–587.
Oak, Mandar P. 2006. "On the Role of the Primary System in Candidate
    Selection." *Economics & Politics* 18(2): 169–190.
Palfrey, Thomas R., and Keith T. Poole. 1987. "The Relationship
    between Information, Ideology, and Voting Behavior." *American
    Journal of Political Science* 31: 511–530.
Persily, Nathaniel. 2015. "Stronger Parties as a Solution to Polarization."
    In *Solutions to Political Polarization in America*, edited by Nathaniel
    Persily, 123–135. New York: Cambridge University Press.
Pew Research Center. 2017. "The Partisan Divide on Political Values
    Grows Even Wider." Technical Report. Pew Center for the People
    and the Press.
Piketty, Thomas, and Emmanuel Saez. 2003. "Income Inequality
    in the United States, 1913–1998." *Quarterly Journal of Economics*
    118(1): 1–39.
Pildes, Richard H. 2015. "Focus on Fragmentation, Not Polarization: Re-
    Empower Party Leadership." In *Solutions to Political
    Polarization in America*, edited by Nathaniel Persily, 146–156.
    New York: Cambridge University Press.
Poole, Keith T. 2000. "Non-parametric Unfolding of Binary Choice
    Data." *Political Analysis* 8: 211–237.
Poole, Keith T. 2007. "Changing Minds? Not in Congress!" *Public Choice*
    131(3): 435–451.
Poole, Keith T., and Howard Rosenthal. 1984. "The Polarization of
    American Politics." *Journal of Politics* 46(4): 1061–1079.

Poole, Keith T., and Howard Rosenthal. 1997. *Congress: A Political-Economic History of Roll Call Voting.* New York: Oxford University Press.

Poole, Keith T., and Howard Rosenthal. 2011. *Ideology and Congress.* New Brunswick, NJ: Transaction.

Poole, Keith T., and Thomas Romer. 1993. "Ideology, "Shirking," and Representation." *Public Choice* 77(1): 185–196.

"Post-Mortem." n.d. Fair Model, Yale, https://fairmodel.econ.yale.edu/vote2016/index2.htm.

Prior, Markus. 2007. *Post-Broadcast Democracy: How Media Choice Increases Inequality in Political Involvement and Polarizes Elections.* Cambridge, UK: Cambridge University Press.

Prior, Markus, Gaurav Sood, and Kabir Khanna. 2015. "You Cannot Be Serious: The Impact of Accuracy Incentives on Partisan Bias in Reports of Economic Perceptions." *Quarterly Journal of Political Science* 10(4): 489–518.

Ranney, Austin. 1951. "Toward a More Responsible Two-Party System: A Commentary." *American Political Science Review* 45(2): 488–499.

Redlawsk, David P., Caroline J. Tolbert, and William Franko. 2010. "Voters, Emotions, and Race in 2008: Obama as the First Black President." *Political Research Quarterly* 63(4): 875–889.

Rehm, Philipp, and Timothy Reilly. 2010. "United We Stand: Constituency Homogeneity and Comparative Party Polarization." *Electoral Studies* 29(1): 40–53.

Rogers, Steven. 2016. "National Forces in State Legislative Elections." *Annals of the American Academy of Political and Social Science* 667(1): 207–225.

Rogers, Steven. 2017. "Electoral Accountability for State Legislative Roll Calls and Ideological Representation." *American Political Science Review* 111(3): 555–571.

Rogowski, Jon C., and Joseph L. Sutherland. 2016. "How Ideology Fuels Affective Polarization." *Political Behavior* 38(2): 485–508.

Rohde, David W. 1991. *Parties and Leaders in the Postreform House.* Chicago: University of Chicago Press.

Rosenberg, Gerald N. 1991. *The Hollow Hope: Can Courts Bring about Social Change?* Chicago: University of Chicago Press.

Rosenfeld, Sam. 2017. *The Polarizers: Postwar Architects of Our Partisan Era.* Chicago: University of Chicago Press.

Ryan, Missy, and Steven Mufson. 2016. "One of Trump's Foreign Policy Advisors Is a 2009 College Grad Who Lists Model UN as a Credential." *Washington Post*, March 22, https://www. washingtonpost.com/news/checkpoint/wp/2016/03/21/meet-the-men-shaping-donald-trumps-foreign-policy-views/?utm_term=.52bfb9c68c87.

Saad, Lydia. 2017. "US Abortion Attitudes Stable; No Consensus on Legality." Gallop, June 9, http://www.aei.org/wp-content/uploads/2017/01/ABORTION.pdf.

Schaffner, Brian F., Matthew MacWilliams, and Tatishe Nteta. 2018. "Understanding White Polarization in the 2016 Vote for President: The Sobering Role of Racism and Sexism." *Political Science Quarterly* 133(1): 9–34.

Schickler, Eric. 2016. *Racial Realignment: The Transformation of American Liberalism, 1932–1965*. Princeton, NJ: Princeton University Press.

Schlozman, Daniel, and Sam Rosenfeld. 2019. "The Hollow Parties." In *Can America Govern Itself?*, edited by Frances Lee and Nolan McCarty, 154–210. Cambridge, UK: Cambridge University Press.

Schlozman, Kay Lehman, Sidney Verba, and Henry E. Brady. 2012. *The Unheavenly Chorus: Unequal Political Voice and the Broken Promise of American Democracy*. Princeton, NJ: Princeton University Press.

Schumer, Charles. 2014. "End Partisan Primaries, Save America." *New York Times*, July 21.

Scobee, Paige. 2016. "Ahoy! The Future of the Filibuster." NCSL, June 29, http://www.ncsl.org/blog/2016/06/29/ahoy-the-future-of-the-filibuster.aspx.

Scott, Dylan, and Sarah Kliff. 2017. "Republicans Have Finally Repealed A Crucial Piece of ObamaCare." Vox, December 20, https://www.vox.com/policy-and-politics/2017/11/14/16651698/obamacare-individual-mandate-republican-tax-bill.

Segal, Jeffrey A., and Albert D. Cover. 1989. "Ideological Values and the Votes of US Supreme Court Justices." *American Political Science Review* 83(2): 557–565.

Segal, Jeffrey A., and Harold J. Spaeth. 2002. *The Supreme Court and the Attitudinal Model Revisited*. Cambridge: UK: Cambridge University Press.

Shafer, Byron E., and Richard Johnston. 2009. *The End of Southern Exceptionalism: Class, Race, and Partisan Change in the Postwar South*. Cambridge, MA: Harvard University Press.

Shear, Michael D., and Ron Nixon. 2017. "How Trump's Rush to Enact an Immigration Ban Unleashed Global Chaos." *New York Times*, January 29, https://www.nytimes.com/2017/01/29/us/politics/donald-trump-rush-immigration-order-chaos.html.

Shor, Boris, and Nolan McCarty. 2011. "The Ideological Mapping of American Legislatures." *American Political Science Review* 105(3): 530–551.

Sides, John, Chris Tausanovitch, Lynn Vavreck, and Christopher Warshaw. 2018. "On the Representativeness of Primary Electorates." *British Journal of Political Science*: 1–9.

Sinclair, Barbara. 2006. *Party Wars: Polarization and the Politics of National Policy Making*. Vol. 10. Norman: University of Oklahoma Press.

Snyder, James M., and Tim Groseclose. 2001. "Estimating Party Influence on Roll Call Voting: Regression Coefficients versus Classification Success." *American Political Science Review* 95(3): 689–698.

Snyder, James M. 1992. "Artificial Extremism in Interest Group Ratings." *Legislative Studies Quarterly* 17(3): 319–345.

Snyder, James M., and David Strömberg. 2010. "Press Coverage and Political Accountability." *Journal of Political Economy* 118(2): 355–408.

"Statement by Former National Security Officials." n.d. National Secuity Letter, https://assets.documentcloud.org/documents/3007589/Nationalsecurityletter.pdf.

Stephanopoulos, Nicholas O. 2011. "Spatial Diversity." *Harvard Law Review* 125: 1903–2011.

Stewart, Josh. 2016. "McCutcheon Decision Has Allowed at Least $39 Million More in Presidential Election So Far." Sunlight Foundation, August 29, https://sunlightfoundation.com/2016/08/29/mccutcheon-decision-has-allowed-at-least-39-million-more-in-presidential-election-so-far/.

Stroud, Natalie Jomini. 2008. "Media Use and Political Predispositions: Revisiting the Concept of Selective Exposure." *Political Behavior* 30(3): 341–366.

Sunstein, Cass R. 2018. *#Republic: Divided Democracy in the Age of Social Media*. Princeton, NJ: Princeton University Press.

Tajfel, Henri. 1970. "Experiments in Intergroup Discrimination." *Scientific American* 223(5): 96–103.

Tajfel, Henri, and John C. Turner. 1979. "An Integrative Theory of Intergroup Conflict." *Social Psychology of Intergroup Relations* 33(47): 74.

Tausanovitch, Chris. 2016. "Income, Ideology, and Representation." *RSF: Russell Sage Foundation Journal of the Social Sciences* 2(7): 33–50.

Tausanovitch, Chris, and Christopher Warshaw. 2013. "Measuring Constituent Policy Preferences in Congress, State Legislatures, and Cities." *Journal of Politics* 75(2): 330–342.

The Economist. 2014. "Powering Down." November 8.

Theriault, Sean M. 2008. *Party Polarization in Congress.* Cambridge, UK: Cambridge University Press.

Theriault, Sean M. 2013. *The Gingrich Senators: The Roots of Partisan Warfare in Congress.* New York: Oxford University Press.

Thomsen, Danielle M. 2017. *Opting Out of Congress: Partisan Polarization and the Decline of Moderate Candidates.* Cambridge, UK: Cambridge University Press.

Toobin, Jeffrey. 2003. "The Great Election Grab." *New Yorker.* December 8.

"Trump in 1999: I Am Very Pro-Choice." 2015. NBC News, July 8, https://www.nbcnews.com/meet-the-press/video/trump-in-1999-i-am-very-pro-choice-480297539914?v=raila&.

Tversky, Amos, and Daniel Kahneman. 1981. "The Framing of Decisions and the Psychology of Choice." *Science* 211(4481): 453–458.

Valentino, Nicholas A., and David O. Sears. 2005. "Old Times There Are Not Forgotten: Race and Partisan Realignment in the Contemporary South." *American Journal of Political Science* 49(3): 672–688.

"Vital Statistics on Congress." 2018. Brookings Institution, https://www.brookings.edu/multi-chapter-report/vital-statistics-on-congress/.

Voorheis, John, Nolan McCarty, and Boris Shor. 2015. "Unequal Incomes, Ideology and Gridlock: How Rising Inequality Increases Political Polarization." Social Science Research Network.

Waldman, Paul. 2018. "The Next Big Thing for Democrats: Medicare for All." *Washington Post*, April 19, https://www.washingtonpost.com/blogs/plum-line/wp/2018/04/19/the-next-big-thing-for-democrats-medicare-for-all/?noredirect=on&utm_term=.e0d22fcad897.

Walter, Amy. 2013. "Primary Colors: To Change Congress Start with the Primaries." *Cook Political Report*, October 16.

Waugh, Andrew Scott, Liuyi Pei, James H. Fowler, Peter J. Mucha, and Mason A. Porter. 2009. "Party Polarization in Congress: A Social Networks Approach." arXiv preprint arXiv:0907.3509.

Webster, Steven W., and Alan I. Abramowitz. 2017. "The Ideological
    Foundations of Affective Polarization in the U.S. Electorate."
    American Politics Research 45(4): 621–647.
Weisberg, Herbert F. 1980. "A Multidimensional Conceptualization of
    Party Identification." *Political Behavior* 2(1): 33–60.
Wire, Sarah. 2018. "Why Centrist Diane Feinstein Is Moving So Much
    to the Left That She Now Opposes the Death Penalty." *Los Angeles
    Times*, May 23, https://www.latimes.com/politics/la-pol-ca-
    feinstein-election-strategy-20180523-story.html.
Wittman, Donald. 1983. "Candidate Motivation: A Synthesis
    of Alternative Theories." *American Political Science Review*
    77(1): 142–157.
Wright, Gerald C., and Brian F. Schaffner. 2002. "The Influence of
    Party: Evidence from the State Legislatures." *American Political
    Science Review* 96(June): 367–379.

INDEX

Figures are indicated by an italic *f* following the page number.